WALLACE STEVE

WALLACE STEVENS AND THE DEMANDS OF MODERNITY

TOWARD A PHENOMENOLOGY OF VALUE

CHARLES ALTIERI

CORNELL UNIVERSITY PRESS

Ithaca and London

Permissions are to be found at the back of the book.

Copyright © 2013 by Cornell University

First published 2013 by Cornell University Press
First printing, Cornell Paperbacks, 2013

Printed in the United States of America

Library of Congress Cataloging-in-Publication Data

Altieri, Charles, 1942–
Wallace Stevens and the demands of modernity : toward
a phenomenology of value / Charles Altieri.
        p. cm.
    Includes bibliographical references and index.
    ISBN 978-0-8014-5167-6 (cloth : alk. paper)—
    ISBN 978-0-8014-7872-7 (pbk. : alk. paper)
    1. Stevens, Wallace, 1879–1955—Criticism and
interpretation. 2. Phenomenology in literature.
3. Value in literature. I. Title.   .

    PS3537.T4753Z557 2013
    811'.52—dc23
                                                    2012030749

Cornell University Press strives to use environmentally
responsible suppliers and materials to the fullest extent
possible in the publishing of its books. Such materials
include vegetable-based, low-VOC inks and acid-free
papers that are recycled, totally chlorine-free, or partly
composed of nonwood fibers. For further information
visit our website at www.cornellpress.cornell.edu.

Cloth printing   10 9 8 7 6 5 4 3 2 1

CONTENTS

PREFACE

This book came as a surprise to me. I had written various essays on Wallace Stevens but could never figure out what held them together. It turns out that nothing I was doing held them together—except the fact that I was fascinated by the power of Stevens's imagination, especially its dialectical desire to assess where his poetry positioned him and how it might more deeply engage the forces that were driving it. That fascination had to be temporal, if not fully historical. So I came to think that this tracking of dialectical movement had to lead the way toward a more comprehensive framework for understanding Stevens's relation to modernity than just a series of essays.

But for a considerable time I worried that I was not up to the task. I could do a decent job of reading poems and even distinctive stylistic features of individual collections, but I did not trust any conceptual frame I thought I could develop. Then I read Peter Nichols's praise of the copulative verb in his terrific book on George Oppen. Persuasive as Nichols is on Oppen's relation to Martin Heidegger's and to Georg Wilhelm Friedrich Hegel's relation to the copulative, I could not value as he did the naming relation that the copulative celebrates. Dante had taught me to love "the intricate evasions of as." But only under the pressure of thinking through Nichols's approach to Oppen did I begin to see how fully Stevens deploys "as" instead of "is" to establish equivalences rather than names. And then I could better appreciate the various ways Stevens had irritated critics who idealize denotation (like Hugh Kenner), critics who honor fact as a means of getting a historical purchase on the world (like Fred Jameson), and critics who want poetry to develop stable, competing voices so that dialogical positions might unfold (like Gerald Bruns). Conversely, I came to see how the workings of equivalence led the reader of Stevens back to Stephané Mallarmé, but by a route that did not have to accept the deconstructive versions of those equivalences, which sought their authority in Mallarmé's idealizations of textuality.

At this point I knew I had to write this book. How could I pass up an opportunity to oppose so many elaborate and powerful critical positions and, in the process, perform what I take to be an educational and aesthetic service to the field? Nonetheless, I still found myself searching for a substantial enough thesis to justify a book-length work. What kind of work does equivalence do? Why might it matter for engaging the intellectual traditions shaping modernity that one thinks in terms of "as" relations rather than descriptions? At this point I got lucky. I was asked by our dean, Janet Broughton, to participate on a committee exploring the possibility of an Institute for the Study of Value at Berkeley. I immediately saw an opportunity. I wanted this institute to emphasize phenomenological aspects of values because, as I see it, the major threat to the humanities in our culture is the tendency of fields of study in the sciences or in ethics or even in aesthetics to imperialize the complex domains in which we experience the world as something to value. However, I had little success in persuading my colleagues until we found online the programs of other institutes for values in the academy—and there are several. All of them equated the study of value with ethics and/or public policy.

As the group turned toward phenomenological approaches to value, we decided we needed a much sharper vision of just what possibilities and just what limitations such an approach might entail. This is where I turned to Stevens's efforts to write a philosophical poetry that put significant distance between its interests and those of professional philosophers. What could we learn from those differences? And could we harness those differences within the confines of at least a loosely philosophical language? The verdict is still out on whether it is feasible to organize the life of an institute on values around what calls for poetry as its fullest means of being philosophical. Still, I am ready to seek a verdict on what those lines of questioning have afforded me as a means of providing a conceptual overview of Stevens's career. In this book I argue that Stevens's career can be characterized by the articulation of three basic responses to what I describe as the crisis with the empiricist models of value that shaped modern intellectual life during Stevens's career. The first is Nietzschean—creative work has to turn from dependency on facts so that the imagination can establish what might become facts as people learn to explore where their wills to power lead them. The second is idealist—built primarily on the power for dialectically negating what history seems to dictate as the conditions of public life. The dream here is that the mind can elaborate and build on human capacities to envision worlds characterized by a richer continuity between one's sense of what matters to the imagination and the often dreary facts determined by hegemonic social conditions.

Eventually Stevens would see that both of these first two models become problematic because their pursuit of values is ultimately mediated by beliefs. These models assumed that values are mental objects and so exist because there is a corresponding mental act that interprets and acknowledges their power. This corresponding mental act is the act of belief: the value of democracy resides in the belief that people ought to determine their own political destinies. In contrast, Stevens chose to elaborate in poetry the possibility that some basic experiences of value do not depend on concepts. Instead, they exist as aspects of states of being that poetry can display but not describe in ways that might satisfy even moderate strictures on what we take cognition to involve. Such values both depend upon and extend what I call complex processes of equivalence, which afford moments where the world becomes temporarily enchanted or at least quickened. Poetry for Stevens could make present such values. Perhaps more important, poetry could dramatize a second-order sense in which we recognize how such values affect our sense of our own powers as individuals and as social beings seeking agreement on what stands out as aspects of life worth living for. I came to think that Stevens is the American poet who offers the richest mediation on equivalences produced by a constant concern for resemblance. And it is largely for this reason that he is arguably the most influential of the modernists on the course of American poetry after the Korean war.

At this point I knew I had a book project. I could structure a graduate course on relations between modernist poetry and modern philosophy. I could also begin to acknowledge the contributions of my students and colleagues as I tried to work out these intuitions about the roles values played in Stevens's imagination. Let me mention first Dean Broughton and now Dean Anthony Cascardi for their intellectual and financial support. I am also eager to thank my much-beloved colleagues in the English Department at Berkeley, who make it in my view far and away the best place in the world to study modern American poetry—Dan Blanton, Geoffrey O'Brien, Eric Falci, Robert Kaufman, Lyn Hejinian, and Bob Hass (whose keen observations have been helping me read Stevens for more than forty years). Other colleagues like Dori Hale, Stephen Goldsmith, Steven Justice, Celeste Langan, Susan Maslan, Kate van Orden, Whitney Davis, Nikko Kolodny, and Namwalli Serpell have posed lively challenges to my efforts to work out my thoughts, while never ceasing to respect those efforts. In the world beyond Berkeley, Charles Molesworth, Anne Luyat, Jeanne Heuving, Allen Dunn, and Brian Glaser seem to have always been there with their kindly supporting criticisms that did not always seem so kind but now deepen my sense of gratitude. In addition, I want to thank Bart Eeckhout both for the clarity and scope of his work on Stevens and for his continuing support of my efforts to bridge literature and philosophy. My debts to other Stevens critics will be evident in my endnotes.

One reason that I believe Berkeley is a great place to teach modern poetry is that the graduate students are remarkably intelligent, learned, and imaginative. I cannot thank all of the students who have made a difference in my understanding of Stevens, but I would be remiss not to mention Natalie Gerber, Omri Moses, Charles Tung, Joe Jeong, Warren Liu, Joel Nickels, Jennifer Scappetone, Charles Sumner, Monica Gehlawat, Maude Emerson, Rebecca Gaydos, Christopher Miller, and Jeff Blevins. Ayon Maharaj has done even more because he is willing to read almost everything I write, and he is utterly fearless and devastatingly precise in his criticisms. Special thanks go to Jane Gilbert and to Ted Alexander for serving as research assistants while I was working on this book.

The world beyond Berkeley cannot go unmentioned even though I am fond of forgetting that there is a world beyond Berkeley, especially a political one. I am indebted to all the editors who worked with my essays on Stevens listed in the bibliography. I have to give more elaborate thanks to an audience at Boston University that struggled through my efforts to adapt the semantics of "as" to Stevens (and especially to Bonnie Costello and Will Waters for their support) , to audiences in Oxford, Leuven, and Paris and the Stanford-Berkeley Graduate School Colloquium) for comments on a version of my opening chapter (especially to Reena Saastri, Sascha Bru, Isabelle Alfandary, and Axel Nesme), to Ulla Haselstein for a glorious four months of writing at the Languages of Emotion Cluster for Excellence at the Freie Universität in Berlin (where I was able to renew conversations with Heinz Ickstadt and enter new ones with Hayden White). Peter Potter, my editor at Cornell University Press, was always available and helpful and a master at revising my awkward prose even when he had to communicate bad news. And the staff at the press more than lived up to the high expectations I had developed from working with them in the past.

Finally, I want to mention one important test that this book has already passed: I came out enjoying and appreciating Stevens more than when I began. And if the gods give me luck, he will be important to the next book I write on the concepts of realization, expression, and appreciation. The gods have already given me the immense good luck of having my daughter Laura become a close friend and having been married for the past twenty years to Carolyn Porter. It is simply amazing to me the difference her patience, her love, and her understanding have made in my capacity to experience life as a series of moments to value in large part because she dispels any sense that I live only in a world of fact. The more difficult I make it to be loved, the more striking are the ways she finds to continue and deepen her love. I hope that in this book at least the author can repay that love by showing what it has made possible.

Abbreviations

AD	Jacques Rancière, *Aesthetics and Its Discontents*
BGE	Friedrich Nietzsche, *Beyond Good and Evil*
CPP	Wallace Stevens, *Collected Poetry and Prose*
CV	Ludwig Wittgenstein, *Culture and Value*
Early Stevens	B. J. Leggett, *Early Stevens: The Nietzschean Intertext*
FI	Jacques Rancière, *The Future of the Image*
GB	Ezra Pound, *Gaudier-Brzeska*
LE	Ezra Pound, *Literary Essays of Ezra Pound*
LWS	Wallace Stevens, *The Letters of Wallace Stevens*
Norton	Arnold Matthew, in *The Norton Anthology of English Literature*
PA	Jacques Rancière, *The Politics of Aesthetics*
PI	Ludwig Wittgenstein, *Philosophical Investigations*
TLP	Ludwig Wittgenstein, *Tractatus Logico Philosophicus*

WALLACE STEVENS AND THE DEMANDS OF MODERNITY

CHAPTER 1

Philosophical Poetry and the Demands of Modernity

> We have never understood the world less than we do now nor, as we understand it, liked it less. We never wanted to understand it more or needed to like it more. These are the intense compulsions that challenge the poet as the appreciatory creator of values and beliefs. That, finally, states the problem.
>
> (*LWS* 526)

> We have been a little insane about the truth. We have had an obsession. In its ultimate extension, the truth about which we have been insane will lead us to look beyond the truth to something in which the imagination will be the dominant complement. It is not only that the imagination adheres to reality, but also that reality adheres to the imagination and that the interdependence is essential. . .
>
> (*CPP* 663)

Philosophical poetry is not to everyone's taste. But such poetry can make two major contributions to intellectual life, especially in cultures where philosophy retreats into refined insularity. This poetry can remind us how important philosophical questions about value and meaning and purposiveness can be to those wanting simply to bring intense efforts at comprehension to their own experiences. One need not have professionally defensible answers to these questions in order to enjoy the perspective they create and the experiences they produce. Many of us care a great deal about the affective contours of our own self-reflexive activity and about finding imaginative paths that enable us to feel that we share the ways in which others reflect on their experiences. Then there is the promise of the content the philosophical poet engages. Even though poets typically are not primarily concerned with producing arguments, they constantly test in imagination the consequences of an intellectual world shaped by the arguments of others. For we look to philosophical poets—to Dante, Andrew Marvell, Samuel Taylor Coleridge, and Paul Valéry—to construct speculative situations that articulate and

1

struggle with the consequences of dominant beliefs. We also look to them to extend the world of the lyric by bringing imaginative vitality and multiple rhythmic densities to traditional modes of discursive thinking.

This book reads Wallace Stevens as one of those philosophical poets. But I cannot make this assertion without providing answers to several questions. Why does Wallace Stevens in particular deserve this exalted status (for those who admire philosophy at least)? If one replies that he talks about philosophical issues, one might reply that we then have to wonder whether there is any serious twentieth-century poet who is not in some sense "philosophical"? Louis Zukofsky, the American poet most committed to the concrete music of verse, wrote the fascinating *Bottom: On Shakespeare,* largely devoted to Baruch Spinoza. Yet we also have to wonder there is any modernist poet sufficiently philosophical to deserve that label, as if that poet's work could take on anything like the status we confer on "philosophy" in our culture? Who among the modernists can be trusted to provide the scope or rigor of thought we commonly associate with philosophy?

Perhaps we have to alter our expectations. Perhaps "philosophical" is a term we apply to modern poets not because of their content but because we recognize in their work a certain kind of ambition to take philosophy seriously as a discipline and so as a constraint on the imagination, which also becomes a stimulus for the imagination. From this perspective Stevens might stand alone among the major American modernists, although he takes on substantial affinities with William Butler Yeats, who tried to persuade the philosopher George Moore of the importance of his ideas as ideas. T. S. Eliot and W. H. Auden wanted a transcendental philosophy that could interpret what in poetry could be only figural. Ezra Pound and William Carlos Williams took the opposite position: they had an abiding faith that art could occupy positions capable of transcending philosophy's bondage to prose. Even Stevens never treated his work as a contribution to philosophy. His work was mostly presented as listening to philosophy so as to elaborate two modes of response—developing states in which the poet has space to celebrate the poetry within philosophy and developing states in which poetry could extend philosophy by testing the feelings and the acts of valuing that might accompany the pursuit of certain ideas.

There is little to say on this matter with regard to Stevens that he does not say for himself in his brilliant late lecture, "A Collect of Philosophy." I refer to this lecture on several occasions within this book, so I now simply summarize his general sense of the relation between the two practices in a way that I hope will help withstand certain popular critical attitudes toward

Stevens's interest in philosophy. One major theme in this essay is how the two practices pursue different orientations even as their modes of questioning overlap.

The philosopher tries to secure a particular analysis of facts and structures; the poet, in contrast, to develop the imaginative possibilities for how people might inhabit those facts and structures with a sense of appreciation and commitment:

> It may be said that the philosopher probes the sphere or spheres of perception and that he moves therein like someone intent on making sure of every foot of the way. If the poet moves about in the same sphere . . . he is intent on what he sees and hears and the sense of certainty of the presences about him is as nothing to the presences themselves. The philosopher's native sphere is only a metaphysical one. The poet's native sphere . . . is what he can make of the world.
>
> (CPP 863)

This and related statements make it clear that by this point in his career Stevens was highly suspicious of the epistemic orientation in modern philosophy. It would be foolish to deny that Stevens sometimes talks epistemologically about what is real and what just a fiction. However, he turned increasingly from overt concerns for the truth to issues of the values made possible by various models of philosophical attention. Moreover, even in his earlier work one might argue that he understood "fiction" not quite as "illusion" but as "something made by the mind." So it is misleading to accept the standard assumption in Stevens's criticism, put superbly by Bart Eeckhout:

> Much of Stevens' work is epistemological in orientation. Its central question, in philosophical terms, is that of the knowledge relation between subject and object: How can we know (and, no less important for a poet, describe and represent) the external world around us?[1]

Stevens could not escape addressing the relation to knowledge that pervades our language about subjects and objects: objects anchor subjects in the world, and the lack of such an anchor is felt in various forms of doubt, insecurity, and what Jacques Derrida would call the endless supplementarity of trying constantly to shore up what will pass as accurate description. But one can also worry about subject-object relations in a very different arena—the arena of values. There the danger is not in misunderstanding the subject's roles in perception (as Eeckhout suggests) but in yielding to a misconceived and reductive objectivity. For Stevens, stabilizing those epistemic relations requires the work of the philosopher to make "sure of every foot of the way." Nonetheless, it takes poetry to express how subjects can interact with objects so as to establish "presences" and challenge reductive accounts of value. That is the level of reality that matters for poets as Stevens conceives them. Their aim is to elaborate forms of life that establish modes of valuing continuous with the world philosophers establish.

So I suggest exploring the degree to which Stevens's later poetry turns from epistemically focused philosophical concerns to these questions about values. Then we might at least partially avoid several traps that beset philosophically inclined critics of Stevens's work. Pragmatist readings of Stevens, for example, have little to offer beyond pragmatism's sensitivity to how nineteenth-century thought developed modes of inquiry suited to a culture no longer wedded to picture theories of knowledge. It would be foolish to say that William James and John Dewey were not interested in values. But, tellingly, James anchors this interest in the epistemic language of belief, and Dewey anchors it in what science can posit about values as objects of knowledge. A short quotation from a recent essay expanding Patricia Rae's work provides a practical case in point. Julianne Buchsbaum tries to steer her readers back from Richard Rorty's neopragmatism toward "the American pragmatist belief in the all importance of the empirical real and in the belief that, although we may not ultimately know the empirical real in and of itself, we can by the process of continually revising our beliefs, come to decide what descriptions of it are more satisfactory." She goes on to give a reading of "An Ordinary Evening in New Haven" as fulfilling a "commitment to the pragmatic strategy of re-seeing, testing, and revising its own propositions and of tethering the imagination to descriptions of the empirical real, the ordinary and the actual."[2] There is precious little discussion of the possibility that this poem might be one of Stevens's greatest achievements in articulating the values possible in a particular way of thinking not fundamentally devoted to empirical inquiry.

Buchsbaum's claims are not false. They are simply not very generative because a secular modernist poetry seems to have no choice but to be provisional and bound to constant revision. In addition, these claims misplace what matters in the poet's efforts to attach the imagination to the eye without subordinating it to "the eye's plain version" as "a thing apart" (*CPP* 397). Yet pragmatist critics repeat them because their primary focus has been countering the success of deconstruction. They are right about pragmatism as a useful alternative to deconstruction. Yet Stevens would have been amused by the irony that deconstruction gets its philosophical force primarily for its skeptical version of almost the exact same epistemological considerations governing pragmatist readings. "Constant revising of its own propositions" becomes the recognition that "the ex-centricity of the writer . . . produces an instability; it disrupts our thinking of the chain of substitutions or orderly movement of centers."[3] Deconstruction is primarily concerned with ontology as it continues forms of inquiry developed by Martin Heidegger, but the foundation for the ontology is a skeptical epistemology.[4] Because language has no anchor in the world and because presence is always subject to difference and deferral, philosophy has to move from the pathos of epistemology to the cruel yet liberating lucidity of shifting our ontology from the search for foundations to the acceptance of groundlessness. (What might be called late deconstruction then grounds an ethics of letting be on the basis of this ontology.)

At best pragmatist and deconstructive criticism can be interesting about particular poems by Stevens, but neither can capture the spirit of his commitment to philosophy. That would require changing the question from "what does it take to know the world?" to "what difference does it make for our sense of the world to be concerned with knowing it in particular ways?" Furthermore, changing the question would probably involve a very different way of approaching Stevens's career. This leads to a second basic consequence of my taking seriously his understanding of the poet's relation to philosophy in "A Collect of Philosophy." Typically criticism that centers around Stevens and philosophy stakes out a particular thinker and shows how that thinker applies to what is usually a given period in Stevens's career. (Or, worse, Stevens's career is telescoped into the ideas of a particular philosopher.) But even the title "A Collect of Philosophy" indicates that at least in 1951 Stevens was simply not interested in writing poetry under the auspices of any commitments to particular bodies of philosophical work or school of thought. And if one reads Stevens under the auspices of any particular thinker, one has to recognize how often he modifies his guiding concerns. (Robert Leggett is one rare critic who honors this by concentrating on the role Nietzsche's thinking plays specifically in *Harmonium*.) For me the thrill of reading Stevens's relation to philosophy is engaging in the way his own constant self-questioning leads him to modify his own views.

I was going to structure this book in terms of relations I could construct between Stevens and four philosophers—Friedrich Nietzsche, G. W. F. Hegel, Edmund Husserl, and Ludwig Wittgenstein. However, I reread "A Collect of Philosophy" and decided that if we want to get as close as possible to Stevens's thinking and affective investment in relations between poetry and philosophy, we have to alter our approach. We have to shift from questions about what Stevens believed or how his poems want to affect our beliefs to questions about what poetry can do to intensify those mental activities that might be sponsored by an interest in philosophical reflection. Only then we will put ourselves in a position to appreciate the kinds of values that this thinking both establishes and enables.

The quest for truth demands belief. For Stevens, though, poetry manages most fully to engage such philosophical questioning by putting imagination to work on what various affective registers within philosophy might entail or involve. He presents himself as a poet who is on a quest to find what is humanly capable in various thinkers or in his own loosely philosophical analyses of the issues involved in particular situations. For example, he praises Plato for defining the idea of Idea. Then he can suggest that Neoplatonic poetry shows what difference that definition can produce when shaping our accounts of desire. That in turn allows the poet to develop concepts like the Platonic notion of "participation" to make it fit contemporary experience without having to worry about what one has to take on to become a Platonist. Accordingly I make participation a central motif in this book without worrying about its Platonic heritage.

Stevens's mode of addressing ideas allows a perspective that few philosophical critics except the deconstructionists honor (and they honor a very limited version of it.) I refer to concerns about how an interest in philosophy might sponsor interests in matters of style. One can ask how style works in philosophical texts, and one can ask how poetry can best develop stylistic modes that can take on the work of complementing philosophical reflection. I argue that ultimately Stevens had to find a style that could honor what it meant for the mind to live continually in the sense of change and variation honored by both pragmatism and deconstruction. However that style would not just embody a version of epistemology. It would become a self-conscious medium by which to reflect on and demonstrate the values involved in thinking when it comes to distrust description, proposition, and system. Ironically, the fact that so few philosophical critics attend to style tempts me to think that, from one perspective at least, the best philosophical critics of Stevens may be Helen Vendler and George Lensing. Both critics almost completely distrust philosophical argument but pay close attention to Stevens's passions even as they turn to the domain of ideas.[5] They also care about style, which ultimately is what the poet can bring to the work of appreciating what philosophy makes it possible to see.

I

This book tries to show how intelligently and complexly the poetry of Wallace Stevens makes a distinctive contribution to the lineage of significant philosophical poets in the West. He offers one of our richest demonstrations of the pressures that Enlightenment attitudes impose on our ways of thinking, especially on our ways of formulating values that will not seem outdated or evasive of the powers of science. In addition, he fosters modes of pleasure that are themselves explorations of what powers we can still take as distinctively human even as he demonstrates for us the need to develop third-person distance from our fantasies that the world will honor or should honor those powers. The question of what capacities humans have to establish values becomes inseparable from the question of what powers poetry has to convert lyric utterance into modes of intensifying experience in domains of mind inseparable from our sense of the world. I explore the concrete working of those powers because this working presents demands for close reading of Stevens's visions and revisions of how it might be possible to align the imagination with a world of fact.[6]

Although Stevens does not offer arguments, and critics probably ought not construct conceptual arguments out of his work, I will emphasize how his poetry develops auras of significance made possible by the arguments of professional philosophers. Stevens gives a pulse to philosophical thinking not only through the literal pulse of his elegant rhythms but also by inviting his audience to share the pleasure and the excitement of states in which we momentarily resolve tensions or manage to change our angle of vision. Then values emerge as small ecstasies where managing to correlate mind and world affords charged moments in which one feels at home in imaginative activity.[7] Stevens's richest statement of his vision is again in "A Collect of Philosophy": "the habit of forming concepts unites" poets and philosophers; "the use to which they put these ideas separates them":

> The habit of forming concepts is a habit of the mind by which it probes for an integration. . . . We must . . . go a step farther and look for the respect that separates the poet and the philosopher in the kind of integrations for which they search. The philosopher searches for an integration for its own sake [i.e., for its truth value] . . . ; the poet searches for an integration that will not so much be sufficient in itself as sufficient for some quality that it possesses, such as its insight, its evocative power or its appearance in the eye of the imagination. . . .
> The philosopher probes the spheres of perception and he moves about

therein like someone intent on making sure of every foot of the way. . . .
[The poet] is intent on what he sees and hears[,] and the sense of the
certainty of the presences about him is as nothing to the presences
themselves. . . . The poet's native sphere is what he can make of the
world.

(*CPP* 862)

II

My primary intent in this introductory chapter is to place Stevens's efforts
to develop a philosophical poetry within an overall modernist sense of crisis, with its accompanying aspirations that poetry can in fact change the spiritual climate. The crisis was how to establish the place of value in a world of
fact. At stake was human comfort with its efforts to establish values, given
the strong prospect that they might be simple fictions making self-interest.
At stake, too, then, were assumptions about the powers of poetry to participate in these valuations even though philosophers and scientists thought they
had to separate observation sentences from unstable and ungrounded projections of subjectivity.

There were many different formulations of this tension between facts
based on unequivocal propositions and values that could at best be mere
feeling or opinion. In my view Wittgenstein's *Tractatus* offers the most succinct rendering of that tension: "The sense of the world must lie outside the
world. In the world everything is as it is, and everything happens as it does
happen: *in* it no value exists—and if it did it would not have value" (*TLP*
6.41). Others, quintessentially A. J. Ayer, whom Stevens read carefully, had
somewhat different formulations of how value and fact simply occupied
two different and incompatible discursive worlds. However, for my work
the specific formulations of this belief by philosophers matter less than the
simple currency of various versions of this position among intellectuals.[8] In
contrast, Stevens's changing orientations toward this tension will matter a
great deal. I am especially interested in the Stevens who eventually understood this problem as a means for developing fundamental differences between the tasks of philosophers and of poets: "The philosopher's world
is intended to be a world which yet remains to be discovered," while the
poet's world is intended to be a world which yet remains to be celebrated"
(*CPP* 864). On the basis of these distinctions he was able to imagine that in
the poetry of Valéry the ultimate significance of poetry is to serve as the
realization of the excitement of meaning "as it is revealed at once in thought

and in act" (CPP 892). The experience of meaningful states of intense participation in the world can offer a direct response to the philosopher's tendency to make meaning a matter of propositions that have to be verified in an
objective world. For Stevens's later work, value is not something built on fact
but a condition of awareness of what sensibility can establish while being respectful of the constraints basic to empiricist thinking (see CPP 867).

A poem's version of meaningfulness depends on its capacities to link attitudes toward the perceived world and toward how we manage self-
consciousness about our powers to characterize perceptions. So my focus in
Wallace Stevens and the Demands of Modernity: Toward a Phenomenology of Value
is on how Stevens makes self-reflexive the experience of valuing aspects of
the world (or the self in the world) by developing modulations of feeling
that eventually produce intricate constellations among related states of mind.
In order to elaborate this modulation I embrace the most elemental definition of phenomenology. There are many variants of phenomenological
methods. But I think we can isolate three traits of this approach to philosophy that are shared by these variants. First, phenomenology is presupposi-
tionless: it tries to avoid explanations of how the world is and therefore can
also avoid taking positions on a host of philosophical questions. Instead of
arguments it proposes to exhaust itself in a description of how consciousness
comes to appear as it participates in or constitutes various elemental states of
awareness.[9] Thus there can be a phenomenology of time-consciousness or
of intentionality or of anxiety. Finally, the goal of phenomenology is not
explanation or argument but changes in the direction of self-reflection so
that one can articulate how certain mental states come into being. This
ideal ,in turn generates the fundamental differences in phenomenological
method: Does it pursue the empirical self as it reflects on these fundamental
modes of being, or does it seek a transcendental position by which we see
how states available to everyone appear because of a disciplinary commitment to achieving more fundamental states of reflection than a differenti-
ated ego can engage?[10] For me then the crucial significance of phenomenology
is that it can claim to attend to values as they emerge in these states of mind.

This sense of how Stevens elaborates a phenomenological perspective on
experience requires our insisting on the importance to Stevens of his frequent critiques of the romantic tendency to put desire before fact. But we
also have to resist the temptation to let ourselves be consumed by the need
for skepticism about these romantic tendencies. Relying on imagination
does not entail simply dealing with fictions. Rather, imagination becomes
for Stevens after Harmonium a power enabling us to align our desires to everything that must remain as it is:

I am a native in this world
And think in it as a native thinks,

Gesu, not a native of a mind
Thinking the thoughts I call my own,

Native, a native in the world
And like a native think in it.

(CPP 147–48)

To think like a native (not just to live like a native) demands that any poetry eager to be modern face two basic crises. First is what we might call the crisis at the origin, virtually demanding that the poets make new not only their sense of the lyric but also their sense of what cultural work the lyric can perform. If there is not a clear path from fact to value, poetry itself has to rethink its possible social roles. So we will have to attend carefully to the major directions of inquiry by which modernist poets faced this problem. Then we should be able to flesh out more fully why it matters that Stevens be able to project a plausible state where one can feel a native in the world and, more important, feel that status earns the possibility that thinking need not stop with the satisfactions of providing accounts of states of affairs. Rather, it can focus on eliciting the many senses of what it means to dwell in this native condition and so be in a position to reflect on its roles in attributing value to what emerges. The section of "The Man with a Blue Guitar" from which I have just quoted ends this way:

Here I inhale profounder strength
And as I am, I speak and move

And things are as I think they are
And say they are on the blue guitar.

(CPP 148)

The imagination's task is to unfold the many layers composed by the power of this situated "as" to produce equivalences between the productive and receptive aspects of what we experience; then the imagination can also try to embody a sense of what we can share by virtue of its powers of composition. In Stevens's terms, the theory of poetry must be tested by the theory of life, and the theory of life must be tested by the kinds of poetry it might legitimate.

Then there is a more figurative and projective sense of crisis involving what a poet's readers can make of the work in relation to how what demanded modernist innovations now affects their culture. Can poetry's bearing witness to history also shape emergent possibilities for how imaginations might conduct themselves in the future? I find Stevens providing for me a phenomenological stance by which to formulate alternatives to the various ways that moral thinking or practical public policy drive our academic discourse about values—if only because such discourse is woefully inattentive to the possible consequences of elaborating the "intricate evasions of as" (CPP 415). So I argue that Stevens's poetry managed to address the specific historical form of the crisis of relating value to fact in such a way as to deserve to influence contemporary discussions of that issue.[11]

For now I reserve generalizations until sufficient context has been produced and turn instead to the pleasurable task of trying to represent how Stevens's philosophical poetry explores feelings surrounding issues of valuation. I have chosen "The Latest Freed Man" (1938) because this poem offers one of his earlier and most directly discursive efforts to face what he saw as the dangers inherent in the then dominant positivist isolation of facts from values. It also matters that this poem is not entirely successful in grappling with the problems posed by positivism. The problems plaguing this poem indicate how Stevens will have to keep modifying his central tension between what ideas can claim and the specific conditions of experience positioning readers through their participation in the movements of the poem:

> Tired of the old descriptions of the world
> The latest freed man rose at six, and sat
> At the edge of his bed. He said,
>   "I suppose there is
> A doctrine to this landscape. Yet having just
> Escaped from the truth, the morning is color and mist,
> Which is enough: the moment's rain and sea,
> The moment's sun (the strong man vaguely seen),
> Overtaking the doctrine of this landscape. Of him
> And of his works I am sure. He bathes in the mist
> Like a man without a doctrine. The light he gives—
> It is how he gives his light. It is how he shines,
> Rising upon the doctors in their beds
> And on their beds.
>
>   (CPP 187)

This opening for the poem is manifestly the cry of its occasion, the cry of a mind balancing skepticism about the speaker's own accomplishments (because he is aware that his formulations offer only the latest of a string of postures) with an intense celebration of what it means to be free from having to anchor one's values and passions in the descriptions and propositions that must justify them. There are values that need not and cannot be justified except by the felt relationship to the world they offer. At one pole these felt relationships are established simply by how the poetry renders the emergence of the details to which it attends. At the other pole, a sense of value resides in the acts of figuration that posit ideal metaphoric significance for the encounter. The gathering takes place through how the sunlight emerges to pervade details of the scene, eventually composing an expanding constellation of related manners of involvement that emerge with the light. Light establishes the "how" of practical knowledge. But the mind processing that light also wants something more than subsuming particulars into concepts or testing the validity of those concepts. "How" is also a qualitative term. "The moment's sun" proves inseparable from what seems an older archaeological level of the text, where it still tries to align the bare sun with metaphorical echoes that offer a figure of background human presences.

Stevens offers an analogy of the sun with a "strong man" even as he qualifies the metaphor of distinctive human power to concentrate on the celebration of sheer presence. The poem subsumes sun and human figure into one giver of light that is at once dependent on figural meaning and free of anything but the production of a liberated presence. Overcoming modern philosophy's reliance on description is not easy, especially when poetry has so much figural baggage that derives from trying to satisfy outmoded romantic criteria for seeing values in facts. Part of Stevens's greatness is his recognizing how difficult it is to establish any philosophical credence for poetry, given the need to purify itself of this figural baggage while remaining faithful to something that gives confidence about its own powers, if only to register in subtle fashion the persistence of desire along with its problematic dependencies. Another feature of his greatness is how fully he can marshal the resources of rhythm and diction and timing to make present conditions of desire that are almost but not quite sufficient indices that the focused energy of the quest is all but a guarantee of its success.

We need now to listen to how the rest of the poem raises the rhetorical stakes until it almost succeeds in replacing ideals of description with what we might call "conditions of encounter." This focus on how states emerge promises both a sense of one's own freedom and an opportunity to identify with sheer self-exulting power. Yet at its final moment the poem seems to realize that these idealized conditions of encounter cannot provide a sufficient ending, at least in relation to traditional expectations of endings as satisfying conclusions to a sequence of investments in imaginative thinking:

And so the freed man said.
It was how the sun came shining into his room:
To be without a description of to be,
For a moment on rising, at the edge of the bed, to be.
To have the ant of the self changed to an ox
With its organic boomings, to be changed
From a doctor into an ox, before standing up,
To know that the change, and that the ox-like struggle
Come from the strength that is the strength of the sun,
Whether it comes directly or from the sun.
It was how he was free. It was how his freedom came.
It was being without description, being an ox.
It was the importance of the trees outdoors,
The freshness of the oak-leaves, not so much
That they were oak leaves, as the way they looked.
It was everything being more real, himself
At the center of reality, seeing it.
It was everything bulging and blazing, and big in itself,
The blue of the rug, the portrait of Vidal,
Qui fait fi des joliesses banales, the chairs.

(CPP 187)

I claim this is philosophical poetry not because it is shaped by a version of argument (which it is) but because it is intent on having the text produce affects elicited by this argument so that the affects themselves become crucial aspects of the text's claims to relevance in the world. Here these affects become so critical that they can be said actually to constitute the states of value in question—preeminently in the contrast between the "ant of the self" and "being an ox." Ultimately questions about manner and the "how" of states of affairs become inseparable from the focus on how poetry composes and rewards our attention. But Stevens was not yet ready to trust this shift in sensibility. The mind here seem not entirely satisfied by these gestures of its own making. The title forces us to come to terms with the ironic possibility that this speaker is as deluded in his visions of possibility as his precursors were in their visions of freedom. Moreover, the focusing on the "joliesses banales" may make the point too well—do we really want attention to how light hits the chairs to replace the culture's obsession with truth? However, this irony is less a means of dismissing the overall claims of the poem than of qualifying them. If one recognizes that this may be another myth, one might be freer to focus on the specific values this shift in sensibility affords. It also might be worth risking banality to have a vital sense of participation in the sensual world. At the least one can say that such questioning dialectically requires Stevens's next volume. There the title "Parts of a World" indicates how the imagination will have to explore all the resources of the grammar of "part" and "participation" in an effort to better balance the claims of "man" and the claims of "manner."

III

In attempting to appreciate Stevens's efforts as a philosophical poet it is obviously helpful to recognize the degree to which he participates in a shared sense of the demands placed on poets eager to represent modern possibilities for their art. Then we can worry about specifying what makes his contribution distinctive. In this case I concentrate on what the writers inherited as the dominant attitudes toward the place of poetry in articulating values. Then I rely on Ezra Pound to exemplify how the modernists thought they could provide a very different model of the values a modern poetry could make available for its culture. Eventually we will see how Pound provides a very useful contrast to Stevens. But first we have to work through the four parts to my sketch—a treatment of how value for the romantics was conceived as an extension of fact and hence a fulfillment of epistemic culture rather than a challenge to its authority, some examples of how the slippage between fact and value proved devastating within Victorian efforts to use lyric for philosophical reflection, the contrast Pound established to that past, and an analysis of how Pound's relation to Nietzsche shows how Nietzsche's nonepistemic way of discussing value had significant parallels in modernist poetry. As Pound said of related matters, these historical elements "move together, though they do not, of course, move in step" (GB 85).[12]

Few would quarrel with a description of romantic poetry as fundamentally concerned with what we can feel in relation to coming to know how various features of the world emerge in their actual plenitude. The act of valuing consists primarily in recognizing the fit between what can be known and how that knowledge guides feeling. For a simple example consider these lines from William Wordsworth's sonnet "Composed upon Westminster Bridge, September 3, 1802":

> This city now doth, like a garment, wear
> The beauty of the morning; silent, bare . . .
> Never did sun more beautifully steep

In his first splendor, valley, rock, or hill;
Ne'er saw I, never felt, a calm so deep!
The river glideth at his own sweet will
Dear God! the very houses seem asleep;
And all that mighty heart is lying still!

(285 4–5, 9–14)

Wordsworth's imagination weaves itself into a description of details so that its presence becomes increasingly eloquent as it expands its capacity for discovering the general within the particular. Here the central movement is from the simile of the first line, attaching imagination to fact, to the rich blend of metaphor and symbol afforded by the projection of "heart" onto the scene. And this is complemented by the work performed by the negatives in the poem in order to establish how much the subject can bring to the world as the extension of its sense of accord.[13]

Wordsworth's sense of fitting knowledge to feeling becomes more dramatic and more philosophically suggestive as he confronts a moment when that sense of fit seems irreparably sundered. I refer to the famous passage in the *Prelude* (most dramatically in the 1850 version) when he realizes that he has already crossed the Alps so that his dreams of a sublime continuity with nature at its most exalted have failed to materialize.[14] This moment dramatically calls attention to how deeply Wordsworth assumes that imagination is fitted to fact. Lost and still hoping for every dimension of ascent, Wordsworth records his asking a peasant who informed him his path now had to be a descent:

And, that our future course, all plain to sight,
Was downwards, with the current of that stream.
Loth to believe what we so grieved to hear,
For we still had hopes that pointed to the clouds . . .

(Book VI, n585–88)

How that "all plain to sight" must have been a torment! The next twenty-five lines present a strange hymn to imagination as it works itself free from the character who in his actual situation feels completely lost:

Imagination—here the power so called
Through sad incompetence of human speech,
That awful power rose from the mind's abyss
Like an unfathered vapour that enwraps,
At once some lonely traveler.

(591–95)

For Wordsworth, though, the descent from the high pass proves a dialectical means of recovering the world of fact (the fathered world of fact) and making it suffice as the space for providing new access to the sublime without the emergence of allegory until the very end of the passage. Each renewal of attention becomes an intensification of the imaginative significance that the details can bear. That "slow pace" seems inseparable from how the world rewards the meditative state it spawns:

> The melancholy slackening that ensued
> Upon those tidings by the peasant given
> Was soon dislodged. Downwards we hurried fast . . .
> The brook and road
> Were fellow-travellers in this gloomy strait,
> And with them did we journey several hours
> At a slow pace. The immeasurable height
> Of woods decaying, never to be decayed,
> The stationary blasts of waterfalls . . .
> Tumult and peace, the darkness and the light—
> Were all like workings of one mind, the features
> Of the same face, blossoms upon one tree;
> Characters of the great Apocalypse,
> The types and symbols of Eternity,
> Of first, and last, and midst, and without end.
>
> *(619–40)*

Being forced to confront fact provides for Wordsworth an even richer basis for approaching the sublime—this time not as contrast between flesh and spirit but as their absolute coexistence.

No such coexistence was possible for Matthew Arnold. He uses the assumption that his readers have read Wordsworth as an economical and telling means of measuring his sense of the pathos of Victorian culture. In his view the Victorians had to look back if they were to find any positive belief in imaginative values. But they could never conceal the fact that this way committed them to illusion. Perhaps his most despondent rendering of that situation occurs toward the conclusion of "The Scholar Gypsy." At first Arnold's speaker imagines including the gypsy within his world, as Wordsworth found ways of including marginal figures like his leech gatherer, who threatens initially to divorce nature from culture. But when the speaker reflects further on his world—with the ascendance of positivism, the transparent proliferation of capitalist wills to power, and the domination of mob rule in the name of democracy—he decides that the only self-respecting option is to encourage that figure on the margins to flee any further contamination by the speaker's social context. For Arnold these descriptions of his world simply will not evoke any penumbra of values that will appeal to the imagination. Both the natural and the social worlds could offer only mockeries of what once had been a world that opened continually into something like spiritual presences:

> But fly our paths, our feverish contact fly!
> For strong the infection of our mental strife,
> Which though it gives no bliss, yet spoils for rest;
> And we should win thee from thy old fair life,
> Like us distracted and like us unblest.
> Soon, soon thy cheer would die . . .
> *(Norton 1367, 221–26)*[15]

The speaker imagines being "unblest" because there is nothing to sustain "cheer." In his world, description has conquered. But the Victorians still had a way to compose a sense of value, one that plays perhaps the most important role in how my story about Stevens will come into the present. If one cannot find value linked to description, one can establish values by going directly to the source. One can find value in one's own capacity to love other people or, lacking that, to externalize the desire to treat others with the sympathy and the decency that one feels entitled to receive from them. Lacking grounds for one's feelings in nature, one can examine one's own capacities to make moral judgments. However, these hard-won moral commitments then have a tendency to take up the entire domain of values. Look again at how the quoted passage from Arnold cultivates a bleak honesty whose only justification can be how it maintains the speaker's dignity even as he despairs of adapting that dignity to anything that will alter the prevailing bleakness. It is as if a general morality had to be invented to domesticate and dignify what Wordsworth saw as the awful unfathered power of imagination. But this morality born in bleakness can feed only on itself since it banishes everything else to the domain of illusion or confusion. It is the moralizers themselves who seem to invite Nietzsche's pleas for an extramoral sense of the world.

I would worry that I was overgeneralizing were I not about to cite a passage from "Dover Beach," the locus classicus for Victorian desperation to find within bleakness some alternative to despair. I hope my contrasts with Wordsworth will help restore these all-too-familiar lines to the full power of an eloquence generated by careful attention to social context:

The Sea of Faith
Was once, too, at the full, and round earth's shore
Lay like the folds of a bright girdle furled.
But now I only hear
Its melancholy, long, withdrawing roar,
Retreating, to the breath
Of the Night Wind, down the vast edges drear
And naked shingles of the world.

(Norton 1368, 21–28)

I think this sounding of melancholy counts as substantial philosophical poetry. The scene seems to absorb the human into this elegant overture of
interlocking vowels that in turn seem to constitute all that can appeal to
human consciousness in the experience of how faith withdraws. And that
withdrawal—of nature as well as faith—intensifies the fear of loneliness
that is nakedly the only possible reason that the speaker can even dream that
the man and woman might be willing to try to love one another. In other
contexts Arnold replaces love by dreams of moral commitment to "the best
that has been thought and said." But the need to adapt directly such models
drains the pleasure from the seeing and the thinking, leaving it largely an
empty imperative, so needy that it is deprived of the very authority Arnold
so desperately wants.[16]

IV

Modernism has its echoes of Victorian self-patheticizing bleakness: one
needs only to think about *The Waste Land*. Eliot's text renders intensely the
pressure of a Victorian heritage suspicious of the possibility that the domain
of value is substantially larger and more capacious than the domain of the
moral. But now I cannot pursue Eliot because I suspect that his intense
Christian resolution to the problem of embodying values in fact is more
part of the problem than part of any workable imaginative change in our
relation to our world. Eliot must be useful here primarily as a contrast to the
very different case of Nietzsche's timeliness. I want to sound various notes
of Nietzsche's reflections on values because he gave modernist writers at
least a diagnosis of their situation: so long as reason had to be separated from
human capacities for creativity, the world would seem a bleak site reduced
to market values on the one hand and an increasingly strident and impotent
moralism on the other.

Nietzsche was not the only thinker attempting to reorient the way that art can present and mediate compelling values by challenging claims that values should be based on facts. Henri Bergson and Martin Heidegger resist the idea that facts can be independent of values in the first place. William James, John Dewey, and F. H. Bradley all stress the domain of prior and projective human actions that give values a useful place within cultural frameworks. However, only Nietzsche, I believe, fully sponsors the spirit of combat and the quest for the ecstatic that becomes possible when we see Victorian laments about the divorce between fact and value as terrifying failures to respect human powers to create values or dwell in value-laden contexts. This indeed is why he has such visible affinities with the poets. And this is why these affinities do not require careful attention to his specific arguments. The striking feature to me is how thoroughly the popular Nietzsche, the figure of cultural revolution, is the one echoed in the poetry and also at times transfigured by that poetry. Nietzsche provides one basic path for interpreting the poets' senses of their historical situation. He also helps readers to understand why these poets had to take critical stances toward the process by which ideals of morality had come to dominate what the culture sought from philosophical attitudes. By affording those perspectives, Nietzsche also helps makes clear the continuing importance of what the poets were trying to achieve since in my view the greatest threats now to what art can do for society derive not from those who reject imagination for facts but from those who align imagination with the questions that obsessed the spirit of Victorian moralism.[17]

Nietzsche's role as exemplar for the modern poets can be best elaborated by assembling three of his major themes. All the ladders start in Nietzsche's acute and compelling critique of the epistemic culture that had dominated Western intellectual life since the Enlightenment. He made clear that the philosophical practice of concentrating on how facts might carry truth value did not so much celebrate the mind's analytic powers as threaten to impoverish experience by reducing it to the endless observation and testing of largely isolated phenomena. Then on this basis he could suggest a philosophical approach to art whose significance is still rarely discussed: there could be an aestheticism that was not at all beholden to formalism. Nietzsche's emphasis on the aesthetic does not address the shape of the aesthetic object per se but concentrates instead on the work the object does in fostering appreciation for various existential conditions. Third, this constellation of critique with the celebration of multiple modes of experiencing values made it possible to propose a withering account of how morality had become the sole philosophical guardian of the place of value in the world. Or, to put this case in a more Nietzschean spirit, he skewered the processes

Victorians used to evade their shame by cultivating the importance of moral identities while surrendering to positivist views of the world—ironically thereby making the pursuit of such identities complicit in the culture's impending surrender to nihilism.

Let me say just a few words about each of these topics because they also dramatize more inchoate concerns among modernist writers. Nietzsche's critique of epistemic culture concentrates on two main points. First, philosophical approval for the cultivation of truth values based on practices of representation had left Europe on the brink of total nihilism because it had given authority to empiricism's strength—its capacity to secure objective and unequivocal descriptive terms. For Nietzsche that meant the return of Christian asceticism in empiricist guise:

> They [philosophers] all pose as if they had discovered and reached their real opinions through the self-development of a cold, pure, divinely unconcerned dialectic . . . ; while at bottom it is an assumption, a hunch, indeed a kind of "inspiration"—most often a desire of the heart that has been filtered and made abstract—that they defend with reasons they have sought after the fact.
>
> (*BGE*, sec. 5)

In his view empiricist thinking ignored both the interests that generated our representations and the struggles for power constituted by those representations. Observation is under the control of the will, perhaps especially when it hides itself as objective and so need not take responsibility for the specificity of its interventions. Moreover, the cult of observation and description makes valuation seem marginal: the force of empiricist descriptions depends on the role static observations play in a practice rather than on the specific satisfactions of will and intelligence that they are capable of displaying. There is no sense in these descriptions of "physiological demands for a certain type of life" (*BGE*, sec. 3) and so no way to register the kind of nobility that "experiences itself as determining values; it does not need approval; it judges . . . It knows itself to be that which first accords honor to things; it is *value-creating.* Everything it knows, as part of itself, it honors" (*BGE*, sec. 260).

The role of the arts is to make manifest our capacities for such creation. Rather than describe or represent phenomena, the primary task of art is to "realize" states of being by eliciting what power these states can offer for the sensibilities that engage them. So making must take priority over interpreting, and the concern for what can be willed as engaged inspiration for conditions of making replaces the concern for how willing might be justified by knowing.[18] The primary question for an art released from what Jacques? Rancière calls "the regime of representation" becomes not whether a statement is true but whether the energies of its making can be exemplary and can specify domains where particular stances become valuable for what they bring to the world. The emphasis on individual making might become a theater for displaying the possible capacities of the individual will.

Nietzsche elaborated how the will in art could work primarily by adapting Kant's arguments about the purposiveness of the art object. But he transformed that picture of purposiveness so that the primary role is not producing objects that supplement knowledge but rather producing powerful images of what the psyche might become in any process of creating values. Both Stevens and Nietzsche came to think that nobility might depend simply on the self's coming to treat "everything it knows as part of itself" (BGE, sec. 260). Then this gathering allows the maker to experience the power to "become who one is": The individual artist is "obliged to give himself laws and to develop his own arts and wiles for self-preservation, self-enhancement, self-redemption" (BGE, sec. 262). The actions of such individuals might even be capable of rebuilding an aristocratic culture that philosophy had been trying to destroy for two thousand years:

> Every artist knows how far from any feeling of letting himself go his most "natural" state is—the free ordering, placing, disposing, giving form in the moment of "inspiration"—and how strictly and subtly he obeys thousandfold laws precisely then, laws that precisely on account of their hardness and determination defy all formulation through concepts (even the firmest concept is, compared with them, not free of fluctuation, multiplicity, ambiguity).
>
> (BGE, sec. 188)[19]

For modernist artists and writers the most significant aspect of this view of the arts was the position it encouraged them to take toward the residues of Victorian moralism still dominant in their culture. Nietzsche's link of empiricism with nihilism made necessary radical changes in attitude. To the extent that morality was based on self-denial or even on empathy with suffering, it seemed a paramount triumph of that same Christian asceticism shaping the values of science, but in another, even more egregious guise because it poisoned the dynamics of everyday life. Moreover, the more one can free aestheticism from formalism (and hence from disinterest), the better it can be separated from even the notion of formal rules to allow full engagement in the work of realization.

Nietzsche's critique of his culture's reliance on morality as its model for values begins at the most elemental level:

> The existence of the world is justified only as an aesthetic phenome-non. . . . Nothing could be more opposed to the purely aesthetic in-terpretation and justification of the world which are taught in this book than the Christian teaching, which is, and wants to be, only moral and which relegates art, every art, to the realm of lies.
>
> (Nietzsche, The Birth of Tragedy, sec. 5.)

For Nietzsche the "ethical" is wrong from the start. It entails separating human life into domains like ethics and aesthetics, which then must posit some external criterion that has the authority to make such divisions. In addition, ethics must explain how an analogous external authority usually attributed to reason or to inner law can take priority over the individual's specific valuations in particular circumstances. In contrast, if value resides primarily in how agents become or realize who they are, the domain of the moral can only haunt the expressive as its negation, as a mark that the indi-vidual has conformed to some version of the pressure of the general and subsumed action into making a copy of something:

> Man, a manifold, mendacious, artificial, and opaque animal, uncanny to the other animals less because of his strength than because of his cunning and shrewdness, has invented the good consciousness to en-joy his soul for once as simple. The whole of morality is a long undis-mayed forgery which alone makes it at all possible to enjoy the sight of the soul. From this point of view much more may belong in the concept of "art" than is generally believed.
>
> (BGE, sec. 219)

Morality is forgery because it claims authenticity while reducing the respon-siveness of an individual to some category sustained by impersonal reason. There is only attuning the self to the idea rather than to the situation.[20] The entire domain of expression, then, for Nietzsche must be conceived as the antithesis to the nihilism inherent in binding the self to models of generaliza-tion that are built on ideals of truth. If, on the other hand, we recognize that value resides in an individual's expressive acts, we can appreciate how "much more may belong in the concept of 'art' than is generally believed." Art for Nietzsche does not simply register conditions characterized by a multiplic-ity of sensual registers cut free from conceptual controls. Rather, art uses that fluidity and multiplicity to allow for the possibility that one can fold many of the fundamental concerns of traditional moral thinking within ideals of self-expression because both responsibility and giving rules to the self are still necessary—but on the basis of immediate relations to the forces at play in situations rather than to general concepts that he thinks fraudulently evade individual responsibility. Art is not an escape from the moral but the vehicle by which expression enters into mortal combat with morality to determine what the ultimate models of valuation will become.[21]

V

Modernist poetry would probably have taken pretty much the same shape if Nietzsche had not existed. But with eyes trained by Nietzsche's sense of cultural crisis it is much easier to see what was at stake for the modernist poets. Obviously one of the primary stakes was to reject everything that smacked of romanticism. And while we have good accounts of various aspects of those rejections, I think we do not have a very good account of the underlying logic that called for these rejections. But my brief account of Wordsworth suggests one way to approach that underlying logic. Romanticism sought to cultivate the range of emotional states that Enlightenment thinking considered impractical and mostly ephemeral because they insisted on cultivating individual powers rather than securing social solidarity. Nonetheless, the romantics (with the obvious exception of Blake) for the most part remained committed to the very Enlightenment empiricism that they were also trying to temper. Romantic affective intensities remained bound to epistemic judgments so that lyric values could be considered extensions of how knowledge could stage the world. Then when epistemology became more strictly positivist, lyric sensibility was cut off from any anchor in fact. It was abandoned to the Scylla of Tennysonian fantasy and the Charybdis of Arnoldian despondency.

Now look at what Ezra Pound accomplishes in his best imagist poems, without Nietzschean overstatement or corresponding mixtures of self-irony and self-pity:

April

Nympharum membra disjecta

Three spirits came to me
And drew me apart

To where the olive boughs
Lay stripped upon the ground:
Pale carnage beneath bright mist.

(92)

I am fascinated by the distribution of sounds in the closing line. The passage moves from stressing the *a* sound to the long *i* of the closing, mediated by the alliteration with *b*. But the emphasis throughout the poem on woven sound effects also suggests a major philosophical shift noticed by Hugh Kenner in his magisterial *The Pound Era* (although Kenner had way too much taste and suspiciousness of abstract language to make the assertions I make).[22] These sound effects are not products of the rhetorical eloquence cultivated by Wordsworth. They do not seem to intensify as the speaker's consciousness grows more comfortable and vital within the world given by the senses. Rather, sound patterns are insistently constructs, figures of authorial will from the start and not based on naturalized versions of intensity. Furthermore, this sense of change is even more striking in how the poem actually deals with objects of the senses. Why does it take spirits to lead the speaker to the vision of "pale carnage beneath bright mists"? Perhaps the poem is less interested in "carnage" as a visual figure than an aural one. Perhaps the poet has to expand ordinary seeing in order to appreciate poetic space as something that does not emerge only from intensified perception but instead is a kind of spiritual gift given by the discovery of what *le mot juste* can actually afford perception.

Let me make the same observations in more pretentious language—after all we are talking about one of the most ambitious writers about writing to emerge in English literature. Where is fact and where value in this poem? If the value here does not derive from the speaker's investment in fact, where does it come from? Why might epistemology have become an inadequate model for what poetry depends on to have its effects in the world? We could say simply that Pound wants to call attention to how art is a distinctive mode of composing that does not so much emerge from experience as make experience worthy of attention for the three spirits. (And in so doing he could make concrete sense of Nietzsche's claim that from the point of view of the critic of morality "much more may belong in the concept of art than is generally believed.")

I think Hegel best provides a model for the force of terms insistent on verbal excess like "carnage." Neither Pound nor his peers like Gertrude Stein, Mina Loy, and Marianne Moore read Hegel, but their sense of the powers of language substantially modified how poetry treats the kinds of substance sense experience can produce in ways that lead us to Hegelian metaphysics. Most interpreters of Hegel focus on transformations of the subject as it modifies the conditions of self-consciousness—for example by moving from unhappy consciousness to reason. But Hegel is equally interested in the transformations to our ideas of substance in the processes by which spirit alters its modes of self-consciousness.

Poems like "April" do not present the world as preexisting the language that rises to the challenge of representing it adequately. Instead, the poem makes it seem that we begin not with the world but with a certain condition of emotion that is inseparable from the language composed for the poem. The poem produces a scenic sense of April for which the word "carnage" is constitutive. Here intense materiality is completely aligned with how the imagination can do its work in the world. The interrelation of April with "carnage" gives a quite different sense of substance because the object is no longer something afforded by description and supplemented by imagination. The object just is what language confers on the scene for the reader: the emotions and reflections language composes completely establish what spirits can see in April. And it is our task to learn to see and to feel as those spirits see and feel. *Le mot juste* is not a state of description but rather of celebration that we can experience the substance of April through the mediation of what the three spirits see in the scene. Their attention provides a figure for how the making of the poem transforms substance to include the objectifying of what is typically merely inchoate for human consciousness.

There are traces of such constitutive activity in various aestheticist writing, from Stephané Mallarmé to Samuel Beckett. However, Pound's imagism is distinctive because he shares Nietzsche's refusal to align aestheticism with formalism while manifestly not seeking escape from the griminess of the world. Form is a gift to the world, introducing into fact intensities and values that cannot be derived from independent and objective descriptions. That quest for expressivist alternatives to description goes a long way toward helping us see the relationship of making in art to the cultivation of various versions of Nietzsche's extramoral senses in the domain of existential values. Pound shows the way to this larger theater in which something indubitably "spiritual" seems inseparable on a constitutive level (rather than an interpretive level) from the immediacies of sensation. In addition, Pound attunes us to how thoroughly Nietzsche pervaded the writing of *Harmonium*, although that text is much freer than Pound in exploring states of subjective will. But for Stevens Nietzsche is only a first step in an intellectual adventure that ultimately presents very different strategies for resisting the claims of empiricism—based less on the will to power than the will to analogy. Eventually Stevens would make adjustments in our sense of substance not by emphasizing the creative power of form but by displaying how the mind can participate in developing possible imaginative extensions of description. As Dora Zhang shows in relation to modernist fiction, writing can shift from an effort to describe objective phenomena to rooting description in what aspects of the world "feel like." Stevens then does the work of imagining how poetry might offer distinctive modes of these likenesses.[23]

Because I think it is crucial to understand how thoroughly this modernist work revolutionizes poetry's relation to the world, I want to offer the more elaborate case of Pound's second Canto before we turn to Stevens. Let me set the scene by commenting on the passage that opens the canto and sets its fundamental motifs:

> Hang it all, Robert Browning,
> there can be but the one "Sordello."
> But Sordello, and my Sordello?
> Lo Sordels si fo di Mantovana
> So-shu churned in the sea
> Seal sports in the spray-whited circles of cliff-wash.
>
> *(Cantos 6)*

Notice that Pound again refuses to treat his poetry as Wordsworthian rhetorical energy extending what a natural scene offers to an attentive eye and needy "I." Instead, the poem tries out different modes of organizing itself until it comes up with an alternative register not tormented by self-consciousness. If we imagine the primary role of "Sordello" to involve reference to the character, there seems to be no way to avoid invidious comparisons to Browning. But when these feelings arise why not just turn to the register of sound associations that the poem can pursue? Here one can fully participate, without a sense of inadequacy, in the movement from "Sordello," via Italian, to "So-shu churned in the sea," to the sea as the focus of associated links enabling the poet to get well beyond Sordello, to the reenactment of Homeric emotions themselves based largely on the ear. Making has its own entry into a full sensuality sufficient to defeat the negativity of self-consciousness.

I skip Pound's lovely lyric expansion of these marine motifs so that I can go directly to the mimetic and narrative central panel of the canto. The action begins with a ship in Scios picking up a young boy, who turns out to Dionysius. The boy gets assurances that this is "straight ship" from the captain, Acoetes, who narrates the events. The crew mutinies, taking Acoetes prisoner. Later the boy comes on deck, sees that the boat is taking a course different from the one promised to him, and releases Dionysian magic, to which the captain is extraordinarily attentive:

> God-sleight then, god-sleight
>> Ship stock fast in sea-whirl
> Ivy upon the oars, King Pentheus,
>> grapes with no seed but sea-foam,
>>>> Ivy in scupper-hole.
>>> Aye, I, Acoetes stood there
>>> And the god stood by me,
>> Water cutting under the heel . . .
>>>> (7)

Sound has given way to a visual register, although that giving way is amply recompensed in the aural riches of this reporting. Then another sense enters, and the details grow more intimate and more dynamic:

> Heavy vine on the oarshafts,
> And, out of nothing, a breathing,
>> hot breath on my ankles,
> Beasts like shadows in glass,
>> a furred tail upon nothingness,
> Lynx-purr and heathery smell of beasts. . . .
> Lifeless air become sinewed,
>> feline leisure of panthers.
>>>> (8)

Precision of detail here relegates the self to a purely reportorial role: it is as if the fullness of the senses demanded the suppression of the self-interpreting energies that make for Wordsworthian eloquence (and Arnoldian despondency). The interplay among the senses virtually replaces an interplay between scene and viewer. But this condition is by no means experienced as lack. Rather, it is a kind of plenitude where the energy of sensation opens into another dimension of experience sharply contrasted to what had been only the nothingness of "lifeless air."

The climax of this scene occurs seventeen lines later as Acoetes offers in two clipped sentences what I take to be an emblem of modernist ambition. These sentences allow no room for the poet's rhetoric or the critic's interpretive speculation. Instead, they provide a succinct and cogent shift from the space of narrative to the literalizing of theophany:

And I worship.
I have seen what I have seen.
    When they brought the boy I said,
"He has a god in him,
    though I do not know which god."
And they kicked me into the forestays.
I have seen what I have seen: . . .
        . . . And you, Pentheus,
Had as well listen to Teiresias, and to Cadmus,
    or your luck will go out of you.

        (9)

This passage stages a conversion but is not based on any dramatized sequence of attempted interpretations. The self is not the source or the center of value. It simply registers the value consequences of inhabiting a distinctive register of sensation. The dramatic moment renders an incarnation. But there is no transcendence, and the god makes no demands or revelations. The focus is all on the force by which the human figure represents how his own life has changed. Devotion to seeing and refusal of the temptations of the slave trade suffice to put him in a position to affirm something close to absolute commitment based simply on what becomes available to the life of the senses, without doctrine.[24]

Pound's version of learning to bear witness certainly echoes passages where Wordsworth confirms his faith in nature. Yet I think the direction of fit with the world is quite different, largely because attention from the start is focused on what the god can do to transform nature and what the poets can do to match that transformation by their timing and by their intricate play of monosyllabic signifiers established by that same overwhelming present tense. The poem extends nature by first cutting itself off from the natural and then making positive that potentially negative state. This insistently composed fullness of detail seems to erase the need for interpretation that tries after the fact to fuse the division between fact and meaning. Instead, these two Poundian passages seem to activate a sense of value coming into existence primarily because of poetry's capacity to reach beyond itself through itself. Or, to make the same point another way, the emphasis on the aural in the beginning casts poetry as not describing sensations but extending them and transposing them into a register where the god dwelling in them becomes visible. This sense of power sanctions Acoetes's advice to Pentheus—not as moral wisdom but simply as respect for sheer power without any qualifying evaluative concerns that derive from social intercourse.

VI

Stevens's values are quite different from Pound's: even though Stevens shares Pound's commitment to intensity and to power, his poetry is more concerned than Pound's with the nuances of how that power adapts to what Stevens calls "reality." For Pound the artist figure is the fundamental bearer of values because the artist can begin with the visionary imagination and then test the degree to which reality might be made to adapt to these projections of human possibility. For Stevens the relevant possibilities do not derive from art, although art is our greatest means of acknowledging and celebrating them. The creative domain of valuing simply occurs as we feel our intimate desires being engaged in the world or giving shapes to situations. In both cases values are not derived from fact but give shape to implicit possibilities in being human. Pound thought we could gain access to these possibilities only by following the path of Nietzsche from alienation to "becoming who one is." Stevens shared that attitude in *Harmonium,* but he gradually domesticated the entire process of valuing, so that awareness of values increasingly became not a grandiose enterprise but an intricately intimate attachment to the dynamics of our capacities to feel we can belong in the world by negotiating its rhythms of satisfaction and dissatisfaction.

It was only late in his career that Stevens took up the task of clarifying in discursive terms what he imagined to be the stance on value that governed his work. But the relevant essay, "Imagination as Value" (September 1948), looks both backward and forward. I will eventually show that its basic definition of value goes back to *Harmonium* while also providing a fulcrum that helps explain how Stevens explores alternative means by which the lyric not only refers to values but also invites our participation in the imaginative forces that embody them.

Stevens's definition is simple but also remarkably precise and capacious in its abstraction and indeed in its demand for abstraction in poetry.[25] This definition suggests why value is not derived from fact but testable against it:

> The imagination is the power of the mind over the possibilities of things; but if this constitutes a certain general characteristic, it is the source not of a certain single value but of as many values as reside in the possibilities of things.

> (*CPP* 726)

Then the essay turns immediately to two problems implicit in this definition. The first problem is defining "the possibilities of things" so that there remains significant pressure to be realistic without seeking to justify one's sense of possibility by turning to the simple analysis of the manifest empirical conditions. The second problem derives from this attempt to reconcile realism and possibility. Does the relevant sense of possibility reside in the things themselves or in the mind's capacity to elaborate possibilities because of how it finds itself positioned toward the things? To address this Stevens develops a contrast between the force of imagination that results in "a certain single" image of what can be valued and the force of imagination that manifests itself as a process continually altering the domain of images without allowing itself to become allied with a specific set of images. This distinction was crucial for him because it enabled him to distance himself from the dangerous tendency of romantic desire to naturalize these possibilities by fleshing out particular representational content for them (*CPP* 727).

This romantic desire reflects habits of thinking that are basic to Western civilization and are not specific to a given period, although the given period may become locked into this sense of possibility and close off its competitors. Perhaps Stevens's richest example of that disposition and its problems occurs in "The Noble Rider and the Sound of Words," where he takes up the question of how societies imagine nobility. Verrocchio could make the ideal concrete through a statue that looks out over the bay from Venice of a horseman deftly and proudly controlling his horse. But this concrete image must necessarily be a victim of the historical forces for which it tries to provide a shape. Now the figure of a horseman would only be kitsch or the conscious irony of the tin horse and rider that sits on the plaza overlooking the city of Albany in a museum Nelson Rockefeller built in the 1960s. This work reminds us that our previous images of nobility become commodities that land in the dump, warranting only tin replicas of bronze originals. However, it also reminds us of how artists can reconfigure our sense of what counts as substance for a given image. In the contemporary work, the substance is not the image in itself but the critical activity of the author, reminding us that the idea of nobility may be capable of outlasting the images it generates.

For Stevens the romantic is admirable insofar as it brings feeling to the foreground of our experience. Nonetheless, its versions of feeling prove inseparable from that sentimentality that testifies ultimately to "a failure of feeling" (*CPP* 727–28). So we see in the romantic both the sense of the imagination as "the liberty of the mind" and the effectual "failure to make use of that liberty" (*CPP* 727). Sentimentality wants to make a self-flattering theater of the facts of feeling rather than looking toward the contexts that allow feeling to provide a mobile dynamic force running through a variety of concrete situations.

Therefore the romantic defines by contrast what for later Stevens has to be the aspiration of a truly modern art. The mind manifest in such art must be sufficiently abstract to project the power of mind over the possibility of things by continually maintaining a productive tension between the domain of possibility and the domain of things. If images tend to become mockery of our powers of establishing values, perhaps something like the voice in poetry can preserve our access to the underlying forces that grapple to re-place one image with another.[26] In addition, if ultimately any "metaphysical content" for the imagination is doomed to the dump, perhaps art can align us with the kind of valuing that takes on a body by abstracting from the specific images the sense of quality that motivates our affirmations:

It was how the sun came shining into his room:
To be without a description of to be,
For a moment on rising, at the edge of the bed, to be,
To have the ant of the self changed to an ox . . .

(CPP 187)

Imagination has to be abstract in Stevens because it must go beyond indi-vidual fictions to stage "time and . . . place, as these perfect themselves" (*CPP* 728), and so call to our attention "the extent of the artifice within us, and, almost parenthetically, with the question of its value" (*CPP* 729). The relevant images now apply to the process of valuing rather than to specific "metaphysical" content so that they can focus on "the extent of artifice" resulting from those aspects of life that depend on the mind. Ultimately the imagination's status as the power over the possibilities of things emerges in poetry as the felt sense of a fit between a vocabulary voiced and an occa-sion in which the imagination finds a plausible place as the power we need to address something like an abstraction of need itself.[27]

Stevens differs substantially from Pound here because Pound places the force of abstraction within how the artifice fuses with the concrete world—hence his idealization of beauty. Stevens's later work on the other hand typically has the concrete world fuse into the subject by making the speaker self-consciously embrace the role of "orator" in order explicitly to invite audiences to specific kinds of social identifications.[28] This entails simultane-ously invoking a political theater and displacing it into abstraction. But however one judges Stevens's politics, I think one has to respect the direct-ness and the intelligence in his acknowledging that acts of valuing within the lyric have to take account of how the needs of social agents have changed along with their images. In his view the primary human concern for values had for a long time been involved in how the imagination could find a place within the interactions between human and natural worlds . But for modernity these struggles take place primarily in relation to the forces involved in the efforts of the "great masses of men" to provide dignity and meaning for their lives. In addition, one cannot plausibly identify these struggles with the versions of nobility and rank that drove Verrochio. That is why Stevens can say "the great poems of heaven and hell have been written and the great poem of the earth remains to be written" (*CPP* 730). This poem will be written only when the poet's imagination manages to find "the most momentous scale" of the sense of possibility appropriate for these great masses of men" (*CPP* 730): "It was how he was free. It was how his freedom came."

Stevens saw that in his time Communism presented itself as speaking for those possibilities. But in his capitalist view Communism was romanticism writ large: it turned out to destroy the imagination by believing so completely in only one of its products that it sought to restrict imagination to practical content aligned with questions of government. Thus he felt we could learn by comparison with Communism how the Bible has the more intimate and capacious sense of needs, aspirations, hopes, and fears. However, we also see that ultimately such states involve activities that cannot be reduced to beliefs about the human. Rather, we need faith in an imagination that enacts and exemplifies "the life of the faculty itself" (*CPP* 731). This imagination cannot be satisfied by politics but "tries to penetrate to basic images, basic emotions, and so to compose a fundamental poetry even older than the ancient world" (*CPP* 732). (Pound's efforts to realize the theophany of Dionysius would be a significant instance of this point.) Composing this fundamental poetry will take appreciating the complex relations between "the operation of the imagination in life" (where imagination often works within social forms, like costume) and "its operation in or in relation to" arts and letters (*CPP* 733).

There remains a pressing danger for the modern poet that brings me back to my concern with Victorian writing. The Victorians treated these operations of the imagination as fundamentally engaged in the struggle for moral identity by individuals. Looking back on the challenge modern poetry faces, Stevens sees that we have been trained to let the domain of values be equated with morality because this was the only way that the Victorians could see "arts and letters" making a difference "in relation to life" (*CPP* 734). But for his culture Stevens thought that the authoritarian claims of the Communists to speak for society's interests too nakedly revealed their origins in this Victorian sensibility. So the task of modernist writing was to shift from this focus on morality to the more abstract, but also far more concrete, demonstration that another kind of authority was available if we could learn to identify with how poetry struggles against the dominant social forms:

> The poet tries to exemplify it, in part, as I have tried to exemplify it here, by identifying it with an imaginative activity that diffuses itself throughout our lives. I say exemplify, and not justify, because poetic value is an intuitional value and because intuitional values cannot be justified.
>
> (*CPP* 735)

Insofar as the primary struggle of our time is "the conflict between man and organized society" (*CPP* 735), the work of the poetic imagination becomes "part of our security" and so "enables us to live our own lives" (*CPP* 735). Perhaps only an insurance executive would align poetry with "security," but this was not a minor concern for a society that had just come out of a long economic depression.

Two further elaborations are necessary for Stevens to flesh out what is involved in the work of imagination enabling us to locate value in the manner by which we come to live our own lives. First, it is crucial not to set reason in opposition to what imagination can afford for individual lives. The two can complement each other: "when does a building stop being a product of the reason and become a product of the imagination?" (*CPP* 735)—again a powerful reminder that Stevens is not concerned primarily with epistemic understandings of fiction contrasted with "reality." More metaphysically, imagination is "the moderator of life as metempsychosis was of death": "Nietzsche walked in the Alps in the caresses of reality," and "we ourselves crawl out of our offices and classrooms and become alert at the opera" (*CPP* 735). Imagination moderates life by providing "a way of thinking by which we project the idea of God into the idea of man" (*CPP* 736). For it creates images whose roles are not primarily referential or descriptive. These images enter into vast and mobile assemblages of other images all capable of carrying affective weight and complexity as figures for qualities by which the subject complements what is given to the senses. Stevens gives the example of a Giorgione portrait as "an instance of a real object that is at the same time an imaginative object": "It has about it an imaginative bigness of diction" (*CPP* 737). So one feels a productive presence, a source of imaginative vitality, that becomes inseparable from the "diction of the portrait" (*CPP* 737).

Second, imagination is a value in social life because it correlates what we might envision as abnormal with what is possible to treat as embedded in the normal. This distinction is crucial because for Stevens it is too easy for poets to opt for celebrating the abnormal. Such identifications seem parallel to "identifying liberty with those that abuse it" (*CPP* 738). The cost is immense when we fall for this temptation because our art then lets reason be the only claimant to "an appearance of normality to which it is not solely entitled" (*CPP* 738). The rise of positivism is a failure of the arts to make their own claims on the real and on the normal, based on the possibility that "we live in concepts of the imagination before reason has established them" (*CPP* 738). Here Stevens's theory comes around again to its initial assumption— that the romantic is the failure of imagination because it is a failure to maintain the imagination's commitment to the normal so that it can keep reason in its place:

> To be able to see the portal of literature, that is to say: the portal of the imagination, as a scene of normal love and normal beauty, is, of itself, a feat of great imagination. It is the vista a man sees, seated in the public garden of his native town, near by some effigy of a figure celebrated in the normal world, as he considers that the chief problems of any artist, as of any man, are the problems of the normal and that he needs, in order to solve them, everything that the imagination has to give.
>
> (*CPP* 739)

VII

I have quoted a great deal from Stevens's essay because this entire book is devoted to his various ways of putting the lyric imagination to work rendering "the mind's power over the possibilities in things" so as to make manifest "the life of the faculty itself." Several questions will have to be addressed. How do various stages of that work show what he means by "the power of mind"? How can it be plausible to envision the mind's power over the possibility of things as something other than what can be represented by formulating specific beliefs? How does his poetry make manifest and significant these powers—as imaginative diction, as eloquence, as control over metaphor, as what his essays call powers of resemblance and analogy, as what I will compare to what Wittgenstein does in his analyses of aspect-seeing, and as an often brilliant expansion of what is involved in our powers to explore the many facets of the grammar of "as," which mobilizes this sentence? On an even more general expansive level we will have to ask how the interplay among Stevens's responses to such questions can produce dialectical pressure challenging and refining all the specific elements of his poetic theory. Finally, we will have to isolate for careful attention Stevens's basic claim that attention to the most elemental aspects of artifice in our lives can substantially modify our understanding of and appreciation for what can be considered "normal." Here we have to see how this strange equation of artifice with normality allows us not just to recognize the normal but also to register it as valuable because of how that normality modifies the states of consciousness by which it comes to appear.

All of these questions are based on the assumption that Stevens's poetry has its maximum force when it is considered an elaborate phenomenological enterprise exploring states where one feels oneself responding to what engages our sense of values. This is why he sees abstraction in poetry as closely linked to an understanding of the normal. Abstraction is the cutting away of the specific contents of value in order to focus on the qualities that constitute how we value. This is also why he emphasizes intuition and exemplification over the power of concepts. In this he shares ideas with a range of significant modern philosophers who resist the domination of reason over practical life—quintessentially Heidegger, Bergson, and James. Unlike these philosophers, however, he can not only characterize feelings but also continually try to make them present by shifting the energy of poetry from dramatic scenes to what orators do, then inviting his audience to identify with the energies of the rhetorician. The basic drive in Steven's later poetry is to make discursive reflection compelling as a way of giving energy, specificity, and complexity to the life of the mind within the normal. It is no accident that the title of Stevens's essay is "Imagination as Value" rather than "imagination of value." This enables him to call attention to quiet modes of valuing by drawing equivalences that are built into our practices of using language.

The ground for drawing out these equivalences is later Stevens's fundamentally phenomenological approach to experience. His focus is primarily on subjects *as* they value rather than on the specific and historically variable objects to which they attribute value. Stevens's mode of attention uses abstraction to lead us to concrete but sharable processes that create a sense of how life might provide its richest satisfactions. Yet it is all too easy to lose sight of such processes when one is concerned primarily with practical judgments about general welfare or moral judgments about what can be exemplary in the domain of actions involving relations with other people.[29] Therefore, I want to close this section by proposing a radical elemental mode of phenomenological attention that is not quite Stevens's but is derived from his work and may be helpful in emphasizing what is powerfully fundamental in that work. I think of what follows as reducing a Stevensian phenomenology to its most basic senses of possibility.

This version of phenomenology would try to locate affective states in our self-reflexive attention to the basic grammatical forces that adapt language to the world and the world to language. For Stevens such grammatical considerations are the ladders where all eloquence begins. Eloquence is that mode of artifice capable of letting us treat the normal as not just conventional but as a domain shaped by quiet but powerful passions.

Consider then the potential for imaginative life if we become aware of the space that we inhabit when we produce meaningfulness within three fundamental linguistic structures. First, there are the values implicit in each of the pronoun positions that indicate directions of agency—the conditions of first-person consciousness of the powers to shape actions and confer significance, the conditions of possible address by which we share these feelings, and the conditions of anchoring that can occur as we recognize the potential for third-person accounts of what has been experienced. Let us call these the positions constitutive for the experience of value as a subject open to the world.

Second, analogous fundamental states are available from our ways of punctuating sentences since these reflect how modulations of voice make "being without description" available to us. Assertion, interrogation, and exclamation are not just indications of what we mean but also manifest how we are capable of making personal investments in those meanings. We can consider these three modes of expression to be the elemental structure of our feelings for how the world emerges in language.

Most important, Stevens leads us to recognize how our most basic verbs can become modes of habitation in their own right—as conditions opening self-reflection on how subject and object seem inseparable from one another. These become the fundamental interfaces by which we actively perform our own powers within the world we encounter. Or we could say that these interfaces allow us to give shape to how the world elicits our performances. For example, Heidegger's ideal of being as *phusis* or "self-blossoming emergence" (*IM,* 11) indicates just how much distance there is between our typical copulative verbs and the sense that they can carry when "to be" is not just a predication but a recognition of and participation in what acts of attention can offer. We can make similar attributions about the force of Hegel's "not" since it marks an elemental difference between simple negation and responsiveness to the work dialectic can do. Finally, Wittgenstein's "as" introduces us to the often complex chains of equivalence giving value to our recognitions of how thoroughly feelings that derive from recognition of likeness pervade our existence. These range from the simple sense of fit that memory produces to the condition of satisfaction by analogy that both Stevens and Wittgenstein elaborated near the end of their careers. I cite Stevens in the text and Wittgenstein in the endnote:

> Take the case of a man for whom reality is enough, as, at the end of his life, he returns to it like a man returning from Nowhere to his village and to everything there that is tangible and visible, which he has come to cherish and wants to be near. He sees without images. But is he not seeing a clarified reality of his own? Does he not dwell in an analogy? His imageless world is, after all, the same sort as a world full of the obvious analogies of happiness or unhappiness . . . In any case these are the pictorializations of men, for whom the world exists as a world and for whom life exists as life, the objects of their passions, the objects before which they come and speak, with intense choosing, words that we remember and make our own. Their words have made a world that transcends the world and a life livable in that transcendence.
>
> (CPP 722)[30]

VIII

I am tempted to offer a summary of this book's account of Stevens's career on the basis simply of which of these three linguistic forms seems to dominate the affective fields within his works at any given time. At first, in *Harmonium,* Stevens emphasized what seemed the often horrifying force of the copulative. At one end of the pole the bare copulative is the mark of mortality for Stevens. Sheer predication becomes also the register of absolute vulnerability to everything that we cannot control:

> Here is the cheek on which that lid declined,
> And, finger after finger, here, the hand,
> The genius of that cheek. Here are the lips,
> The bundle of the body and the feet.
> Out of the tomb we bring Badroulbadour.
>
> (CPP 40)

However, that sense of mortality also provides the pressure by which we come to appreciate the force of the metaphoric naming that can make this blankness bearable:

Donna, donna, dark,
Stooping in indigo gown
And cloudy constellations,
Conceal yourself or disclose
Fewest things to the lover—
A hand that bears a thick-leaved fruit,
A pungent bloom against your shade.

(CPP 39)

In the 1930s Stevens often turned to a version of Hegelian negation—to establish how abstraction works in preserving the force of imagination from the romantic desire to provide content for its images and so to secure the power to place oneself within history while escaping any concrete fealties to the ideologies it inculcates. But then he had to flesh out how abstractions could mesh with one another to elaborate equivalences and allow audiences fully to participate in the energies driving the poems. So he spent a great deal of imaginative energy exploring the powers of "as" and hence of "resemblance" for what I think of as his most complex and timely and intricate and dialectical working out of how experiences of value pervade the normal. This labor eventually brought him very close to the range of significances Wittgenstein brings out in his discussion of aspect-seeing. Moreover, because Stevens manages to anchor aspect-seeing so thoroughly in the "normal," he can treat aspects as if they were themselves the grounds for attributing copulative verbs.[31] The aspects by which we see are as real and as significant as the facts that they frame:

We live in a constellation
Of patches and of pitches,
Not in a single world
In things said well in music,
On the piano, and in speech,
As in a page of poetry—
Thinkers without final thoughts
In an always incipient cosmos,
The way, when we climb a mountain,
Vermont throws itself together.

(CPP 476)

Climbing a mountain is one way to envision our aspect-seeing, making it possible to see the earth again, as if for the first time, every time.

IX

I feel obligated also to give a more elaborate map for this journey. *Harmonium* matters for my story because it presents one of the richest engagements I know in the problems created by empiricist models of value. And because Stevens is so attuned to the problems produced by that model, he finds himself experimenting with attitudes that come close to Nietzschean positions. It is as if he had to exhaust those positions before he could stop fighting battles created by empiricism and begin actually working toward feasible alternatives for projecting the powers poetry could provide for cultural life.

More precisely, the crucial Nietzsche for Stevens was the radical naturalist who recognized how the death of God destroyed our culture's values and tried to find in human creative powers an alternative model for coming to terms with a naturalist version of the real.[32] Stevens took that hyperempiricism as inseparable from the glaring pressure of the fact of mortality on any possible projection of human values. So for him the primary testing of imaginative power is in the elaboration of specific intricate lyric attitudes that both realize and deflect everything that mortality comes to involve in this world that cannot rely on religion's promises of rewards for lives well spent and deaths accepted with dignity and hope. Stevens's lyrics call attention to their strange and exotic qualities and then use these qualities to test the possibility that only an imaginatively intense and focused strangeness in this culture has the necessary resources to avoid failed public rhetorics while still finding a position from which to engage various kinds of emotional turbulence. Such strangeness then sets a benchmark for the work of reenchantment that poetry has to accomplish, while also revealing limitations that require Stevens's later stylistic emphases that increasingly concentrate on the work of analogy rather than metaphor.

I also begin with Nietzschean aspects of *Harmonium* because I think Stevens's version of tragic gaiety allows us to see how he staged his own bid for attention as a major voice in responding to the conditions of modernity. He explicitly criticizes Williams and implicitly criticizes imagism because they do not do sufficient imaginative work to differentiate their poetry from any fealties to a romantic past. Consequently this work enters into critical dialogue with the heritage of French symbolist poetry, from which I think Stevens borrowed his cult of exotic attitudes and strange angles of vision on the real. The poetry of Jules Laforgue in particular defined for Stevens a mode of defamiliarization oriented toward the inner life rather than the domain of perceptions. Laforgue exemplified for Stevens strange kinds of intimacy that can stem from a subject's looking at itself in ways that enable it to take responsibility for aspects of the psyche typically repressed by our postures of high seriousness. What can feeling as a giant undone by maidens whispering heavenly labials do to one's fantasies of manhood? How can it make a difference if one envisions desire for beauty though the figure of an oddly meditative Peter Quince? But Stevens also seems to have thought that this work was too effete and mannered or at least that its ways of being mannered were insufficiently vigorous and critical. There again Nietzsche's epigrammatic mix of distance and pointedness could provide a different path by sponsoring attitudes that had more conceptual spine and "virile" assertiveness than the dandyish stances cultivated by Laforgue.

During the years after *Harmonium*, when Stevens wrote very little poetry, he seems to have realized that the exoticism necessary for poems to mine the virtues of defamiliarization left them at too great a tangent from the most intense challenges facing the imagination—not challenges to escape the normal but to recast it or recuperate how aspects of a life shared with others might take on imaginative intensity. And to turn to more typical situations is also to have to confront something more oppressive than the sense of mortality that haunts *Harmonium*. It is to have to confront more directly the general sense that the triumph of empiricism in Western culture risks the leveling of all values and the cultivating of what Stevens saw as mere individual interests that could be pursued with very little accompaniment by the reflective mind.

So Stevens began experimenting with how poetry could engage the limitations of empiricist attitudes shaping his culture's typical concerns about meaning and value. Yet the more he felt he was succeeding in that project, the more he felt substantial tensions between the possible directions that new enterprise could take. At one pole Stevens explored possibilities for treating what he called the "theory of life" as a fundamental resource for developing aspects of lyric experience. Poetry could have an abstract reach without imposing discursive structures upon concrete situations. But defamiliarization would have to go—or least be substantially reduced. Where defamiliarization had been, the three volumes after *Harmonium* could offer powerful uses of explicit negation. They could seek a dialectical relationship between what was in the process of becoming mere history within common experience and what could open up into intuitions of something like a heroic figure or major man or supreme fiction at the core of those desires that seemed to persist. Many of these poems rely on a model of fictionality that casts the poet as someone who articulates a common plight: poems show how our "inner lives" push against the domain of what empiricism sanctions as fact and in that pushing constitutes possible values for the society. The fictive would not be just the testing of attitudes but also the testing of what in our making, in our desires, seemed a fundamental demand that showed the path to possible abiding satisfactions for the spirit of poetic inquiry. Presenting and negating images makes us aware of a condition of shared desire for meaningfulness, which Stevens elaborates as the quest for major man or the supreme fiction with a capacity to bring out what is shared at the deepest levels of human concern (or the deepest levels of our concern for humanity). The ideas defining this quest could be discursive and yet also "inherently poetic" (*CPP* 855) so long as they are put in the service of "some quality" that the "work possesses, such as its insight, its evocative power, or its appearance in the eye of the imagination" (*CPP* 862; cf. 864).[33]

However, at the same time there are sufficient delights and attunements taking place in the concrete poems to breed an eventual dissatisfaction with those abstract formulations about value.[34] Stevens never repudiates the discourse of fictionality. Yet I believe I can show how those poems that rely on the grammar of "as" develop an increasing interest in a quite different form of abstraction based on processes of analogical thinking that display interpersonal modes of valuing. Beginning with "The Man with the Blue Guitar," Stevens manifests a substantial and growing interest in how the "interaction" or "inter-relation between things" becomes the crucial "source of potency" in the lyric (*CPP* 867). This sense of multivalued equivalences leads Stevens to what the grammar of "as" can offer. With the help of his essay on "Effects of Analogy," I can characterize that mode of attention as an "aspectual thinking" that dominates the poetry of *Auroras of Autumn*.

The forms of valuing elaborated in aspectual thinking can be related to fictionality because they share Stevens's sharp distinction between describing the world and making situations that literally become parts of the world. But some of the properties of the new poems make the language of fictions seem unnecessarily abstract and somewhat misleading primarily because these poems produce intimate continuities between how we experience the world and what we can say to articulate the actual force of these experiences. Stevens more than any other modernist manages to produce a sense that making is manifestly an aspect of living and therefore is as concretely situated in the actual world as any other feature of behavior. Therefore the values attendant on these conditions of experience need not be considered as somehow constructs composed by the mind. Instead, the values seem inseparable from the kinds of care and attention that poetry brings to that actual world as accompaniments of its capacity to produce a "quickened" sense of ease and fluidity within what occurs to us.

In order to develop what is at stake in Stevens's aspectual thinking I follow chapters on *Harmonium* and on how negation works in *Ideas of Order* and "The Man with the Blue Guitar" with three chapters concentrating on what he does with what I call the grammar of "as." "As" performs two primary functions, but in an intricate variety of ways. Unlike the copulative verb, it stages equivalences that mark the activity of the subject in the formulation of the object, and it uses those equivalences to define the role audiences are asked to play *as* they realize the opportunity to see *as* the language of the poem performs its place in the world.

The first of these chapters offers a nonlinguist's mapping of the particular imaginative work that this grammar of "as" can perform. I trace how "the intricate evasions of as" (*CPP* 415) provide a form of inner dynamics in poetry that Stevens derived from his sense of how the mind is active in perception without any longer inviting idealist accounts of that activity.[35] Stevens is fascinated by "as" constructions primarily because they have the capacity to treat manner as also matter and so establish equivalences among processes in time and in space:

There he walks and talks as he lives and likes.
(*CPP* 449)

This sentence invites reflection on the work that thinking is doing both to modify the appearances it engages and to create a present tense for thinking and for living that the poem can make available to the reader in its full concreteness. On the basis of passages like these I argue that the work Stevens has equivalences do makes his poetry distinctive within American modernism— for its suspicion of images as privileged modes of lyric expressivity,[36] for its capacities to flesh out what Hegel meant by a new romantic lyricism that locates the sensuous in the dynamics of psychological life, for its cultivation of an intimacy with the actual feel of an imagination at work to engage that pressure of reality, for its ability to move cogently from developing particular equivalents to treating extended poetic thinking as inherently aspectual, for its efforts to preserve a sense of the transpersonal qualities of imagination that the poem makes actual in the present tense of the reading, and for its ability to make lyricism of his own overhearing the shifts in registers that his voice undergoes.

The next two chapters simply develop Stevens's own practical awareness of how such equivalences can be put to use in projecting philosophical significance for poetic projects. The first of these chapters moves from isolating characteristic uses of grammatical strategies for expressive purposes to spelling out how Stevens's concern for "resemblances" generates an overall style for presenting lyric voice that I call *aspectual thinking.* Aspectual thinking, which is fully realized in *Auroras of Autumn,* differs from traditional lyricism in its refusal of dramatically developed situations and in its foregrounding of the processes of thinking "as" situations shift and perspectives open up. Aspectual thinking also creates different (and ultimately very influential) models for acts of mind than we find in the two basic modes of thinking promoted by modernist lyrics. It seeks a presence located in the speaking voice confronting a metamorphic reality rather than seeking the presence in how the constructed object embodies the work of imagination. Furthermore, it seeks not the elaborate analogues of the symbolist tradition but the constant modulation of analogical presences. I cannot escape hopeless abstract summaries at this stage in the book, so I offer only this promissory note: we will attend to how Stevens seeks at every moment a sense that a poet's eloquence can participate in a spirit of discovery. The work of imagination becomes a mode of participating in the reality it encounters, so Stevens can plausibly believe that this new style affords a possible union between the states of making and of finding that most modernist poetics labors to reconcile.

The second of these two chapters focuses on one particular value for which aspectual thinking proves especially congenial. I begin by asking why *Auroras of Autumn* concludes with a relatively minor though fascinating poem, "Angel Surrounded by Paysans." That question introduces an elaborate reflection on how Stevens handles the forces of pain and suffering and loss in that volume—as if the entire volume might be seen as taking its tonal key from Stevens's dissatisfaction with his own grappling with those issues in "Esthétique du Mal." In my view "Angel Surrounded by Paysans" makes explicit in concrete form the volume's efforts to treat as complements the sense of constant loss and the constant feeling of the mind finding its anchor in how it engages the present tense.

But for Stevens this emphasis on process ultimately does not suffice because it does not establish a sufficient stage for self-reflection on the second-order states that poetry can bring into action, like making acts of will or aligning the self with the necessity of change and loss. So he develops a different dimension of our capacity to use the grammar of "as." I cannot avoid a clumsy terminology here: Stevens's last volume, *The Rock,* changes from ideals of participation in the flux of experience to a model of second-order aspect-seeing that parallels Wittgenstein's thinking on this topic. In one sense Stevens turns back to the logic of *Harmonium* (which many of his late poems echo). A sharp distinction between spirit and fact, reflective inner life and the poverty of a naturalist perspective occupies many of the poems. But now the imagination is not seen as the antagonist of the natural—its task to build attitudes that resist subordinating the self to mortality. Rather, imagination has to find ways to identify with that mortality, as if imagination were the artifice within the real that allowed us to understand how we play a part in what refuses all our fantasies. This artifice boils down ultimately to our capacity to see one condition as another, as the sun provides Penelope the power to substitute for Ulysses or as the possibility of addressing an old man asleep, or Matisse at Vence giving "a new account of everything old" (*CPP* 948), or an old philosopher in Rome in a way that can identify with his capacity to see "the figures in the street / Become the figures of heaven" (*CPP* 432).

I stress how Stevens utilizes "seeing as" to afford a way of attaching the mind to the world that does not submit to description and depends on a particular relationship that invites self-reflection. That self-reflection in turn establishes something like an irreducible human element within the world because one can will as necessity what creates immense pain for the desiring self. Here Stevens finds a satisfying imaginative stance that can acknowledge the reality of evil without self-congratulation or other theatrical effulgence. *The Rock* treats suffering as if it were simply inseparable from the affirmation of the moments that define what acceptance of limitation can involve for typical sensibilities. There is almost no aboutness in most of these poems, almost no sense that the poems comment on situations to which the poem refers. Descriptive and anecdotal orientations are replaced by figures of pure access to the imaginative richness of states so utterly concrete that there seems almost no difference between the subject responding to the world and the world eliciting these responses. The developing of resemblances occurs within the very conditions of perception, as if it were impossible to separate the substance invoked by the copulative from the equivalences generated by the analogical imagination.

Stevens offers these last poems as illustrations of what it might take for poetry to be in time but beyond the history that relegates its figures to the dump. There must be a sense of abiding substance. But the poetry that pervades that sense also retains the dynamic equivalences that make it possible for us to treat this achievement of substance as a significant model for valuing human life. The relevant model of substance just becomes the world of elemental and recurrent imaginings that frame the most basic aspects of mortality as possible conditions for wonder.[37] Poetry can restore something like the power of the copulative simply by virtue of how the *as* develops sufficient force to intensify the plain sense of things without displacing it into the manifest rhetorical eloquence of the staged image. The imagination serves entirely as a means of habitation rather than as a force asked to produce value on its own. Thus fact, and the generalization from fact that constitutes necessity, needs no supplement that is not an intensification of specificity. There is no need to displace that world by seeking ancillary values or human forms. Imagination is still desperately needed—denying this is where Simon Critchley goes wrong—but it is an imagination purified of anything but the capacity to put the pressure of need on what turns out to satisfy that pressure because the world composed is suffused with a sense of sufficiency, all displacement spent. The reader encounters here something very close to early Wittgenstein's version of the mystical—the sheer presence of the facticity of the world as a bound whole. But Stevens is fascinated by the poet's capacity to manifest the force of that binding. This was not available for the logical empiricism of the *Tractatus.*

CHAPTER 2

Harmonium as a Modernist Text

The chief defect of humanism is that it concerns human beings.
Between humanism and something else it may be possible to create
an acceptable fiction.

(*LWS* 449)

This year it [summer] did not belong to us and was like a foreign
oppressor and this has made me low-spirited and blank: or perhaps
I should say reduced me to a state of unrelieved realism.

(*LWS* 760)

"Being conscious" is not in any decisive sense the *opposite* of what
is instinctive: most of the conscious thinking of a philosopher is
secretly guided and forced into certain channels by his instincts.

Behind all logic and its seeming sovereignty of movement, too,
there stand valuations, or, more clearly, physiological demands for
the preservation of a certain type of life.

(*BGE,* sec. 3)

The letter from which I take my first epigraph for this chapter was written
in 1943. I like to imagine that it took many years for Stevens to be in a position to add its second sentence. For the first sentence taken alone seems to
provide a perfect rationale for the distanced, abstracted, and ironic playfulness
that characterizes most of the poems in *Harmonium.* More important, this
first sentence provides one index of why this volume stands as a major modernist achievement—despite the many critics who argue, largely on stylistic
grounds, that Stevens never achieved the intricacy or depth of true modernist montage styles. Those critics not sympathetic to Stevens grudgingly admit that *Harmonium* differs from Stevens's more conservative recapitulations
of romantic themes in his later work. But they see the poems in Harmonium as all attitudinizing and all stylistic glitter without much substance—a
modernism manqué without the power to transform readers' sensibilities or
posit challenges that would bind poetry to a truly modern world.[1]

In my view, Stevens's efforts to adapt symbolist attitudes and styles is sufficient to earn for *Harmonium* the status of distinctively modernist American

poetry. But the case for Stevens's modernism—in this early work and throughout his career—does not depend primarily on matters of style. His significance as a modernist stems from the way he melds style into a full engagement
in ideas of what modernity requires—as complicity and as resistance. The
more fully we appreciate the ambitions of *Harmonium,* the better position
we will be in to recognize and perhaps to honor how the conservative dimensions of Stevens's later work stem from his effort to think through essentially the same problems that he articulated in this first book. The better
we recognize the terrifying force of fact for early Stevens, the more we will
appreciate the need he felt to grapple with providing convincing models for
how values might appear against that background.

   Harmonium is not just a congeries of self-indulgent bravura performances.
Rather, the volume offers a rich exploration of how such aesthetic commitments can positively engage a world in which it was difficult to tell "desire . . .
from despair" (*CPP* 286). In this volume Stevens was obsessed with being
adequate to his historical moment, a moment defined by the triumph of an
essentially secular and typically empiricist worldview. This milieu created
two basic challenges for Stevens. How could he develop stylistic traits that
acknowledged modern skepticism about traditional values yet nonetheless
possessed the ability to redirect that skepticism to accord with the capacities
of imagination that poetry might display? And how could poetry's modes
of statement accommodate themselves to the fundamentally naturalist ontology attuned to these empiricist perspectives while calling on resources
that empiricism tended to ignore? I think one short answer to both questions is that Stevens' realized he could learn a great deal from Nietzsche—
stylistically from his brisk ironic mode of writing, which seemed a forceful
alternative to symbolist efforts to meld the secular and the transcendental,
and thematically from his version of a naturalism that included the imagination within its ken and therefore could deal with questions of power and
invention without leaping into humanism. The best sign of Nietzsche's at-
tractiveness as a thinker might in fact be his capacity to show how even
empiricist versions of naturalism feed off humanist models of postulating
the importance of the conceptual mind and the rhetoric of self-knowledge.
For then Stevens could establish attitudes that proclaimed their indepen-
dence from those models, so that the mind could feel its capacities to reconfigure how it makes its claims on the world. Attitudes in *Harmonium* are
stances by which the poet self-consciously stages the imagination's struggles
to deal with the sheer otherness of what seems to come through perception.

   Ideally the negative freedom from the authority of various traditions
could combine with a positive freedom that Stevens figured as the ability of

the young girls in "The Plot against the Giant" to undo whatever plays the role of giant by whispering "heavenly labials in a world of gutturals." It takes self-irony of course to dream of poetry having force in that kind of world, but self-irony, too, must find its ways of separating itself from nihilistic self-satisfaction. By ironizing irony, by eliminating all its self-theatricalizing postures and much of its sense of pathos, one could explore the active power that lyric attitudes might possess. Ironizing irony allowed the poet to get beyond the feeling that the spirit is trapped in a world composed solely of mere facts that deny all of its basic desires to care about what comes in the form of fact. And then the poet might begin to test how those attitudes that the imagination formulates might spread into the actual world and promise to make differences—not only in how we stand toward "reality" but also in what we demand from the attitudes that we are tempted to adapt. At the least, poetry could offer a sense of imaginative freedom whose limitations were not yet entirely grasped and therefore whose positive work could not yet be circumscribed. Imagination fosters modes of protecting ourselves from the beliefs imposed upon us; it fosters the shaping of stances that allow for mutual recognition of desires that have no place within the dominant culture; and it allows us to stage modes of awareness of our bodies that produce attitudes allowing us to accept what no abstract formulation can justify.

There has been very good criticism showing how Stevens uses specific Nietzschean ideas in *Harmonium*.[2] However, I am less concerned with matching Stevens and Nietzsche in terms of those specific ideas than with characterizing how Stevens took on one aspect of what he saw as Nietzsche's basic project—to correlate an aggressive naturalism with a faith in the possibilities of self-creation and so to free the imagination from the felt imperatives of both humanism and empiricism.[3] For Stevens this naturalism involves questions about value because it insists that lying behind his culture's obsession with fact was the barely recognized need to come to terms with mortality.[4] Naturalism entailed fully grappling with everything that had been concealed by religious faith, especially the now apparent fact that human lives simply ended with the demise of the body. Thus one of Stevens's basic concerns about imagination was how it could adapt to being deprived of all the values that depended on hopes of immortality and on justification by the caretakers of morality. There is of course the haunting concrete case of the woman in "Sunday Morning" whose religious convictions make it difficult for her to connect with all that the world around her offers—as opportunities for ecstasy as well as demands that she take on the final stanza's adapting to mortality through the figure of "casual flocks of pigeons" descending "Downward to darkness, on extended wings." However, I hope to show that the entire volume expresses a pervasive need for versions of Nietzschean gaiety as a workable alternative to religious sensibility (*CPP* 284). More important, I develop ways of our valuing that enterprise even though Stevens never really achieved an impressive sense of tragic individualism.

I

I begin with two poems that show the Stevens of *Harmonium* at his most philosophical and at his most critical of all traces of humanism. "Nuances of a Theme by Williams" deserves pride of place in this context because it so fiercely contests what is involved in developing an unblinkingly secular and naturalist stance. This ferocity was perhaps necessary if Stevens were to arrogate those qualities for himself since it took considerable insouciance to so openly to criticize Williams at a point when Williams was one of the leaders of the New York literary avant-garde. Stevens deploys very little nuance in focusing his attack:

It is a strange courage
you give me, ancient star:

Shine alone in the sunrise
toward which you lend no part!

I

Shine alone, shine nakedly, shine like bronze,
that reflects neither my face nor any inner part
of my being, shine like fire that mirrors nothing.

II

Lend no part to any humanity that suffuses
you in its own light.
Be not a chimera of morning,
Half-man, half-star.
Be not an intelligence,
Like a widow's bird
Or an old horse.

(CPP 14–15)

Stevens strikes at the core of Williams's self-image as the poet more aware of the demands of modernity than even his expatriate friend Pound. Here Stevens claims that Williams is still trapped in a kind of humanist romanticism that has no chance of addressing the depth of dispossession demanded by modern thought. It is not enough to make stylistic gestures like *Spring and All*'s lament for how modernity makes it so difficult to establish vital harmony with nature. One has to adapt oneself to modernity's demands for self-consciousness about every metaphor, especially when the metaphor seems to allow the possibility of metaphysical solace or psychological identification with what were in fact nonhuman forces.[5] Once the boundary or difference between human and nonhuman is breached, every excess of romanticism can return in concealed and therefore more virulent terms. Even Stevens's first responding stanza seems deliberately contaminated as he allows himself all manner of similes in the effort to break from Williams while eliciting emotions for characterizing nature without analogies to the human.

Stevens's second stanza sounds the necessary notes by shifting the primary figure from simile to negation. That shift ironically allows him to return to his usual practice of capitalizing all the first words in his lines. For as he feels his way to letting a different rhetoric define the field of play that is the poem, he also recognizes that, if a modern poetry is possible, it will not be a matter of externals like capitalization. Rather, it will have to find a way out of the self-hatred deriving from his offering imperatives that have to rely on very much the same analogical grounds he criticizes in Williams's poem. The final turn comes when the speaker can find a way of speaking that seems less the victim of romanticism than the witness to his culture's failures to replace a romantic logic he cannot but observe is doomed to contradiction. Stevens can will a poetry whose metaphors are self-consciously as tired as that old horse. Changing to a modernist style will not in itself resolve the dilemma of having to find alternatives to humanism. But unlike the Williams poem it criticizes, this text manages to save at least the intricacies of self-consciousness as an uncontaminated space that may eventually afford a new Nietzschean theater for celebrating capacities of that consciousness.

If sneaking human values into nature betrays bad faith in the poet, the opposite pole provides no more gratification. For once the arts start a process of purifying their practices, one has to ask where that level of scrutiny is likely to end, and what values are likely to survive? "Metaphors of a Magnifico" offers one basic answer to that question. Among the several poetic visions that the poem ironizes, Pound's dream of constative presentation by focusing on the constitutive power of images dominates the scene:

Twenty men crossing a bridge,
Into a village,
Are twenty men crossing twenty bridges,
Into twenty villages,
Or one man
Crossing a single bridge into a single village.

This is old song
That will not declare itself . . .

Twenty men crossing a bridge,
Into a village,
Are
Twenty men crossing a bridge
Into a village.

That will not declare itself
Yet is certain as meaning . . .

The boots of the men clump
On the boards of the bridge.
The first white wall of the village
Rises through fruit trees.
Of what was it that I was thinking?
So the meaning escapes.

The first white wall of the village . . .
The fruit trees . . .

(CPP 15–16)

Presentation served for many modernists as a plausible alternative to a mi-metic art devoted to copying and interpreting the real. An ideal of presenta-tion promised that poetry could take on a reality in its own right by making manifest the energies of apprehending and reconfiguring what perception offers. But Stevens did not quite share this ideal. This poem suggests that im-agist idealizations of presentation might just replay the romantic cult of nature while surrendering the grammatical and conceptual resources on which pre-vious generations could rely for poetry's efforts to make its images perspicuous and resonant.

The first stanza proposes treating the men crossing the single bridge in terms shaped by two kinds of idealism—first, subjective idealism, and then its transcendental cousin. These songs can celebrate each agent producing a world, or they can define how something like spirit establishes the same world for all. Both of these options seem "old song" because both stances are shopworn and predictable. Neither alternative will declare itself to compose an adequate account of the phenomena. So the poem turns to realism, which is certain as meaning but also cannot declare itself because it provides no news for the imagination. Imagination seems stymied by tautology.[6]

With the failure of classical epistemology, the poem has to try on what seems a modernist style, bound to the order of perception and taking up the challenge to root consciousness there without postulating a specific locus of reflexive agency. This imagist mode avoids tautology because there are no overt claims to meaning. But that success exacts a significant price. When the world is reduced to perceptions, we lose any sense that the rendering might have a purpose beyond the effort to make objects declare themselves. Perhaps this faith in sheer objectivity will at least silence complaint since then there is also no room for a romantic rhetoric of alienation to dominate the scene. But rendering the objects this way also prevents any liveliness of declaration. There is only the otherness of the world. Whatever its appeal—at least it does not suffer human analogies—not even sheer naturalism can erase or cancel the effect of those ellipses and hence those traces of human desire for something more. Poetry can, however, ironically match the increasing objectivity by not interpreting the ellipses but by casting them as the only gesture of feeling capable of defining what is lacking in the scene. The first two ellipses suggest that nothing more need be said; the final two suggest nothing more can be said because of the limitations of the commitment to evocative concreteness.[7] In the end there is no power to correlate images and meanings—except for the poem's own capacity to offer a vocally nuanced space where it can celebrate its own tonal capacity to "declare itself" by offering intense and precise modes of self-consciousness about our dilemmas.

II

These two poems make manifest what Stevens thought it meant to be a poet consciously responding to a distinctively modern condition. One had to confront what I call a "radical naturalism," which brooks no humanistic consolation—either from relying on analogies that align humankind with nature or from imagining that art could establish something like an alternative site of grace, where one could experience a pure presence or distinctive integrity provided by formal synthesis. Neither Williams nor Pound could suffice as a model, and Eliot's daunting lament for the possibilities of the integrity that modern culture had destroyed seemed not a promising path for cultural renewal. Science had made convincing cases that explanation must be in terms of general laws rather than distinctive purposes by any kind of agency. And democratic politics made the explanation of values a matter of fashions and inclinations, with very little sense that heroic action was possible or, if possible, likely to be noticed or have much influence. Poetry had to deal directly with a flattened world everywhere haunted by reminders that we die alone and with very little to show for the time we managed to stay alive. The past becomes a tissue of illusions that poets can rely on only to make clear those roads that could no longer be taken.

However dark the situation, the poet still had considerable control over how choices about language could compose attitudes capable at least of successfully resisting empiricist models of inquiry without becoming merely evasive fantasy. Attention to how one might see or to how one might put language together had to serve provisionally as the source of a content that could engage the imagination and lead it back to the world. The imagination did not have to mime or copy the actual world but could play within it, testing the capacity of play to sponsor satisfying modes of self-reflection.[8]

In fact, the poet could treat an entire volume as an expression of the imagination's constructive abilities to make these invented attitudes converse with one another. Stevens had to rely on individual poems to develop a sense of encountering the variety of claims the world makes upon us. However, he could also organize patterns among the poems that thickened this particular sensibility by manifesting how fluid and how persistent it could be in trying to exercise its claims to participating in what modernity entailed. The poet could build an imagined repertoire of stances by which inner dialogue across poems replaces the modes of connection within poems that were once established by argument or by models of social coherence. Then the poet could visibly confront the most obvious consequence of modernity— the sense of fragmentation leaving consciousness trapped in the ironic condition of enforced awareness that it did not possess the powers to provide the meanings it seeks. While individual poems emphasized aspects of this fragmentation and a more general sense of desperation before all that made mortality terrifying, the poems as a collection might at least manifest the ability to bring order to one's own imagination even if that only intensified the painful disorder of what the subject could not control. If one could not penetrate appearances to establish a satisfying underlying reality, one could try to match the variety of appearances by providing an intricate set of tests for the reader's imaginative flexibility. All of these poems require reading against traditional assumptions about lyricism because the agency involved is not overtly expressive but embodied within shifting relations between sensation and abstraction. What else could embody a radical naturalism?

So far as I can tell, the kind of unity Stevens gave *Harmonium* in arranging previously independent poems does not quite warrant attributing a plot to the volume. Rather, the volume is organized by collocating series of poems that emphasize the capacity to develop varieties of affects in response to analogous situations in neighboring texts. There is also what seems a deliberate progression among these sets of poems that displays increasing self-confidence in transforming bitter ironies into more playful modes of confronting the bleakness of fact. Here I concentrate on what I consider two clear units—the first ten poems and the last five.

The first ten poems constitute a remarkable achievement. They reject dramatic realism of any kind (with the partial exception of "Le Monocle de Mon Oncle," a poem with its own considerable tonal strangeness). There is nothing charming or sentimental in these poems—nothing that invites readerly identifications because the primary trait is a Nietzschean distance from ordinary humanity. *Harmonium* begins by insisting that a truly modern consciousness has to take up a radical version of impersonality and abstraction that is less a stylistic device than an attitude toward what had been the characteristic stances of traditional lyric poetry. As Pablo Picasso's friend André Salmon put it, the new emerging modernism in art "set apart the men who were beginning to look at themselves 'on every side at once' and thus learning to scorn themselves" (in Chipp, *Theories of Modern Art,* 204). Such looking puts Stevens's readers in positions approximating the roles of anthropologists invited to participate in some unfamiliar culture whose lyrical rituals seem as enticing as they are shorn of discernable roles. Stevens made sure no other poet could write a "Nuances of a Theme by Stevens."

Perhaps, then, it is no wonder that Stevens needs to end his volume on somewhat different notes. I am fascinated by how Stevens seems to put the last five poems of the volume together as positing a much richer way of thinking in the face of the problems with naturalist models that oppress the book. Early on Stevens proves himself the master of ambiguous concluding gestures that manage at least some playful transformation of the bleakness presented: no poem ending with "Out of the tomb, we bring Badroulbadour" (*CPP* 40) can be content with the bleakness of the situation described. Yet readers might wonder at the value of letting so much depend on imaginative gesture rather than sustained thought. The last five poems gesture toward a response to this complaint. The first two poems in that final group are as intricate and as Nietzschean as Stevens gets in transforming the volume's tendencies to revel in how irony can play upon pervasive despondency. But all this strength and all this complexity only intensify the question, why add the concluding three very direct and simple poems? We have to figure out how these three poems feed off and complement the energies elicited by such complexities. These five poems, not incidentally, also inaugurate Stevens's reflections on the work that simile, resemblance, and equivalence can perform in shaping readerly emotions and in locating values poetry can address.

III

The opening ten poems of *Harmonium* seem to me a clear instance of how certain attitudinal qualities in Nietzsche's work probably influenced Stevens. The poems are not sponsored by any particular Nietzschean ideas. Rather, they offer an amalgam of sharply rendered versions of late romantic world weariness. But their excessiveness and sharpness are hard to imagine without Stevens's having internalized the spirit of this philosopher. There is here a distance from the human, a willingness to imagine humanity as a class of foreign beings, that is substantially deepened if we recognize its parallels with Nietzsche's capacity to put an entire race on trial for what it has let itself become. The sense of trial in turn deepens the force of Stevens's strange concreteness that so manifestly seeks to avoid fealties to the past in order to determine what might still be viable in our fictions about human values.

This way of reading *Harmonium* casts that book as trying out a Nietzschean freedom to begin with the inhuman and then make that inhumanity dazzlingly human in its play of compassion and startlingly lucid yet strange insight. By departing from the human we become able to see some aspects of it as if for the first time. Moreover, by departing from any capacity of rhetoric to establish what we take as values, value becomes itself an immediate condition of how the mind manages to give a shape to elemental forces of being that consciousness has yet to parse. Perhaps a radical naturalism has resources we overlook when we take our version of naturalism from the sciences. We might ask, for example, whether there is a stranger opening poem to a volume of poetry than "Earthy Anecdote." The title itself promises that this text seems unexpectedly casual for an introduction to the volume. Perhaps being earthy requires turning from the sublime to the anecdotal.

In order to enter this volume we have to be willing to place ourselves in this stripped-down space where we confront competing forces in their bare structure, with all social and personal details suppressed as irrelevant:

Every time the bucks went clattering
Over Oklahoma
A firecat bristled in the way.

Wherever they went,
They went clattering,
Until they swerved
In a swift, circular line
To the right
Because of the firecat.

Or until they swerved
In a swift circular line
To the left,
Because of the firecat.

The bucks clattered.
The firecat went leaping,
To the right, to the left,
And
Bristled in the way.

Later, the firecat closed his bright eyes
And slept.

(CPP 3)

Everything putatively "human" in this opening seems merely a figure in some flattened and opaque quasi allegory. There is only a distanced perspective before which there unfolds an apparently timeless and mechanical abstract scenario. But that perspective is decidedly not just reportorial. The poem revels in subsuming the world of reference under the imperatives to pleasure afforded by lyric form's capacity to undermine the apparent simplicity of assertion. The wildly varying trimeter is supplemented by an internal feminine rhyme between a preposition and the tail of a place name. In addition, the imaginary bucks are placed in what seems a real space but they subsume that space into the bizarre domain of sheer anecdote. The firecat, when it emerges, seems by contrast a principle of order brought to this clattering, and the verse mirrors that order by giving equal time to the swerve to the left and to the right—that is what "because" can do to an initial clattering over Oklahoma.

After that exercise in bringing order, the firecat can internalize causality and begin to revel in its power over the clattering. In the penultimate stanza the cat exercises something like subjectivity as the poem's means of preparing for the contrast established by the second long line. The opening was a matter of harsh sounds and brittle activity. The final stanza begins with a harmony of vowels all gathered into a state that embodies the opposite of clattering, so that the cat's sleeping comes to seem the essence of satisfied desire. It is as if the language were miming the force of the firecat even to the extent of not having to reveal anything about itself or about the allegorical situation except what manifests itself as quiet confidence in how it can produce effects on other beings.

Talking about free verse and structure can defer the question of what the actual allegory is in this poem, but it will not make the question go away. A reader has to determine what the bucks and the firecat represent since their relation is all that the poem offers. Are the bucks mere humanity driven by imagination? Or do they represent an imagination desperate to align itself with an endlessly shifting reality able to sleep secure in its difference from its pursuers? As I pose these alternatives I wonder whether the reader must actually choose between them. Why should we get a key to an allegory or submit it to a binary logic? Why can it not be enough to know that whatever the cat comes to represent, it satisfies our desire to identify with the position that possesses power and enjoys the narcissistic fruits of that possession.

Perhaps the audience for the poem is invited to concentrate on the structure of oppositions and so take up a somewhat playful mode of abstracted inhumanity in relation to its own fantasies. The refusal of standard hierarchical structure may itself provide the meaning because then we might learn something about ourselves that is not the standard fare of allegorical contrasts. This hypothesis is probably the only way we can make sense of the fact that the scene seems to allow for no hope of change or fulfillment. If we could resolve the allegory, we could think we escaped that level of fatality. But without a key to the allegory beyond the effects of sound and syntax, the poem challenges us to accept the discipline of trying to understand why it might matter that there appears to be no adequate principle for identifying who the victim is and who the victimizer. This sparseness asks us to shift from whining about powerlessness to being able to share a fascination with the cat's ultimate self-absorption—for the sake only of recognizing the effects of power whatever the contents attributed to it.

Allegory itself then serves less to interpret the world than to facilitate a mode of generating value not available if we insist on decoding meanings. Allegory makes it possible to identify with the cat's narcissistic repose because even if we do not know quite what it represents, we know that it stems from successful resistance to everything the bucks come to symbolize. In this reading the quasi allegory allows the writerly energy to manifest human intentionality without the promise that such signs of intentionality need to be backed by proposed resolutions for our uncertainties. How else might we position ourselves to heed those aspects of human life that are subjected to forces beyond our control?

IV

The rest of the *Harmonium*'s opening sequence explores subject positions and related possibilities of evaluation that emerge as consciousness pursues this fascination with inhuman perspectives. There is no drama of self-expression and no reach toward "profound" thematic resolutions. Yet these refusals are not without a sense of new permissions. The poems invite us to try out modes of participation that have no clear ethical correlates and no obvious way of reaching beyond what the senses activate, although there is a constant striving for something more than appearances yield. Value must reside in finding ways fully to inhabit the attitudes generated by maintaining differences from the typical human emotions that seem called for by the underlying situations.

Once "Earthy Anecdote" has defined the imagination's dilemma in relation to physical reality, it seems perfectly plausible to attempt directly addressing the soul. So the next poem, "Invective against Swans," begins with a Laforguian self-consciousness having to deal with a world in which swans have become ganders. A modernist poet who uses the figure of swans virtually has to play with self-contempt, so Stevens stages this situation to leave this soul only the fantasy of total escape:

> The soul, O ganders, flies beyond the parks
> And far beyond the discords of the wind.
>
> A bronze rain from the sun descending marks
> The death of summer, which that time endures,
> Like one who scrawls a listless testament
> Of golden quirks and Paphian caricatures,
>
> Bequeathing your white feathers to the moon
> And giving your bland notions to the air.

Notice that the first simile in the volume completes an embedded relative clause modifying "the death of summer." It is ganders who worry about the weather, and it is ganders whose texts become "Paphian caricatures." But the abilities of the ganders extend only so far. They do not control the soul. Instead, they motivate the soul to try to escape the world that they do control:

> Behold, already on the long parades
> The crows anoint the statues with their dirt.
>
> And the soul, O ganders, being lonely, flies
> Beyond your chilly chariots to the skies.
>
>   *(CPP 3–4)*

The one trace of human emotion, "being lonely," both interprets the soul's journey and makes it necessary. Here, in contrast to the opening poem, the allegory is all too clear and all too self-enclosed.[9] Allegory becomes the self-definition of a soul in flight from the statues whose dirt prevents satisfying the soul's need for recognition. However, even though we can easily interpret the poem's allegory, I suspect that we cannot identify with it except as a mark of the writers' failures to prove themselves anything different from the ganders they have produced out of swans. This sense of fear at perhaps not escaping being a gander leads us to the level of allegory that most concerns Stevens—not a level for decoding the content but a level in which we try to interpret our own responses to what seems dissatisfying in the ease with which we perform that decoding. Now we have to realize that our primary need for allegory is not to produce a meaning but to find ways of caring for and identifying with how the allegory structures experience. In this case we encounter a continuous tension between the intelligible on the level of cultural code and the meaningful on the level of how we might put that cultural code to work. We cannot not prove ourselves ganders.

As soon as the soul makes its entrance, it seems that the volume has to find a way of addressing the body within the same reductive abstract perspective. But for Stevens, introducing the body also requires introducing gender differences. Thus the volume turns to four poems on different aspects of the feminine as a framing of the sensual world. The last of these, "Infanta Marina," so thoroughly links body with the motions of mind and the uttering of subsiding sound that it prepares the way for the volume's first distinctive lyric speaker in "Domination of Black." This "I," however, is not a psychological being so much as an elemental force, teased out by the play of sound, color, and motion.[10] Stevens's lyric poetry will eventually need a more robust first person. But thanks to this sequence, it seems that there can be an effective first person that emerges simply as an expression of affects extending sensual experience. We do not need anything like a core self trying to work out its identity to appreciate the values involved here. This "I" seems to bring together the abstract soul and the "feminine" body without imposing any psychological pressure to express anything inward. Rather *Harmonium*'s first "I" seems born out of a vague yet intense void that desperately needs to supplement the sensuous order, if only by acknowledging its capacity to produce terror:

> At night, by the fire,
> The colors of the bushes
> And of the falling leaves,
> Repeating themselves,
> Turned in the room,
> Like the leaves themselves
> Turning in the wind
> Yes, but the color of the heavy hemlocks
> Came striding
> And I remembered the cry of the peacocks.

Here there is no allegory. Or, better, whatever allegorical impulse might have existed is swallowed up in how this "I" becomes fundamentally a second-order locus for registering the impact of sensations. Any greater effort to impose meaning would presumably reduce the impact of what is being concretely experienced. Moreover, that effort would have to make determinate what achieves presence only in the form of questions. These questions in fact serve as the poem's vehicle for entering these second-order concerns for responsiveness that make souls of what otherwise reminds us of ganders:

> I heard them cry—the peacocks.
> Was it a cry against the twilight
> Or against the leaves themselves
> Turning in the wind,
> Turning as flames turned . . .
> Full of the cry of the peacocks?
> Or was it a cry against the hemlocks?

> Out of the window,
> I saw how the planets gathered
> Like the leaves themselves
> Turning in the wind.

I saw how the night came,
Came striding like the color of the heavy hemlocks.
I felt afraid.
And I remembered the cry of the peacocks.

                                                    (CPP 7)

Formally the poem asks how we can correlate these activities of the "I."
How do "I fear" and "I remember" differ from the act of seeing? Why are
psychological terms here so allied with sheer sensations? And what is the
structural relation between a first person fearing and that person remembering? The poem's overall fullness of sensual apprehension seems inseparable
from some fundamental ontological lack that the peacocks produce because
they are so deeply responsive to the contrast between the turning leaves and
the immobile hemlocks. What began as the space of potential allegory gets
internalized as this modification of how sensations take on a haunting presence. But this modification is no less alien or uncomfortable, primarily because the resulting state of sensibility suggests that there might be such a
thing as a soul embedded within the sensual order.

"The Snow Man" offers a radical shift in sensibility. I am tempted to say
that the poem moves almost entirely from the realm of the senses to a mind
repudiated by that world. But that is to oversimplify the way Stevens adapts
these elemental binaries of sense and world, neither yet embodied in persons. Probably it is more accurate to say that instead of dwelling on sensibility immersed in oppressive physical detail, this poem explores the feelings of
power that can be mustered by pursuing as abstract a version of intentionality as possible. This mode of mental act may even afford a quite different
kind of sensuality located in the shaping force of the poem's single intricate
sentence.[11] This is the sensuality of impersonal care being forced to respond
to something like pure negation. Playful allegorical space and flattened detail become the instruments for a new capacity for synthesis that is philosophical precisely because it refuses all imperatives for argument and for
self-congratulation. Here poetry manages to shift from its newly found "I"
to the composing of a "one" able to experience concretely the force of its
constructive abilities. In effect, what had been the synthesizing work of
rhythm now takes on semantic force, and we find in this capacious sentence
a minimalist giant able to resist those "heavenly labials in a world of gutturals." What frames the nothing is not itself without force.

Still, these poems will not be confined to marmoreal structures, however
elegant and capacious. The feminine returns, first in the mode of women

rising from poverty to "puissant speech" that gives resonance to the endless "insinuations of desire." Then, with "The Load of Sugar Cane," the feminine becomes as abstract and as elemental as the mind of winter:

The going of the glade-boat
Is like water flowing;

Like water flowing
Through the green saw-grass,
Under the rainbows;

Under the rainbows
That are like birds,
Turning, bedizened,

While the wind still whistles
As killdeer do,

When they rise

At the red turban
Of the boatman.

(CPP 10)

Where silent immobility had been, now there is a marvelous abundance of clausal and phrasal connectives. And these connectives are not isolated within a distinctive world of language with its own conditions of causality. Rather, the linguistic connectives bring all of nature into conjunction with the sudden emergence of the boatman's red turban. All of nature seeks this possibility of the pure event of emergence, as if that were the crucial value available when we extend the figures of gender to the implicit language of metaphysics.

V

In this context we are in a position to appreciate why, when "Le Monocle de Mon Oncle" presents the volume's first contextualized human speaker, it has to be so wary and so intricate about how expression is possible. This speaker must offer himself as an expressive and purposive agent—the volume finally offers an agent responsible for producing meanings for the fluidity of the senses. However, it is difficult to attribute to this speaker much more stability than one finds in the order of the senses. The poem does offer a speaker manfully persisting in an effort to take responsibility for his situation, emboldened in large part by the pleasures of language that each version of the self affords the speaking. Yet even in the poem's assertiveness, aspects of that self seem to arise unbidden. The "I" seems always on the verge of becoming a mere construct, necessitated by his fear that without that projection the speaker would be even less in touch with his immediate situation, especially with the insistent "you" who must be addressed. In fact, it is only by developing qualities of this interlocutor that the poem can offer something other than solipsism. The self recognizes that it has to take responsibility for the horrors of mortality that provide what may be only a flight from any openness to what cannot be controlled:

> An apple serves as well as any skull
> To be the book in which to read a round,
> And is as excellent in that it is composed
> Of what, like skulls, comes rotting back to ground.
>   *(CPP 11)*

Here the volume has certainly found its way to apply allegory as a means of aping traditional moralizing. The poem becomes an exercise in adapting the wit and invention of the opening sequence to grim lyric cries of pain, but now with a better sense of both the defensive and the self-reflexive resources that emerge when one can speak of one's tears as the expression of "some saltier well / Within me" (*CPP* 13). The "I" has to recognize its bondage to elemental forces that require our turning ironically against our own lyrical impulses. But that turn itself opens significant new lyric possibilities for attaching feelings to our capacity to reflect on the limits of the expressive ego. In producing a lyric "I" for the volume, "Le Monocle de Mon Oncle" also establishes a new aspect of intentionality. This speaker seems capable of dealing with the distances that emerge when we recognize how the "I" is not a site in which we can reside very comfortably: "I never knew / That fluttering things have so distinct a shade" (*CPP* 18). Our need for meanings condemns us to the constant pursuit of shades and shadows that are implicated on the margins of what is sensible.

Here when we do get drama, we find even more irony and distance than we did in the flattened allegories, perhaps because what had been experiments in impersonal distance now become renderings of how far even personality can stray from its own immediate needs and desires. The volume forces upon us the pressure of all those qualities of experience that separate us from any of the forms of self-satisfaction lyric had promised. It also locates value in refusing to surrender to despair about that fact. Instead of despairing, imagination finds itself capable of staging subtle and intense states of mind impossible under more public and discursive expectations about what lyric poetry can afford social life.

VI

What can we say Stevens has accomplished with this opening? How does it announce the coming onto the scene of a modernist poetics to be reckoned with because of its ways of addressing its intellectual culture? We have already discussed one important achievement. There is in *Harmonium* an insistent refusal of traditional modes of attaching persons to their reflective lives because the poems refuse to celebrate their own sensitivity or moral intelligence. We are thrown into positions where the imagination has to learn again to inhabit its own demands for what a satisfying relation to the real might be even if these stances put it in tension with what might be practically feasible. Poems become exercises in defining styles of dissatisfaction and stylizing them so that they become more attractive than the conventional stances allowing us to confirm practical lives. If the negative could make ideals flutter, lyric intensity might give new vitality to the shades and shadows created by that fluttering. A new poetry might find the true giant by dwelling on the gutturals that undo his preferred self-image.

Gutturals after all play their part in Stevens's use of sensations to reverse traditional ironic practices. This is a second distinctive achievement. Irony typically feeds on a gulf between the senses and the mind: the senses seem trapped in error and the mind trapped in fear that correcting the error might produce even more debilitating conditions. But Stevens pushes irony to one of its limits by stressing movement in just the opposite direction. He is fascinated by "gusty emotions on wet roads on autumn nights" (*CPP* 67) that are too elemental for idealization. So he makes it appear that by pursuing such states of sensation we might be able to dwell without irritable reaching for ideas by which to interpret the compelling forces created by lyric rhythm and aural density. Stevens's naturalism is not just a matter of his intense attention to how sensations might be articulated. Stevens's naturalism fosters a radical commitment to something like an ideal of the senses by seeming to make present a significance beyond the details of sensations but nonetheless within them.

Stevensian sound is exemplary here. The words slip and strain semantically. But their commitment to lush musicality seems to afford its own sensual literalness not quite dependent on sense. The imaginary mother has a real existence in her cry:

> The pine tree sweetens my body.
> The white iris beautifies me.
>
> *(CPP 4)*

And there is no escaping the cry of the peacocks, so we have to speculate on what world might be the site of its reality.

Such commitments might make poetry matter not because of how it pursues or celebrates belief but because of how it manages to hold off the temptation to impose belief on sensation, thereby binding the imagination to that concrete world. This observation brings me to the third distinctive achievement in this volume. Critics are right when they characterize the values of this text as aestheticist. But Stevens gives a distinctive cast to aestheticism. For Stevens, aestheticism does not depend on formalism, although there is considerable attention to formal features. I prefer to see his aestheticism as emphasizing at every moment the work that poetry has to do to attach the mind to sensations while insistently refusing to yield to empiricist versions of what is entailed by the life of the senses. Poetry for early Stevens must let the imagination pursue the pleasures of refusing to let philosophy control how sensation releases imaginative energies.

Value resides in the particularity of the invention. For such invention has the capacity to make us care about the imaginative resources of each particular gesture and attitude explored by the poems. This caring for the particular twists and turns of imaginative energy is true of all significant poetry. However, traditionally the imaginative energy is organized and justified by a rhetorical concern for metaphoric significance. *Harmonium*'s distinctive intelligence is its almost total refusal of this route to significance. The significance is all in the process by which the imagination manages to keep its inventions engaged while putting off any sense that interpretive authority can be produced by projecting onto the text typical situations, emotions, and judgments. The poems both create distinctive stances and embrace the task of justifying or celebrating them in their particularity as inventions within the world rather than in their capacity to secure any kind of "truth" about the world. Poetry must insist on its capacities to compose literal equivalents that adapt the world of sensation to the demands of art.

A fourth achievement concerns the displacement of person in the poems for modes of expression more abstract and provisionally inhuman. This is not Eliot's impersonality, which one could say is personality uneasy with self-expression. Stevens makes poems whose expressivity depends on their distance from any typical dramatic scene and their demand that meaning inheres primarily in how characters engage situations. The best way to talk about these traits may be to see the poems in *Harmonium* as inviting readers to alter how they envision what is involved in intentionality, as many of Nietzsche's texts do in another register. As heavenly labials undo the giant, the readers are allowed a glimpse of the imaginative state that makes some-one a giant in the first place. Perhaps there can be structures that fully en-gage the mind precisely because they yield to modes of linkage for which the mind has no categories and no preset expectations. Perhaps the activity of making as an extension of sense can replace making sense as a cognitive enterprise. As the psyche finds satisfactions in poems that do not lead back to traditional imaginative identities for author and audience, it can become fascinated by something close to an inhumanity at the core of its investments in the flesh. Poetry can virtually replace a psychological speaker with sheer conditions of speaking and hence conditions of lush sound make articulate what becomes of the senses filtered through language. In addition, poetry can invite the imagination to take into itself what become figures for its own intensities. Poetry does not interpret the cry of the peacocks but remembers it and transmutes it into a state of fear that brings the subject to the emotion rather than putting the emotion under the control of the subject.

In order to characterize these emotions we have to repudiate any image that they are "about" a specific person struggling to make sense of his or her particular life history and present social situation. Stevens's impersonality is built into the very status of what voice is and how expressivity emerges. In other words, impersonality becomes a specific condition of intentionality that is content to locate this expressivity in the constructive process, without implying any needy and ultimately self-congratulatory presence underlying how the experience is formulated.[12] *Harmonium*'s opening lyrics become experiments in foregrounding versions of intentionality that can stand in themselves as states of agency while refusing to allow the modes for recu-perating purposes we employ when we pursue intentions.[13] We can then speak of the structure of the opening segment of the volume in terms of how each of these models of consciousness needs supplements and adjust-ments if the sequence as a whole is to respond to the sense of challenge Stevens projected as the need to make lyric poetry adequate to twentieth-century realities. If one keeps all these innovations in mind, it seems no surprise that this opening sequence leads directly to the poems critical of Williams and of Pound with which I began this chapter.

VII

Invent as the poet might, reality offered one persistent challenge forcing the poet continually to begin again. The more forcefully the poet's imagination could strip away our typical fantasies about lyric agency, the starker the pressure of a mortality carried by the language of fact that elicited the poetic energies in the first place. One could pose alternative ways of thinking not caught in empiricism's fantasies about reducing all language to lucid and unequivocal statement. But Stevens could not avoid the empiricist core of truly modern thinking—that a world of fact was also a world where mortality appeared in sheer and unrelieved otherness to the projections of imagination. All of the dazzle in *Harmonium* keeps coming back to the demand that the imagination face the unredeemable mortality implied by the sense of rampant contingency. The poet had to recognize that metaphor could not escape this contingency, although even modernity might allow playing with such contingency as one mode of bitter ironic relief for an individual self-consciousness.

"The Emperor of Ice Cream," for example, fuses an ultimately naturalist despair with a metaphoric register that I think successfully repudiates pathos—in part because its bitter impersonal playfulness puts the collective tendency toward self-pity on stage. At least we can see around our fears of mortality and play with them rather than being bound to the pathos of our continuity with nature. What is more, the link between empiricism and mortality is even tighter and more bleakly playful in how "The Worms at Heaven's Gate" stages the path of empirical investigation:

> Here is an eye. And here are, one by one,
> The lashes of that eye and its white lid.
> Here is the cheek on which that lid declined,
> And, finger after finger, here, the hand,
> The genius of that cheek. Here are the lips,
> The bundle of the body and the feet.
> . . . .
> Out of the tomb, we bring Badroulbadour
>
> *(CPP 40)*

Rarely is the depressing ontology of the copulative verb so clearly manifest. Confronting mortality turns out to be also testing the imagination's power to provide alternatives to empiricist thinking. Here each bodily part is so emphatically fact that facticity itself becomes a theme. And as theme it enters the Mallarméan space of writing: these are facts living in imagination and taking on a metaphoricity in their capacity to resist metaphor.

This confrontation with the naturalist spirit of contingency pervades *Harmonium,* so simply registering the nature of the struggle is not news.[14] Nonetheless, it may be newsworthy to treat these observations as a reason for returning to the question of Nietzsche's significance for the volume—in relation to the handling of naturalist themes and, more abstractly, in relation to how Nietzsche might be seen as an influence on Stevens's development of a style that can adapt a Mallarméan stress on the subtle complexity of attitudes to the sharpness and brutality of modern life.

On the most elemental level Nietzsche matters in the reading of *Harmonium* because he is the philosopher who best indicates why Stevens's book can lay claim to a timely engagement with his culture on the level of the history of ideas. Nietzsche articulated conceptually what Stevens also saw quite clearly: the pressures of fact and of mortality could best be confronted philosophically not by an idealistic rejection of naturalism but by a refurbished naturalism capable of adapting many idealist themes, especially with regard to self-expression. More generally, Nietzsche would have mattered most for the Stevens of *Harmonium* because he most clearly addressed what naturalism might become. There were many late nineteenth-century thinkers devoted to developing naturalist alternatives to theology and to the idealism that had come to seem its bastard. But only Nietzsche seemed willing to wage that struggle without forging an alliance with empiricist science. Unlike James or Husserl or Dewey, Nietzsche saw the problem of nihilism as generated by the very ideal of truth that empiricist science had to take as its foundation. Science was not wrong to assert its ability to influence human practices. It was, though, dangerously wrong in tying itself to claims about an apparently objective and impersonal version of truth and then making imperialist claims that it was science that should determine what might count as "truth" in the full range of human practices.

So Nietzsche's naturalism, like Stevens's, does not stop with the divide between fact and value or that between bare mortality and what the imagination might make of one's efforts to become who one is. Nietzsche insisted that an adequate naturalism had to provide a genealogy in which the category of fact had to be linked to power. Moreover, an adequate naturalism had to use this genealogy to diagnose where the dominant empiricist spirit had gone wrong. For Nietzsche and for Stevens the basic mistake was coming to trust in what Adorno would call "identity thinking," by which the primary task was to render individual descriptions unequivocal so that there could be clear relations between those particulars and the categories that subsumed them.[15] Stevens added to Adorno's suspicions of the lack of significant self-reflection in such thinking a critique of the very form of empiricist logic, based as it was on the copulative verb fixed by the mind's capacities for description. Later I elaborate ad nauseam on how Stevens tends to replace the copulative by predications that depend on analogy and resemblance, where "is and as are one" (*CPP* 406).

Robert Leggett has provided a marvelous rendering of how Nietzsche affected Stevens's thematic concerns in the major poems of *Harmonium*. Even with the stunning results Leggett achieves, however, I feel I have to resist his way of reading because I do not trust the direct thematic application of philosophy to poetry.[16] Stevens was to put the contrast between the disciplines this way in "A Collect of Philosophy":

> The habit of forming concepts unites them. The use to which they put their ideas separates them. . . . The philosopher searches for an integration for its own sake . . . ; the poet searches for an integration that shall be not so much sufficient in itself as sufficient for some quality that it possesses, such as its insight, its evocative power, or its appearance in the eye of the imagination.
>
> (*CPP* 862)

Hence Stevens's contrast between the philosopher seeking a world "which yet remains to be discovered" and the poet seeking a world "which yet remains to be celebrated" (*CPP* 864). When a poet like Stevens reads Nietzsche, that philosopher's perspective becomes for poetry something closer to a *habitus* or disposition of imagination than a set of beliefs. Even the naturalism they share becomes more a place for the imagination to dwell than to rest in the comforts of shared belief.

If I am right, this assertion has two oddly balanced consequences—that we should tread lightly in employing specific Nietzschean arguments or intertexts and that we should recognize that taking on a philosophical model as a kind *habitus* is more likely to influence a poet's style and overall values than it is the development of the poet's specific themes. Just as F. H. Bradley provided Eliot a means of adapting the intricacies of symbolist poetics to a more socially conscious disposition of poetic energies, so Nietzsche afforded Stevens the possibility of eliciting more robust philosophical resonances from the nuanced ironies emphasized by symbolist attitudes.[17] These attitudes were sufficiently subtle and complex to stand for modernity but not sufficiently pointed or aggressive fully to express either the poet's needs or the poet's ambitions. So I want to elaborate two ways in which Nietzsche probably contributed to Stevens's own sense of finding styles adequate to the modern world—his way of encouraging an epigrammatic pointedness and assertiveness that does not lose the subtle ironies and correspondences of symbolist writing and his modeling a "masculine" brio that helps explain a temptation Stevens flirts with in the poems on mortality gathered after "Sunday Morning."

It is not sufficiently remarked that Laforgue and Mallarmé were naturalist writers. The Baudelairean correspondences that fascinated them were psychological, not transcendental; alternatively, one could say that spirit seemed a more subtle extension of matter (*CPP* 750). Subtlety and hence spirit had to live in textual presences that refused the apparent naturalness of earnest speech for the denser and more fluid sensibilities presented by the foregrounding of a self-consciousness absorbed in the intricacies of its own self-presentation. Heavenly labials in a world of gutturals might undo the giant of empiricist realism while emphasizing how the writing itself is neither heavenly love nor pity but a mode of presence based largely on the force of its negations. The unseen world is no longer a dream because the poem's music offers the indecipherable as the most palpable feature of what writing makes present.[18]

Yet while we can see in symbolism a lineage for much of *Harmonium,* I think Stevens felt that Mallarmé and Laforgue were impossible to bring directly into an American context. Put simply (and with the necessary touch of irony), they were insufficiently virile. Their characteristic attitudes involved sly manipulations of what Americans would take as effete and decadent postures. Stevens's poems are more elemental in their assertions, more dramatically gestural in their eagerness to draw out explicit yet strange ironies from the situation, and more philosophical in their asking the complexity and delicacy of images to seem to reach beyond and make judgments of the particular situation of the writing. I think Stevens would say that as *Harmonium* develops, his poems become more "masculine" because they are ultimately less caught up in the flourishing of the senses and more driven by something like an epigrammatic brio. This brio provides the presence of an authorial will often drawn to conclusions that project an abstract level of reflection (as opposed to Mallarmé's abstraction, which extends the order of sensation).

I have no independent evidence for the claim that Stevens's break from the symbolist style evoked by the initial poems in *Harmonium* stems largely from his reading of Nietzsche.[19] I could cite Leggett's demonstration that Stevens read a lot of Nietzsche when he was living in New York. However, my claim for Nietzsche's presence in *Harmonium* consists simply in the likelihood of his recognizing that this philosopher affords useful ways to adapt the intricate self-consciousness of the best late nineteenth-century poetry for the twentieth century. Nietzsche brought modernist style from the fine parings of Flaubert and the meditations on champagne bubbles of Mallarmé to the struggle between Apollonian and Dionysian forces for the spirit of a culture. More important for my purposes, Nietzsche's overall tone of tragic gaiety authorizes two basic stylistic gestures that enable the activity of writing to resist its own possible satisfactions in copulative naming. He provides an overall spirit of playful metaphors that carry on a literal struggle for expressive satisfaction in the present tense so that one need not submit to the order of "fact." And his writing relies on well-turned and swiftly delivered surprising and perspicuous phrases that demonstrate the scope and intensity that give such playfulness distinctive power. Aphorism marries subtlety with logic.

We can pursue this comparison of aspects of Nietzsche's style with aspects of *Harmonium* by turning to three Nietzschean characteristics that arguably help establish Stevens's differences from symbolist poetics. There is first the feeling for the epigrammatic even if it is evident in *Harmonium* more in the economy of the writing than in an actual series of epigrams. (That Stevens loved the epigrammatic is evident in his *Adagia,* but this brings us to a different stage in his life.) For Nietzsche, the aphoristic imagination is valued not for its capacities to escape the real or to evoke alternative realities but instead for its capacities to produce equivalences for the real that are not arrived at by empiricist ideals of representation. Exotic points of view turn out suddenly to produce valuations to which even the most practical of consciousnesses have reason to attend. Artifice becomes inseparable from vigorous perception: "If you have your *why* for life, you can get by with almost any *how.*—Humanity does not strive for happiness; only the English do."[20] Such passages simply and compellingly demonstrate that empiricist reason is not the only or always the most powerful instrument for negotiating and regulating perception.

Second, there is a remarkable capacity for self-conscious writerly work to put psychology and metaphor on the same level as sensuous existence while keeping the focus on the mutual force distributed between consciousness and sense. The following passage is casual Nietzsche, yet it shows a way to have abstraction extend a naturalist attitude without departing from the physical world, much as the opening poems in *Harmonium* do: "Perhaps there is nothing about so-called educated people and believers in 'modern ideas' that is as nauseous as their lack of modesty and the comfortable insolence of their eyes and hands with which they touch, lick, and finger everything"

(*BGE,* sec. 263).[21] Here moral language about lack of modesty immediately gets situated in body parts, then in actions with body parts, so that the passage can play with putting abstraction and physicality on the same writerly plane. Nietzsche asks us to see moral behavior *as* a kind of bodily bearing and bodily bearing *as* indicative of moral stature. There is no place for the traditional concept-driven mode of evaluating actions and persons.

Finally, there is in Nietzsche and in Stevens an implicit willfulness in the writing that differs substantially from Mallarme's tendencies to have the writer eventually absorbed within the space of reflection offered by the writing. Nietzsche speaks of author and authority in the same breath: "The noble type of man experiences *itself* as determining values; it does not need approval; it judges . . . It knows itself to be that which first accords honor to things; it is *value-creating.* Everything it knows, as part of itself, it honors" (*BGE,* sec. 260).

This value-creating aspect is crucial for early Stevens because Nietzsche showed how value could be simply a condition of expression, a condition developed within an attitude developed by writing, with no need for supplementary justification. Just think of how "Worms at Heaven's Gate" offers Nietzschean means for transforming pathos into something like transvaluation. The poem evokes two features of authorial will. First, we might notice that while the details build up, the eye has to slow down to register the force of each fact. It seems as if the poem were flaunting its own capacity to examine the facts without submitting to the pressure of reality. Then we have to ask why it is we bring out of the tomb so oddly named a character as Badroulbadour. Why are we not bringing her into the tomb? I think the reason is simple but powerful. Out of all these details we construct a person, indeed a person with an exotic name that calls up how the register of sound need not submit to the register of fact. Perhaps we could reconstruct the spirit of the person by dwelling on those awful details. Then the person as reconstructed and as sounded becomes a figure testifying to the imagination's abilities to make differences within how we perceive the natural world. This quasi-epigrammatic conclusion stresses the reintegration of fact into personhood and so establishes for the poem its own complex attitude that does not resolve either into body parts or into a pathos lamenting what becomes of those parts. Naturalism properly conceived may be compatible with ideals of resurrection.

Another brief poem, "The Curtains in the House of the Metaphysician," allows us to extend this embodied willfulness beyond the poems explicitly devoted to mortality. Here we see Stevens modifying a Mallarméan attitude toward landscape by testing how it can provide a space for a Nietzschean authorial will. Now the encounter is not with bare fact but with a general feeling of nature's resistance to the imagination that Stevens even at this early date feels has to be imagined.[22] In effect this poem offers a second-order naturalism whose stress on the inhuman mocks all efforts to develop romantic analogies. Yet the poem still manages to cast facing that bleakness as a bold expressive attitude whereby the human finds its place in an expanded naturalism:

> It comes about that the drifting of these curtains
> Is full of long motions; as the ponderous
> Deflations of distance; or as clouds
> Inseparable from their afternoons;
> Or the changing of light, the dropping
> Of the silence, wide sleep and solitude
> Of night, in which all motion
> Is beyond us, as the firmament,
> Up-rising and down-falling, bares
> This last largeness, bold to see.
>
> *(CPP 49)*

That largeness is even bolder to hear. "Up-rising" and "down-falling" are at best quite awkward attempts at cleverness. But notice what they set up. "Bares" seems to occupy the point of the poem where several internal systems come together. There is simple alliteration with "bold" and a more complex play of *a* sounds transmitting "firmament" to "last" and "largeness," with the *b* picked up in "bold." More important, syntactic and semantic double meanings in the final lines belie the poem's apparent economy of concise direct description. "Bares" evokes "bears," a brilliant switching of agency so that bareness itself has to take on the capacity to bear up under what it reveals. This move helps set up an intricate contrast between physical and mental motion. And "bold to see" refers both to the object the bareness creates for human consciousness and to the possibility that this bareness seems capable of seeing in its own right, as the ultimate power of continuity. Bareness is the condition allowing the realization that the opening "it comes about" marks a general level of contingency that must replace any allegorical promise for a level within human experience that symbolist poetry might want to render. Yet that contingency does not rule the poem because there is a boldness suggested that is nourished by this last largeness. Seeing itself becomes a heroic act, completed by the fact that this seeing does not even try to interpret itself—it just comes to occupy all of the alien stage set for it.

VIII

I think something strange happens in *Harmonium* after "Sunday Morning." Most of the poems between "Comedian" and "Sunday Morning" explore attitudes toward the imagination's roles in relation to fact, quintessentially "A High-Toned Old Christian Woman," "The Weeping Burgher," "The Curtains in the House of the Metaphysician," "Tea at the Palaz of Hoon," "Disillusionment of Ten Clock," and, at the negative end of the pole "Banal Sojourn" and "Depression before Spring." Here the emphasis is on the range of attitudes and tones that become resources against the pressure of reality. After "Sunday Morning" there seems a narrowing of range and a more perplexing tonal concentration on two basic motifs—what we might call "the poems of the perfect cock" and "the poems of the perfect vagina" (or perhaps of the imperfect vagina). Here I think the Nietzschean resistance to the dandy goes too far because the masculine poems seem pushed to excessive posturing as the absolute threat of mortality refuses to abide. Yet these poems are worth our attention, in part because they deliberately prepare for *Harmonium*'s final group of five poems, which conclude with a more philosophical and expansive sense of how the masculine and the feminine can be brought together in an almost satisfying expansive naturalism.

It is not only self-protection that leads me to confess I have nothing to say about the poems of the perfect vagina—"Stars at Tallapoosa," "Frogs Eat Butterflies," "Jasmine's Beautiful Thoughts," "Life Is Motion," "Colloquy with a Polish Aunt," "To the One of Fictive Music," and, for me most evocatively, "Two Figures in a Dense Violet Light." These poems directly and powerfully register what it might be like to accept fully the relation of what we sense to what we feel, with no added reaching after fact, reason, or gesture that protects us from yielding to bliss possible within "the marriage / of flesh and air" (*CPP* 65):

> Of bliss beyond the mutes of plaster,
> Or paper souvenirs of rapture
>
> Of bliss submerged beneath appearance,
> In an interior ocean's rocking
> Of long, capacious fugues and chorals.
>
> *(CPP 63)*

The "masculine" poses typically come in weaker poems or, more accurately, poems that have as their task contouring to what defeats more direct and capacious forms of imagination. Here Stevens seems to examine the consequences for lyric of stressing stances that refuse to rely on the presentation of images but seek instead the expressive force of an attitude that seems capable of forging alternatives to despair. The basic examples are "Bantams in Pine Woods," "Palace of the Babies," "Cortège for Rosenbloom," "Architecture," "The Wind Shifts," and "Gubbinal."

These poems offer a variety of tones—from postures of unblinking stoical lucidity, to bitter resignation, to bold, self-assured challenge. However, they all share this need to have writing issue in a cross between gesture and attitude that resolves situations simply by finding an emotional stance that seems provisionally to dodge the pressure of reality. There is little internal process of thinking in the poems. Instead, the stanzas stage situations that challenge the possibility of any response from within that might evoke a conventional emotional repertoire. Attitude must provide values that seem unavailable to argument or perception or reliance on tradition. So the poem must rely for psychic survival on manly gestures like setting "I" against the fear of "portly Azcan" and "his hoos" or the sheer acceptance of the failures of imagination in "Cortège for Rosenbloom" and "Gubbinal." Stevens makes such texts grapple with the potential hollowness of the gestures they rely on because the poet cannot but hear how his constructions fail to alleviate the pains of mortality that they have to engage.

I like "Architecture" best as an example of the struggle to find a resolving attitude because that poem turns Mallarmé's constructivist images for writing into pseudo-Nietzschean eugenics. But "The Wind Shifts" is shorter, easier to talk about, and more explicitly attuned to a naturalism gone slightly mad:

This is how the wind shifts:
Like the thoughts of an old human,
Who still thinks eagerly
And despairingly.
The wind shifts like this:
Like a human without illusions,
Who still feels irrational things within her.
The wind shifts like this:
Like humans approaching proudly,
Like humans approaching angrily.
This is how the wind shifts:
Like a human, heavy and heavy,
Who does not care.

(CPP 68)

The boldest feature of this poem is the level of generalization. It flaunts occupying a position where consciousness need not distinguish at all between kinds of humans. The only relevant differences are temporal—between old humans who "still" think "eagerly and despairingly" or indulge a range of affective responses to the uncaring wind and the human (presumably a new type) who is sufficiently heavy not to care. I think this human is heavy enough not to try emotionally reacting to the wind because, rather than treat the wind's lack of care for humans as a threat, the poem simply identifies with that lack. In this poem it matters only that consciousness can adapt a heaviness providing an adequate complement to the wind's tendency to produce meaningless change. Analogously, the perfect cock is one that does not worry that it is only a cock. That refusal of worry may be the only way to achieve an ironic harmony with nature while managing to utter fewer syllables than it takes to refer to the wind. Heaviness of soul does not get much more absolute, especially since it cannot even try to vary the adjectives needed for the rhythm. Why should such frippery as variety matter for a real man? But how can this real man not mock his own need to care about the role of not caring? This mode of acceptance is so flat that I cannot resist hearing an ironic note, although the irony may reside only in the poem's surprise that this simple a gesture might suffice to define the values at stake.

IX

Leggett is terrific on how "Peter Quince at the Clavier" invites a much more subtle and more supple Nietzschean reading that attempts to put together the male and female attitudes that *Harmonium* has separated:

> Music is associated with art in the poem but not as a symbol for aesthetic form. Rather music is identified with the form-destroying Dionysian impulse; it is identified with desire, and music/desire is the force that moves the poem, the agency of change. . . . The shifts in tone and mood correspond to the shifts in imagery, and these suggest the stages of the transformation of the speaker, who moves from Apollonian individuality to Dionysian oneness to the Dionysio-Apollonian affirmation of the world of becoming that ends the poem.
>
> (*Early Stevens* 81–82)

Yet although this statement is true and welcome news, it seems slightly out of place as a summary of the poem. It makes Stevens a poet who imitates philosophy rather than one who uses it for lyric purposes. So I want to shift from what "Peter Quince" says to what the poem does as a performance of capacities distinctive to lyric. I concentrate only on the overall action because this poem seems to me the first in a closing series that finds Nietzschean motifs capable of resolving the basic tensions in *Harmonium*'s coming to terms with naturalism. The resolution is less thematic than it is a matter of stretching and modifying the attitudes carried by the lyrics earlier in the volume. Here philosophical ambitions need no longer be a source of embarrassment for the poet, requiring intricately indirect stances toward abstract statement. These ambitions can be absorbed into dramatic stances toward the world.

Notice, for example, how Peter's tone changes from the dandy solipsist perhaps defensively staging a sensibility in the first section to the confident and dense philosophical tone of the fourth section. Building on equivalences provided by "so" seems to me especially important here. So by the fourth section the attitude generates a complex chain of thinking:

> The body dies; the body's beauty lives.
> So evenings die, in their green going,
> A wave, interminably flowing.
> So gardens die, their meek breath scenting
> The cowl of winter done repenting.
> So maidens die, to the auroral
> Celebration of a maiden's choral.
>
> Susanna's music touched the bawdy strings
> Of those white elders; but, escaping,
> Left only death's ironic scraping.
> Now, in its immortality, it plays
> On the clear viol of her memory,
> And makes a constant sacrament of praise.
>
> *(CPP 74)*

Leggett rightly notices connections between the acceptance of becoming here and in "Sunday Morning." The ideas are much the same, but the tones are very different. In the conclusion of "Sunday Morning" there is a sad acceptance that lingers over the details much in the same way that the extended wings sink slowly downward to darkness. Here "Now" introduces a note of triumphant discovery. Furthermore, the poem concludes not just with acceptance but also with praise, in fact with a sacrament of praise that embodies the praise within the physical world. Naturalism is not denied and death in no way transcended. But there emerges the possibility of letting beauty do its work without requiring self-protective and ironic strategies that protect the poet from the risks of opening language to the world. Now, in fact, there is sufficient ease of mind or certitude of stance to allow an integration of narrative with the expression of significance that "Earthy Anecdote" seemed to have successfully banished from the volume.[23] The dramatic cause of praise is manifestly "the clear viol of" Susanna's memory. Now rather than being in tension with the order of perception, the memory of Susanna extends perception into a second-order domain of generalizations about his sensations that establish possible significance for the narrative.

"Peter Quince" constitutes a reconciliation of conflicting motifs based on the ecstatic powers of the imagination to find its excesses compatible with truth. The next poem, "Thirteen Ways of Looking at a Blackbird," offers a very different kind of resolving movement. It engages the problem of mortality in terms of the most elemental features of time, with none of the lushness or abstract assertion possible in the previous poem. Clearly the poem echoes "Metaphors of a Magnifico," but just as clearly it differs from it in several important regards. The main difference is that "Metaphors of a Magnifico" moves only in one direction—toward increasing incoherence. I think "Thirteen Ways . . ." opens many possible directions for the imagination to pursue. The most important of these introduces ways of dealing with figures of time and death.

Here death begins by occupying its usual mode of presence in *Harmonium*, as absolute other (section VI) and as the strange fear that the shadow of the equipage could be blackbirds (section XI). But the final two stanzas brook no shadows. In a poem mostly about what the mind brings to looking,[24] these stanzas place that mind concretely within its capacity to handle typical circumstances. And that reminder of intimate yet intricate instant calculation offers resonant paths for defining ways to accept and even to treasure the roles that fear of death can play for our imaginations:

XII

The river is moving
The blackbird must be flying

XIII

It was evening all afternoon
It was snowing

And it was going to snow.
The blackbird sat
In the cedar limbs.

(CPP 76)

These passages are elemental because they deliberately fuse intense concreteness with a high degree of abstraction. The force of the inferences matter a great deal because they give the imagination a means of cooperating in the practical world—a state very rare in this volume. Imagination is deprived of its usual playful excesses, but that only intensifies the need to register the forces at work. Section XII embeds complex processes of inference. If the river is moving, the ice has melted, and the blackbirds must be active. Here there is no actual sight of the blackbird. Rather, the relevant theater is how the mind can elaborate the place of blackbirds in the cycle of seasons.

The final section shifts from a combination of temporal and modal relations to a much more dense spatializing and thickening of time. The swift movement of the seasons yields to the ways New England weather can slow time and produce a static scene that invites imaginative dwelling. What we see becomes inseparable from how we know both the present and the future. And we realize that we can make these leaps because we know not just that it is snowing but also that the world produced by the snow imposes its own temporal order. The observer can project with confidence states that are not basically matters of observation. So the blackbird's sitting blends the nothing that is not there with something that is in fact there—with a strange sense that the very fear of death aligns us positively with what is most elemental in our orientations toward living in a physical world.

We could put essentially the same observation in another way by noting that readers seem invited to extend into the metaphoric domain the confidence by which the poem handles temporal relations implicit in the scene. To see the blackbird is to see a figure of mortality. The blackbird cannot not function also as a symbol, albeit perhaps the most fully naturalized symbol in American poetry. There is none of the tension of "Earthy Anecdote" between the physical and the allegorical. The blackbird just sits there in his place, no longer moving, though presumably able to move. The poem "wills" this passivity because it completes the scene and does not disrupt the temporal continuities. Fear of what the blackbird represents seems as natural and as capable of being handled as is this forecast of the weather.

X

Why after these two fulsome poems does the volume conclude with so un-pretentious a trio? We need some distinctions before we can offer an answer. "Nomad Exquisite" is short but not "unpretentious." I see the poem as complementing its two predecessors by focusing explicitly on the possible implications of the linguistic resources these poems bring to bear. "Peter Quince" offers an explicit philosophical coming to terms with death that allows the integration of scene and commentary. "Thirteen Ways" in contrast works imagistically to provide a picture functioning as a symbol that absorbs all discursivity into how the blackbird accepts and even wills its relation to time. "Nomad Exquisite" becomes free to resolve the volume in terms of the poet's rhetorical expansiveness, here built on the capacity of "as" structures not just to contrast with identity thinking but also to exemplify a very different relationship to time. "Nomad Exquisite" repeats "so," much like the conclusion of "Peter Quince," but this time Stevens stresses how "so" can function in an elaborate, formal grammatical structure. Here poetry creates a different temporality, a temporality of complex equivalents where the time of the writing, the time of the reading, and the qualitative conditions of the experience all reinforce one another.

This poem then explores a new model of valuing whose intricacies and possibilities will occupy Stevens for the remainder of his career. The logic of the "as"/"so" relation defines one way poetry endures by establishing its own continually reinforced present tense. There "in me" emerges as something not quite in time because it becomes so fully in its place and indeed in the reader's place—like the blackbird but self-aware as the satisfied creator of how it can live:

As the immense dew of Florida
Brings forth
The big-finned palm
And green vine angering for life,

As the immense dew of Florida
Brings forth hymn and hymn
From the beholder,
Beholding all these green sides
And gold sides of green sides,

And blessed mornings,
Meet for the eye of the young alligator,

And lightning colors
So, in me, come flinging
Forms, flames, and the flakes of flames.

(CPP 77)

Rarely have descriptions in lyric been so resistant to objectifying a scene.[25] This is a poem about orientations toward nature. But what we can take as nature is from the first qualified by relational terms that bring subjectivity and appearance onto one complex plane. And the relations in turn establish audience conditions in which the subjectivity circulates though all persons who are willing to enter the structural demands that elaborate these relational terms. The "as" structure insists on how "in me" the mind can actually participate in the qualities defined by these blessed mornings. The mind does not interpret these qualities but "partakes" of them (to use the language of "Infanta Marina").[26]

I am most fascinated by this poem's capacity to objectify the force of grammar so that as we attend to what we all share by virtue of learning the structure of a language, we also recognize how language can frame a distinctive range of affective connections. Stevens seems not all that subtle about these forces. But even the lack of subtlety becomes profound in Stevens's laboring syntactically to make the entire situation "meet for the eye of the young alligator." Readers are likely to assume that the "beholder" referred to in line seven is human, so the reference to the alligator seems unnecessary or excessive. However, Stevens wants to populate this scene with a mobile kind of consciousness that apparently can be shared by the beholder and the eye of the young alligator. For a naturalist, especially for a naturalist released into playfulness, it is rank presumption to assume that only humans enjoy the entire scene of sunrise. Moreover, it may be folly not to recognize that by attempting to see *as* the alligator sees we may take in a more elemental and satisfying vision than we would if we burdened the scene with human needs for metaphor. What matters ultimately is only that the force of the grammar be itself naturalized so that these various beings can celebrate both the morning and the sense of fitness the alligator experiences. Perhaps there is a version of "so" providing the imaginative extension to the eye of the alligator.

But it is not enough to be oriented toward this scene. Stevens now wants to place the act of valuing this scene within a composed attitude very different from the defensive wariness (and weariness) typical in this volume. Here I think Stevens can give the aura of making a full commitment because the attitude is so fully grounded in objective features of grammar rather than being "merely" subjective interpretation. The attitude itself might be an extension of our capacity to use elemental features of language. The relation of framing attitude to framing grammar is most tested and most forceful in Stevens's refusing to have the third stanza begin with "so." That choice would have offered a tightly balanced relational structure, but it would also let logic take priority over the potential for bounded excess so important to *Harmonium*.

Instead, Stevens relies on "And" for this crucial turning point. Then he reinforces that "and" with three more uses of the conjunction in the final six lines. This is not likely to be an accident. Stevens probably deploys the language of paratactic proliferation because he wants to spell out one possible implication of what it means to sense "hymns" in nature. More important, he wants to elaborate one significant ability of this gathering "so," now made considerably more expansive because it includes both an identification with the alligator and an identification with the power of the grammar of equations to expand exponentially when the world as first term is sufficiently charged. Notice, too, how "Forms, flames, and the flakes of flames" renders artifice and sensation inextricable complements of one another.

By means of the conjunction between the instances of "and" and the "so" Stevens manages to combine the poem's emphasis on witnessing with a sense that the poem itself can establish a locus of Nietzschean volition for that witnessing. The poem ultimately offers a feeling of "so" built on a series of "ands"—that is, it utters "so be it" and gives as the reason for "amen" the ability of the hymns to gather being and not just to describe it. Even though the final reference to subjective agency in the poem stresses the object position of "in me," the poem's intricate use of grammar suggests how thoroughly subjectivity can flourish in the object position when it feels being an object as itself a mode of response and responsibility. This same sense of flourishing is reinforced by the alliterations of the last two lines because they not only combine physical and abstract forms but also mark the transfer from the object position into the affirmations that a positioned writing can express. Now the world of sensations pulsates both in the represented world of the scene and the actual world of the writing—each modifying the other.

XI

Perhaps Stevens's boldest gesture in this bold book is ending the volume with two very brief poems. The only motive I can think of is that he wants to indicate a certain kind of self-sufficiency earned by the book. Any more elaborate lyricism would indicate unresolved needs for yet more verbal invention and complex attitudes. Any expression of hope reveals a corresponding lack and a corresponding inability to accept conditions as they are. So many attitudes have been tested that there might be a point where there is no point in further testing or further complaining. The previous three poems have shown there is still room to think philosophically, still the possibility of coming to terms with mortality as an aspect of a larger picture so that one can focus instead on the pleasures and consequences of bringing the imagination's resources to Florida mornings. Now the brevity of the final two texts brings finality to the accepting of the practical world, a finality crucially free from straining after lyrical effects.

Contrast "Tea" with the straining oppositions in the opening poems between bucks and firecat, between soul and ganders, and between aspic nipples and the honey of expectations in late spring:

When the elephant's ear in the park
Shriveled in frost,
And the leaves on the paths
Ran like rats,
Your lamp-light fell
On shining pillows,
Of sea-shades and sky shades
Like umbrellas in Java.

(CPP 77)

Now there are shades, not shadows. And here the opposition between frost and the indoor plush inventiveness is significantly not marked as irreconcilable or an effort to evade the real. The real is enlarged to include what the imagination can make of it insofar as one can commit to the consequences of that making process.

This is all possible because of the poem's emphasis on the range of linguistic acts taking place and finding a place within this little scene. The opening description could lead anywhere, but Stevens surprises the reader by having it taken up into personal address. I think this suggests that there need be no abstract gulf between the actual scene and what is made of it. Direct address simply assumes the character has made something of how the landscape provides a natural sign of mortality. This is one of the many ways human values attach to the world offered for description. So construction need not be evasion; it is just the possibility of moving from existing in a situation to inhabiting it as the recognition of what can be involved in our careful attention.

The relation between the two primary clauses probably is sufficient to sustain this reading. "When" introduces a public dimension of time and space immediately made psychological and naturalized within conditions of intimate life by the direct address. Then the address clause seems to relax into filling out aspects of the room. The contrasts in syntactic function receive a lively boost from the contrast between the two instances of "like": the first is banal cliché simply completing a description; the second opens another dimension for description. This "like" extends the aura of intimacy to include the work the imagination does in developing equivalences without stress or strain. And "Like umbrellas in Java" both gives the shades concrete existence and exercises the ability of imagination to participate in producing that concrete existence. Because the figure is not elaborated, it does not lead back into the fictionality of making so much as it opens into the intimate projections that make living possible where "fluttering things have so distinct a shade" (CPP 14).

Then there is the even more puzzling choice of making "To the Roaring Wind" the final poem in the volume. Again the conditions of direct address have to play a large part in our interpretation. We also have to appreciate why it might matter that here direct address results in an imperative (which I think echoes the imperatives at the end of "Two Figures in a Dense Violet Light" and "To the One of Fictive Music"). What kind of an imperative is this? In part it has the tone of permission and in part the tone of urgency, as if there might be consequences if the auditor did not speak it. Additionally, why can "it" suffice as the object of the imperative? Just as direct address quickly shifted description to intimate space in "Tea," here the imperative beautifully pulls us out of the initial question with its potentially infinite recesses. Whatever the syllable and whatever the distances of sleep, the only alternatives are endless self-questioning or the confidence to equate what is said with what is sought. That is a modernist revolution against empiricism certainly worth pursuing all the way through a volume of poetry.

XII

I am tempted to apologize for offering a reading that stresses how well Stevens integrates his volume since closure is not much esteemed by critics or poets in contemporary culture. But this is what I find. And this sense of integrating the volume turns out to be fairly standard for modernist work. Consider how "Black-Eyed Susan" celebrates the capacity of poetry to integrate motifs that seem contradictory when uttered by the prose in *Spring and All*.[27] Or consider the way the concluding poem of *A Draft of Thirty Cantos* merges the critique of pity with other possibilities of sensibility connected to the carving of letters. Print becomes a form of carving on the page that makes available the Renaissance culture that has been the major source of the poem's intensities. Even *The Waste Land* honors expectations about closure by offering the ironic inadequacy of the formal ending of an *Upanishad* to provide significant resolution for its dilemmas.

If my reading captures the basic energies of the volume, the conclusion raises a much more important issue than the degree of closure that is established. The basic question is not whether Stevens sought at least this level of resolution to his book but why his subsequent volumes abandon the more radical aspects of what he does to achieve this closure. One possible reason is that he thought the emphasis on sensation and the related world of fluttering things simply could not sustain his ambitions to make a difference in how people viewed their lives. The final poems of *Harmonium* deliberately remind us of how limited a world is afforded by the perspectives taken up in this volume, even as they brilliantly celebrate the syllable's capacity to complete a sheerly visual metaphor intimately linked with experience. Or it might be the case that Stevens needed a different set of possibilities for self-projection. Leading a life in which he felt his poetry had to be hidden may have required from within his isolation projections of something more grandiose than the ambitions to bring language and sensation into marvelously close contact. Whatever the case, it would be silly to lament the philosophical poet Stevens became. But it would be even sillier not to honor the quite different mode of philosophizing that makes *Harmonium* still perhaps the most innovative challenge in modernist American poetry to conventional ways of thinking about lyric speech.

Appendix: *Harmonium* and the Symbolist Tradition

In order to appreciate the stylistic boldness of *Harmonium* one might try to imagine Stevens turning from the earnest abstraction of nineteenth-century American poetry to an imaginative project that might warrant the descriptions of poetics offered by Arthur Symons's great book *The Symbolist Movement in Literature:*

After the world has starved its soul long enough in the contemplation
and the re-arrangement of material things, comes the turn of the soul;

and with it comes . . . a literature in which the visible world is no longer a reality and the unseen world no longer a dream.

(Symons 2–3)

This is not quite Stevens's version of resistance to empiricist ideals of description. But such passages lead us to recognize how deeply Stevens's reading of the symbolist poets affected his style and reinforced his belief that the life of the spirit offered through poetry would have to take forms compatible with naturalism. As Michel Benamou first demonstrated, symbolist poetics taught Stevens how being modern required relying on gesture and attitude as the work's basic resources for engaging a reality threatening to deny everything the poets valued. Stevens learned from these poets how Spirit had to live in subtlety (*CPP* 750). And subtlety had to live in textual presences that refused the apparent naturalness of earnest speech for the denser and more fluid sensibilities presented by the foregrounding of a self-consciousness absorbed in the intricacies of its own self-presentation. Heavenly labials in a world of gutturals might undo the giant of empiricist realism while emphasizing how the writing itself is neither heavenly love nor pity but a mode of presence based largely on the force of its negations. The unseen world is no longer a dream because the poem's music offers the indecipherable the most palpable feature of what writing makes present.

Anna Balakian labels symbolist poetry "semantic transcendentalism" (5) and so stresses how "language in the new poetic sense becomes a place of encounter for analogies that are to the enrichment of personality what an interlining is to a simple cloth garment" (7): "What strikes me in the progression of the symbolist mode is the passage from allegory (unilateral correspondences) to symbol" and hence "from metaphoric closing to the open-ended metonymy" (Balakian 5). Meaning involves "the elocutionary disappearance of the poet, who yields the initiative to words mobilized by the shock of their inequality" (31). But this semantic perspective risks losing Symon's more robust rhetoric of spirit. In his view such self-consciously written work could cast off the "old bondage of exteriority" inescapable within the "the old bondage of rhetoric" (5). For it was the sheer vivacity of the poet's constructive intelligence that could bring the Absolute into the domain of pure saying by refusing the seductive appeal of realistic dramatic and pastoral scenes. Instead of trying to implicate the world, the text would substitute for it and forge its own lines of connection on its own terms, thereby establishing the self-sufficiency of the beautiful. Nothing could be left to implication (3–4); everything had to attain the mastery of precise and indescribable statement so that poetry could animate what empiricists would be content to describe.

Because of this animating power, both poetry and art become "a kind of religion, with all the duties and responsibilities of the sacred ritual" (5). Indeed, it was Mallarmé's major achievement to see how that sense of ritual can be composed entirely through a writing where "every word is a jewel scattering and recapturing sudden fire, every image is a symbol and the whole poem is visible music" (69). How could such a poetry not aspire to music since music is our richest figure for the working of subtle, fluid, and elaborate interactions among the elements of experience that are not usually possible in more practical domains: "'It is not in the elementary sonorities of brass, strings . . . but in the intellectual world at its utmost that, fully and evidently, we should find, drawing to itself all the correspondences of the universe, the supreme music'" (73).

Consider, for example, the first half of Mallarmé's "Les Fenêtres" as it works out metaphoric extensions of light that have rough affinities with Stevens's "The Latest Freed Man," discussed in my first chapter:

Las du triste hôpital, et de l'encens fétide
Qui monte en la blancheur banale des rideaux
Vers le grand crucifix ennuyé du mur vide,
Le moribund sournois y redresse un vieux dos,

Se traîne et va, moins pour chauffer sa pourriture
Que pour voir du soleil sur les pierres, coller
Les poils blancs et les os de la maigre figure
Aux fenêtres qu'un beau rayon clair veut hâler.

Et la bouche, fiévreuese et d'azur blue vorace,
Telle, jeune, elle alla respire son trésor,
Une peau virginale et de jadis! Encrasse
D'un long baiser amer les tièdes carreaux d'or.

Ivre, il vit, oubliant l'horreur de saintes huiles,
Les tisanes, the horologe et le lit infligé
La toux; et quand le soir saigne parmie les tuiles,
Son oeil, à la horizon de lumière gorgé,

Voit des galères d'or, belles commes des cygnes,
Sur un fleuve de pourpre et de parfums dormer
En berçant l'éclair fauve et riche de leurs lignes
Dans un grand nonchaloir chargé de souvenir![28]

Stevens is not unique in his fascination with the horrors of mortality. One can imagine him learning a great deal from how this poem replaces the rhetorical stating of opinion by absorbing the situation into the brilliantly physicalized feelings for the hospital setting. Notice, too, that what begins as a psychological reaction to the hospital and the smell quickly merges into tracing the smell's own agency as it leads us to visualize the room—as if mind and smell had many more similarities than differences. This same strange linkage between subject and the objects of perception reappears in a different key with the mildly shocking sense of the crucifix as bored by the empty wall—here the objects of perception cannot escape the projections of the perceiver, but at the same time this boredom has a metaphysical tinge that goes far beyond the perceiver's consciousness.

The rest of the passage builds on a single action that sharpens a basic contrast perhaps defining what is central to an awareness of mortality. Even for this dying man, or especially for this dying man, the light has enormous seductive powers because of the fullness with which it charges the scene, a fullness that eventually forces the man into the space of memory. Yet that light also has enormous power to set forth the contrast between its capacious force and the pathos of the mortal body desperate to forget its condition. The dying man's appreciation of the sensuous order is all the more moving because even in this drunkenness there can be only his bitter kiss responding to what the readers at least cannot forget is his desperate situation. There emerge two elemental sensuous registers: what the light affords for the senses and what the brain records as the reality of his situation. Perhaps the only way to honor both registers is to switch to memory, where one becomes drunk on the fusion of light and memory and where his dying can be subsumed into the very different temporality of this "grand nonchaloir."

The different temporality has its anchor in the crucial function "telle" plays here. This expression establishes interconnected links between the sense of the present produced by the sunlight and the dying man's memory of when his sense of plenitude was not so haunted by mortality. So there is complete interconnection between what is described as memory and what is felt as immersion in the scene. More important, the incorporation of feeling also produces the possibility of a range of equivalences in the form of correspondences both fleshing out and extending the original situation. There is a contrast between youth and age that modifies the actual feel of the sun hitting the glass to project it as a "long bitter kiss." The time units fuse into a kind of drunkenness that transforms the scene from a site of suffering into the possibilities afforded by the imagination. The dying man lives and forgets *as* part of how sunlight is completed by imagination, and imagination is materialized as drunken will. Analogies are not just expansions of meaning but also sites in which feelings transform possibilities for identification. The poem moves from memory to drunkenness to the realization that the dying man can enter the "grand nonchaloir" that mimes in life what the labors of art offer in the poem. And the poem becomes the site where we enter something like a world constituted and energized by the logic of analogy rather than the binary logic of our epistemic disciplines.

Such poetry is rich and beautifully subtle. But it does not offer abrupt shifts in sensibility that address the pressure of the real and directly combat it. For this Stevens needed Nietzsche.

CHAPTER 3

"Ghostlier Demarcations, Keener Sounds"

The Parts Negation Played in Developing a New Poetic

> For the sensitive poet, conscious of negations, nothing is more
> difficult than the affirmations of nobility, yet there is nothing that
> he requires of himself more persistently.
>
> (*CPP* 665)

When Stevens took up again a serious commitment to writing poetry in the 1930s, he found himself in a position all too frequent in our creative practices. He knew clearly what he did not want to do any longer, but he was not sure what could satisfy him or bring poetry successfully into conjunction with a feasible theory of life. He could never embrace the versions of modernism that *Harmonium* rejected—the trust in the image, in Poundian transcendental presentation, and in any covert form of romantic humanism that evaded the stark realities of naturalist thinking. Rather, he characteristically began by attempts to formulate the dilemma he felt himself encountering. The one thing he could be sure of was that any poetry he could write at that time had to have a strong interest in negation: poetry had to express the sense of confusion and often repulsion that the poet felt in attempting to address society at all:

> This heavy historical sail
> Through the mustiest blue of the lake
> In a really vertiginous boat
> Is wholly the vapidest fake.
>
> *(CPP 99)*

I do not want to give Stevens's version of negation heavy philosophical weight, although it does have significant philosophical parallels. Negation for him is simply the use of certain resources of grammar to suspend any feeling of belonging or identification in favor of an analytic critical attitude toward both social life and the self's stances as it tried to establish relations with that life. He also shares with the Hegelian tradition the idea that such negative attitudes can provide a path whereby new lines of identification with a spiritual potential in society or at least in art become possible. But while negation feeds a version of personal development, he offers no elaborate dialectical process or vision of history as the unfolding of how spirit might inhabit substance. Yet he does use negation to emphasize the capacities of self-reflection to create distance for the self from beliefs that tied his social order to blind and imaginatively destructive practices. And he became fascinated by what we might call the sense of excess that negation could establish for these acts of self-reflection. Not only did negating appearances create a split between the subject and objects that beckoned for imaginative loyalty, but it also gave a sense of sources of energy within subjective life. That sense of energy would also have to be submitted to severe scrutiny, but the critical activity at the least could introduce a force or active principle that the facts could not explain. Negation might find in itself sources of energy upon which the imagination might build. Imagination might use negation to understand its own dissatisfactions and find there a thin but potentially powerful direction for struggling against "things as they are."

Among the many modes of writing that Stevens explored in the thirties and early forties, this chapter dwells on the two that seem to me the richest means of adapting the energies of negation for locating plausible sources of value. Both these modes elaborate a discursive dimension new to Stevens's poetry. At one pole Stevens thought that negation helped struggle against beliefs and social values which that seemed little more than fashion or ideology subject to the forces of historical change. Even on the dump that collects the refuse of that change, one can attend to how consciousness produces the very conditions by which the "the" orients us to the world (*CPP* 186). So it may be possible to imagine something persisting through change, some generative source of values that is not reducible to the historical forms values take in society. If there is this generative power, there is also something beyond politics, beyond the play of forces that dominates public life. There is a force of imaginative judgment that affects the qualities by which we frame what matters for us. And that frame may not be entirely subject to history since it manages to reject what history offers:

If you say on the hautboy man is not enough
Can never stand as god, is ever wrong

In the end, however naked, tall, there is still
The impossible possible philosophers' man
The man who has had time to think enough,
The central man, the human globe, responsive
As a mirror with a voice, the man of glass,
Who in a million diamonds sums us up.

                              (CPP 227)[1]

I call this mode of negation the idealist strain in Stevens because it concentrates on the possibility of clearing a way by means of the negatives to gain access to an ideal figure of imaginative power capable of recreating value for our experiences.

At the other pole Stevens also elaborates idealist motifs by concentrating on the mind's role in the dynamics of predication. But here Stevens does not worry about historical pressures or the construction of ideal figures. He is content with a continuous productive tension between the force of the subject and the authority empiricist thinking gives to the object of thought. For Stevens in the thirties that authority depends on using copulative verbs as if they could fix timeless conditions that lent themselves to descriptions and propositions. Negation matters because it threatens that authority and calls attention to the perspectival conditions that frame and alter what seems the stability of objective conditions. Negation emphasizes the degree to which our sense of the objective depends ultimately on the subject making decisions to accept these descriptions as the limits of our world. This does not entail treating negation in a Hegelian fashion as the mediating force that makes dialectic possible. Rather, it entails treating negation only as calling attention to the roles consciousness and self-consciousness play in our having a world at all, or at least in our having a world that matters to us.

For Stevens this minimal constructivist orientation could be most simply expressed by imagining the degree to which "is" depends on "as."[2] Stevens began to play with this formula in "The Man with the Blue Guitar," where it seemed to offer a radical perspectivism worthy of being conjoined with the principles of collage construction in modernist painting. But as Stevens's ambitions changed, he could not be content with the theatricalizing of perspectivism. That seemed too external a condition. He turned perspectivism inward so it did not express a point of view so much as enable a continual exploration of resemblances allowing a particular subject to participate in what it perceived. That exploration eventually generated what I call the "aspectual thinking" of *Transport to Summer* and *Auroras of Autumn,* where "is" continually gets modified by clauses demonstrating the power of "the intricate evasions of as" (*CPP* 415).

II

These paths for negation run on parallel tracks, so it is difficult to say on every occasion which of the two prevails. Given this problem, it is prudent to begin with the general shifts in sensibility that negation reflects in the poetry Stevens produced during the 1930s. When negatives appear in *Harmonium,* they seem primarily focused on the object rather than the subject. Such negatives define an abiding emptiness rather than serving to release forces that are blocked by the imaginative structures shaping appearances at a given time. Notice how the climax of "The Snow Man" casts its negatives so that the focus is entirely on the present tense: "nothing that is not there and the nothing that is" (*CPP* 8). But there is one striking exception, the closing lines of one of Stevens's most playfully bleak poems, "Cy Est Pourtraicte, Madame Ste Ursule, and Les Unze Mille Vierges":

> The Good Lord in his garden sought
> New leaf and shadowy tinct,
> And they were all His thought.
> He heard her low accord
> Half prayer and half ditty,
> And he felt a subtle quiver,
> That was not heavenly love
> Or pity.
> This is not writ
> In any book.
>
> (*CPP 17*)

Here at least God is given a subjective power of sublime negation that refuses any responsibility to standard human expectations. So the poem defines an admirable power that Stevens would eventually try to capture and to moralize. The first "not" functions metrically to transform the three-stress line to shorter, more constrained lineation. This negative also functions dramatically in the anecdote as a subtle but powerful reminder of the force of God's difference from our moral and psychological predicates. This is negative theology with an ironic twist. For to appreciate God's power we have to register unblinkingly the pathos of the eleven thousand virgins deluded into mistaking for compassion something like bemused indifference. And this sense of God's power along with God's sheer distance from our modes of predication then generates the second negative. Two reasons make this tale impossible to write in any book: we cannot give a positive shape to this divine sentiment, and this God has enough power within history to ban this kind of publicity. Negation proves the only instrument by which we can actually recognize the differences in power allowing there to be a God in the first place.

If we get a decent grasp on what the negatives in *Harmonium* cannot accomplish, we will have something like a ground-level view, making it possible to appreciate the fundamental shifts in sensibility that Stevens elaborated in his subsequent poetry. This appreciation will help us clarify the elements he has to establish if he is to work out more sophisticated ways of having lyric poetry address the crisis of values that continues to haunt his imagination. In *Harmonium* the negative is fundamentally the absence of any positive possibility for meaning or for action. It has no dialectical power, no power to build on the lacks that it registers (even when it indicates a force that cannot be included in our scenic descriptions), and no power to enter complex temporal structures where negating the present implicates a possible future that in turn redirects our sense of the past. There is only the struggle to formulate attitudes by which something can be made of an intensely bleak present:

> The first white wall of the village . . .
> The fruit trees . . .
>
> *(CPP 15)*

Consequently, there is also no way to open up the copulative verb—no hovering half presence or internal division between subject and object that might entail a more complex ontology with a place for competing perspectives and temporalities. *Harmonium* rarely glimpses the path from the "is" or "is not" comprising descriptions to the "as" that introduces differences created by what aspects observers see. But in the thirties Stevens became less interested in the facts that constrain our lives than in the constructive possibilities that might arise if poetry could see itself embodying the processes by which we compose worlds.

III

One major difference in Stevens's next volume, *Ideas of Order,* is the demand that negation help establish alternatives to a poetics caught within the power of fact and of description, which had caused so much pain in *Harmonium.*

Negation helps poetry reclaim the full powers of discursive thinking that had been sacrificed to the various ways romanticism and modernism came to prefer the direct presentation of objects and the feelings they elicit. In particular I show how Stevens develops for these two modes of negation in his poetry from *Ideas of Order* through *Parts of a World* three basic strategies for bringing to bear the force of that figure. Such strategies took him a long way toward shifting his focus from the gulf between description and value central to *Harmonium.*

The first two ways are closely connected. First, negation gives a dramatic grammatical figure for the possibilities of freedom that simultaneously fascinated and terrified Stevens. Freedom begins in the power to say "No" and then to build future tenses that can compete with prevailing ideologies. But what can freedom seek as satisfaction that does not simply repeat its own anxious aimlessness? The second way establishes at least some alternative to that anxiety because of the power to convert the space opened by negation into a productive locus for a more abstract stance toward the negated particulars. Negation can frame and compose hypothetical spaces won from a world of sheer appearance so that persons can recognize common interests and formulate common projects attuned to what the negatives expose as significant underlying forces. Negation encourages a shift from description to self-reflection, with the opportunity then to have self-reflection take a somewhat dialectical cast in accord with Hoon's cry:

> . . . and what I saw
> Or heard or felt came not but from myself;
> And there I found myself more truly and more strange.
> *(CPP 51)*

But In *Harmonium,* from which these lines come, the potential for even this level of dialectic was predominantly individualist in its projections. Stevens had to reimagine this potential when he sought a poetry overtly concerned with social relations. So he returns to abstraction. Now, though, abstraction is not simply a means of deepening self-consciousness. Rather, abstraction provides a level from which to read the forces of historical change without quite being absorbed by that change. Abstraction turns away from the specific images inevitably consigned to the dump in order to focus on more permanent features of need, with the creative power to establish access to alternative values perhaps somewhat less bound to constant historical change.

These redirections of Stevens's imagination became increasingly necessary for him because of his disappointment with *Owl's Clover:* It seemed there that the effort to muster specific political passions for poetry only confined the imagination to the domain of images and appearances. A deeper political poetry would be necessary if writers were to address the conditions by which people determined their satisfactions and dissatisfactions with the political order. Negation might afford a means of making this transition because it provided a possibility for abstracting from practical particulars to the desires and perhaps the historical patterns that underlie them. Then one might deal with force in more concrete and perhaps enduring forms.[3] Fact turns out to have a dialectical complexity well beyond anything imaginable in the world of *Harmonium:*

> In the presence of the violent reality of war, consciousness takes the place of the imagination. And consciousness of an immense war is a consciousness of fact. If that is true, it follows that the poetry of war as a consciousness of the victories and defeats of nations, is a consciousness of fact, but of heroic fact, of fact on such a scale that the mere consciousness of it affects the scale of one's thinking and constitutes a participating in the heroic. . . .
>
> We leave fact and come back to it, come back to what we wanted fact to be, *not* to what it was, *not* to what it has too often remained.
>
> (*CPP* 251; emphasis added)

The desperateness of the political situation required that Stevens also pursue a conceptually less ambitious mode of negation that comprises a third possibility. In "The Man with the Blue Guitar" negation becomes in one sense more limited because the emphasis is not on the work abstraction can do in relocating how the imagination deals with specific social values. But at the same time it is more penetrating because it takes on the various modes of description that depend for their authority on epistemically stabilizing the role of the copulative verb. Negation has the power to help undermine much of this authority because, as Nietzsche saw, negation introduces forces dissatisfied with the positive shape of the copula. Negation makes the minimal claim that what seems absent should be incorporated at least as background into judgments of what is. And negation can point to how its statements set the agent's force against a world that otherwise might be sufficient in itself. Then the imagination can dwell on such force and become fascinated by why such dissatisfaction takes place. There emerges a rationale for preferring manner to matter or, better, for preferring the matter of manner:

. . . Yet, having just
Escaped from the truth, the morning is color and mist . . .
It was how the sun came shining into his room: . . .
It was how he was free. It was how his freedom came.

(CPP 187)

Stevens's concern for manner leads him to emphasize a radical perspectivism, in large part because that perspectivism could be anchored in the same kind of grammatical resources relied on for the work negation does. Perspectivism has its concrete linguistic ground in the figures for establishing equivalence: "like" and, especially, the modes of resemblance that "as" can bring to bear. The power of "as" undermines trust in the impersonal copulative verb because it introduces perspective as an aspect of our descriptions. Unlike the copula, "as" has the capacity to make what we can describe inseparable from how the agent takes a stand toward the world. And that stand can become the most intimate mode by which persons express values. More generally, we can say that the varieties of negation Stevens cultivates in his second book all serve to divide the copulative verb against itself and so prepare for the subsumption of "is" under "as." The negative suggests that identity is at least present in relation to a background of nonidentity. Significant truth might take the form of establishing equivalences between positions in the world—both as ways of recognizing the irreducible force of what subjects bring and as ways of attuning those subjects to how each might experience what the other sees:[4]

Where the voice that is in us makes a true response,
Where the voice that is great within us rises up,
As we stand gazing at the rounded moon.

(CPP 112)[5]

IV

The introductory poem in *Ideas of Order,* "Farewell to Florida," depends for its force on the negatives implicit in the contrast between what had been the speaker's life in the tropics, which he seeks to reject, and what he wants from his journey north to a form of life built on struggle. Since the poem is fairly long, I concentrate only on how the use of negatives differs from that in *Harmonium:*

I

Go on, high ship, since now, upon the shore,
The snake has left its skin upon the floor. . . .
Her mind will never speak to me again.
I am free. High above the mast the moon
Rides clear of her mind and the waves make a refrain . . .

II

Her mind had bound me round . . .
Her home, not mine, in the ever-freshened Keys . . .
How content I shall be in the North, to which I sail
And to feel sure and to forget the bleaching sand . . .

III

I hated the weathery yawl from which the pools
Disclosed the sea floor and the wilderness
Of waving weeds. I hated the vivid blooms . . .
To stand here on the deck in the dark and say
Farewell and to know that that land is forever gone
And that she will not follow in any word
Or look, nor ever again in thought, except
That I loved her once . . . [6] Farewell. Go on, high ship.

IV

My North is leafless and lies in a wintry slime
Both of men and clouds, a slime of men in crowds. . . .
To be free again, to return to the violent mind
That is their mind, these men, and that will bind
Me round, carry me, misty deck, carry me
To the cold, go on, high ship, go on, plunge on.

(CPP 97–98)

Notice first the variety of negatives, all, I think, qualifying and fleshing out the claim for freedom. Freedom for the speaker is the capacity to separate himself from Florida and the female presence from which it seems inseparable. So freedom is in part just the capacity to imagine oneself on a journey to an elsewhere. Then the poem contextualizes this journey by showing how freedom becomes also a capacity to wield the full panoply of tenses that were largely absent in *Harmonium*'s obsession with the oppressive present tense imposed by its apparently inescapable world of facts. In part the negative allows us to reimagine a past as past, as scenes that the agent feels he has transcended. And then the intensity of memory in effect sanctions the investment in the future as possibility despite its bleak violence. Second, this sense of yielding to the violence of a will to change also invites a recasting of the masculinity motif in *Harmonium*. Now the perfect cock cannot just stand and admire its own projected power. It must act; it must plunge on to make a present capable of replacing the feminine order that has held the speaker in bondage. I see here the beginning of a large shift from simply occupying attitudes to insisting on how certain ways of thinking may connect to possible actions.

Finally, this poem introduces a new level of self-consciousness that Stevens's lyrics begin to pursue.[7] "Farewell to Florida" is intensely self-reflexive and recursive because it enacts the "return to the violent mind" that it proclaims. All the negatives are not simply commentary on experience. They involve manifestly violent actions in the service of the effort to free the mind so that it can join what it takes to find value and belonging in a world that is emphatically not Florida. Manner becomes the matter of the poem—not just aesthetically in the sense that form and content are fused but also existentially. The poem approaches being "the cry of its occasion" (*CPP* 404) in the sense that it is less about a situation than the making present of the character's gathering of linguistic energies. Moreover, the poem can be seen to provide a test for those assertions to the degree that he can already manifest the capacity for action the poem idealizes.

Here Stevens finds a way for lyric to have the dual temporality of first-person, present-tense narration that continually tests whether the speaker in the present has learned to deploy what he claims to have learned from what is being narrated. Wordsworth's *Prelude* is one powerful example. But in Stevens's poem there is only a hint of narrative, so the speaker has to synchronize himself with world solely by virtue of how he speaks rather than what he points to in his story of his development. The poem's deployment of this self-reflexiveness still depends on the speaker's own sense of difference from the world. But Stevens will soon see that the same self-reflexiveness about the manner of speaking can serve as an invitation to the audience to take up this stance and in the process demonstrate the strange link between the pronouns "I" and "one."[8]

V

"Sad Strains of a Gay Waltz" achieves similar versions of performative freedom, but the focus is more directly on a specific historical perspective that was to haunt Stevens's search for an adequate level on which to project values. The empiricist fact-value distinction seems no longer simply a static and perennial conflict. Rather, what is valued itself seems inevitably over time to become mere fact no longer capable of engaging feeling for the world. No wonder there is a pronounced and effective range of negations with which the poem must grapple—those affecting values and those affecting the facts that values become:

> The truth is that there comes a time
> When we can mourn no more over music
> That is so much motionless sound.
>
> There comes a time when the waltz
> Is no longer a mode of desire, a mode
> Of revealing desire and is empty of shadows.
>
> Too many waltzes have ended. And then
> There's that mountain-minded Hoon
> For whom desire was never that of the waltz,
>
> Who found all form and order in solitude
> For whom the shapes were never the figures of men.
> Now for him his forms have vanished.
>
> There is order in neither sea nor sun.
> The shapes have lost their glistening.
> There are these sudden mobs of men,
>
> These sudden clouds of faces and arms,
> An immense suppression, freed,
> These voices crying without knowing for what,
>
> Except to be happy, without knowing how,
> Imposing forms they cannot describe,
> Requiring order beyond their speech.
>
> Too many waltzes have ended. Yet the shapes
> For which these voices cry, these, too, may be
> Modes of desire, modes of revealing desire.
>
> Too many waltzes—the epic of disbelief
> Blares oftener and soon, will soon be constant.
> Some harmonious sceptic soon in a skeptical music

Will unite these figures of men and their shapes
Will glisten again with motion, the music
Will be motion and full of shadows.

(CPP 100–101)

I cite the whole poem in part because here Stevens is careful to produce
an intricate rhetorical structure that frames what might be his most discursive and straightforwardly argumentative poem to date. The first two and
the last three stanzas provide different kinds of lucidity about what a sense
of history entails. The first two stanzas simply state the speaker's sense that
the waltz is "no longer a mode of desire." The last three stanzas are equally
direct in stating the likelihood that there will emerge a skeptical music rein-
tegrating the imagination with more perspicuous forms of desire with the
capacity to charge shadows with substance. But for the confident sense of
the future to take on its full lyrical power we have to feel the tension created
by what the present tense renders in the center of the poem. Here we find
two portraits of modes of agency that threaten the poem's discursive calm
by an increasingly intense and almost hallucinatory feeling for the present-
tense qualities within social life. The desperation of "these sudden mobs of
men" reveals the terrors that must accompany the failure of the waltz as a
mode of social imagination.

I love how Stevens's rhetoric here manages an increasingly tight precision
even as the situation comes to seem increasingly disturbing:

These sudden clouds of faces and arms,
An immense suppression, freed,
These voices crying without knowing for what,

Except to be happy, without knowing how,
Imposing forms they cannot describe,
Requiring order beyond their speech.

(CPP 100)

That intensity seems to suggest another kind of negation—one that is not
explicit but juxtapositional. Can the skeptical music built on these characters' unbelief suffice to give them the sense of purpose they need? Or is the
skeptical music more like the music of *Harmonium*, which can produce order through a distanced refusal to make serious commitments to the world?

Once we ask this question I suspect we cannot be content with the concluding satisfaction in this skeptical music. Instead, we have to go back to

the strange two stanzas that allow Hoon another appearance. He is the one figure in the poem dissatisfied with any version of music because it binds the imagination to variations that all ultimately serve only ideological purposes. This figure for the artist seeks a form of imaginative satisfaction he can find only in a solitude able to withstand what happens to crowds. Hoon does not want a meaningfulness for social life that depends on overt musical content. He wants pure states of consciousness so he can place his own intensities into abstract forms that then might allow the poet a sense of social solidarity, even if only on an abstract level. For that abstract level may offer a domain beyond specific needs and beliefs where solidarity might be based on shared ways of constructing and responding to the need for images in the first place. But at this point in Stevens's career Hoon has no dialectical means by which to get a grasp on the nature of those forms. His sense of negation seems limited to the practice of simply replacing one music with another. Perhaps Stevens had to develop the quasi image of an abstract central man in order to give a shape to human desires more stable than the images they pursue.

VI

Critics from Frank Doggett to Edward Ragg have elaborated the idealist strain that connects "Sad Strains of a Gay Waltz" to "The Man on the Dump" to "Montrachet le Jardin," "Asides on an Oboe," "Chocura to Its Neighbor," and "Examination of a Hero in Time of War." Moreover, Ragg is sharp on how the failures of Owl's Clover's version of realistic, socially responsible poetry make that idealism all the more important since it provides a dialectical alternative to the sheer relativism of "Sad Strains of a Gay Waltz" and "Man on the Dump."[9] Idealism allows one to treat these failures as somehow provisional, as paths to our occupying a different level of experience. That level of experience involves something like pure self-reflection on the creative power that underlies the possibility of our having values at all. It is important, then, that Stevens does not attempt a version of Hegel's historical dialectic. His dialectic is psychological. It invites the audience to identify with a mode of self-reflexive creative power that occupies a level irreconcilable with what must submit to history. And because it is psychological it can take form in the quasi image of the hero ("quasi image" because the hero need not have any specific shape). The hero is the mode of self-consciousness of the powers of creativity with whom anyone can identify as a means of recognizing the counterforce to history's endless emptying of value from the particulars in which we invest it. Yet Stevens pays a price for settling on the image of the hero because, as I soon elaborate, this image against images makes Stevens's views victims of the very forces they would surmount.

Since critics have made this aspect of Stevens's work reasonably familiar, I call on it primarily to set the stage for the contrasting path in his career in which negation unmoors the copulative and forces a complex resistance to identity thinking. His idealist vision is most fully articulated in "Examination of the Hero in a Time of War." This poem also realizes that one aspect of this psychological dialectic is the role the poem itself plays. It cannot simply present a series of concepts but also has to issue in an affective process by which the reader is induced to participate in the new mode of self-reflexive thinking embodied in the text. Developing the figure of the hero is intended to elicit feelings that confirm the reader's own sense of creative power. And this sense of creative power confirms in turn the possibility of identifying with the imaginative activity that generates the idea of the hero in the first place.

This process is a lot easier to display than to describe. One can think of stanza XII in "Examination of the Hero in a Time of War" as allowing the character of Hoon, whom we last saw locked into silence, finally to articulate the power of what his refusals gain for him:

> It is not an image. It is a feeling.
> There is no image of the hero.
> There is a feeling as definition.
> How could there be an image, an outline,
> A marble soiled by pigeons?
> The hero is a feeling, a man seen
> As if the eye were an emotion
> As if in seeing we saw our feeling
> In the object seen and saved that mystic
> Against the sight, the penetrating,
> Pure eye. Instead of allegory,
> We have and are the man, capable
> Of his brave quickening, the human
> Accelerations that seem inhuman.
>   *(CPP 248–49)*

Abstraction proves a force capable of shifting the imagination's investments. It can step away from the kinds of images that bind desire to the dump and instead align with the work of feeling accomplished in resisting the force represented by the pigeons. In fact, the poet can use the poem's own acts of abstraction to justify a move from characterizing the "it" to securing the presence of "we." This "we" then provides the necessary awareness of how this quickening extends our sense of human powers. Were this sense of the hero an image, it could be described. But if desire were invested in that form of objectivity, it would become condemned to its own eventual place on the dump, to be replaced by a more skeptical music. So the poem has to find a way to establish a huge difference between believing in something specific that should be done and finding that, in the repeated collapse of specific beliefs, whatever is done can reflect certain qualities of attention and care and embodied creativity. Stevens manages this leap by mining this distinction between image and feeling in order to suggest how subjectivity can be located simply in an essentially transpersonal force of heroic concentration. As feeling, the idea of the hero ultimately depends not on a picture of something that can stand alone but only on this invitation to participate in the opportunity for identification with a way of establishing value. The poet's task is to intensify the wanting that becomes the precondition for pursuing feelings capable of leading beyond the image to the figure of self-reflexive humanity.

And that level of imaginative activity turns out to be so intensely personal that it may bring us to the core of what makes every person a person. If the invitation for identification can be honored, the poem can claim actually to evoke or even to produce a new sense of subjectivity so anchored in its quickening that it becomes available to all. We move from the denial that the hero can be the subject of an image to the discovery that the hero lives precisely as the force that remains vitally collective in the effort to replace the image as the principle by which identifications are secured.

VII

Many critics understand this transformation of desire away from the effects of particular images. Yet they rarely offer convincing explanations of why Stevens abandoned this form of dialectic based on abstracting to the presence of the hero. I do not think we can avoid asking how this ideal of the hero might prove problematic—as an idea of the best way for poetry to perform social roles and as a model for putting to work the quickening produced by lyric feeling. Ultimately the idealist strain in Stevens is oriented toward producing identifications. Poetry brings out the powers to construct a heroic presence in all of us, and that presence provides something deeper and more powerful than the specific objects of belief. But even that level of deep identification produces images against images, and those images, too, are subject to all of the static forces mobilized by copulative verbs. Even if there is an important distinction between an image and a feeling, there is likely to emerge an image from the feeling or of the feeling.

And this likelihood generates a related problem. The passage we have been attending to relies heavily on "as if" constructions. These are certainly appropriate if poetry is to have the status of a supreme fiction. But that status proposes a sharp distinction between the fictive and the real that keeps poetry still bound to essentially epistemic contexts: poetry tells the truth, or it substitutes believable fictions for the truth. Stevens could change this mind-set only if he could find a way of relying less on any version of "truth" and more on fostering literal identifications with the possible values that he posited for the hero. What he projected for the hero did not have to depend on a journey through experience to some kind of source. Rather, the values could simply be immanent in certain qualities of consciousness made possible by how poems invite readerly participation. Then truth becomes not so much a value in itself as a condition for intensity and a quality inducing identification.

Again my point is easier to display than to explain. Consider the difference between "as if the eye were an emotion" and a statement like "as the eye becomes an emotion." An even stronger case can be made for the difference between "as if in seeing we saw our feeling" and "as we see our feelings." Stevens knew the difference even then, as evidenced by how he eventually turns in the penultimate stanza to the "as" of complex equivalence rather than the "as if" relying on the imaginative sites fictionality can sponsor:

This is his day. With nothing lost, he
Arrives at the man-man as he wanted.
This is his night and meditation.
                    (CPP 250)

Here we can see clearly that the alternative expression "as if he wanted to arrive at the man-man" would fail to honor the reality of the state of intense dialectical self-awareness Stevens wants for his hero. This alternative would also give a very different invitation to the audience. He does not want them making comparisons between kinds or degrees of wanting. He wants them to be able to imagine entering states where full identification

with the speaker is possible, *as* he works out his imaginings. The poem has
to capture not just what the state is like but also the capacity of the audience
to will this identification. For the heroism is in the willing, in the proof that
there can be a subjective intensity beyond any images or any descriptions.
That self is inseparable from a manner of wanting and a possibility of audience identification with that wanting.

But Stevens was not ready to commit himself to the modes of participation made possible by the contrast between the kinds of thinking shaped by
"as if" and those facilitated by "as." Stevens probably thought he needed
more overt and powerful idealist measures to engage both his sense of the
collapse of civic society and the horrors of world war, which seemed to
him to require a specific human ideal, however abstract. So he turned to
the gathering force of figures like the hero, central man, and supreme fiction, even if they inevitably reinforced the sense of imagination as producing what is not part of the world but exists only in ideal space. It would be
only after World War II that Stevens would actively and persistently pursue
the possibility that there were richer ways to blend the plural "we" with the
singular "man" on a consistent basis. He could further de-emphasize images
and attitudes in favor of a sense of continual process that I call aspectual
thinking. By freeing "as" from issues of fictionality he could focus on the
values involved in the quickenings that make it possible for us to feel in
ourselves this inhuman core of creative activity.

VIII

"Restatement of Romance" offers a subtle beginning for a very different use
of negation and recuperation of values that would eventually lead to postwar
Stevens:

> The night knows nothing of the chants of night.
> It is what it is as I am what I am:
> And in perceiving this I best perceive myself
>
> And you. Only we two may interchange
> Each in the other what each has to give.
> Only we two are one, not you and night,
>
> Nor night and I, but you and I, alone,
> So much alone, so deeply by ourselves,
> So far beyond the casual solitudes,

That night is only the background of our selves,
Supremely true each to its separate self,
In the pale light that each upon the other throws.

(CPP 118)

Here there is no abstract source of identity between two agents, whether the agents be persons or a dialogue between romance and its restatement. Even the subject of the poem is dual, so that we are constantly adjusting for differences and equivalences between strongly held identities. Rather than pursuing identification by a process of abstracting from the image, the poem tries to let the supposed content of images come through as a process of mutual reflection. We can have contingent equivalences between worlds rather than shared identities.

In effect this poem defines one implicit logic that would eventually shape many of the poems in Stevens's *Parts of a World*.[10] We have to accept parts and partiality and participation as the fundamental terms of our ontology. And art then provides not the quickening of a shared spirit but quickenings that arise from the partial convergence and swerves of beings intent on their own specific freedoms. One can accept this freedom without projecting solipsism just because that freedom itself can never be whole, can never be generative without finding its place always within some "background." We arrive at a social and semantic world that is always incomplete but always at least potentially caught up in the play of that pale light that each upon the other throws. And we arrive at a sense of history capable of seeing what need not be consigned to the dump. Romance might be very remote from our historical situation. But just that fact casts a pale light upon that very situation. The fact offers a glimpse of what our bleak world is not. That vision in turn might allow us to see the persistence of romance in mutated forms, in skeptical music perhaps. After all, is not the basic role of romance simply to forge possible relations among agents that provide a level of imaginative being that need not yield to despair?

IX

The pale light that the figures throw upon each other offers a view of social relations that, for Stevens, would eventually dismantle the authority of the copulative verb. Identity thinking gives way to making identity depend on this working out of equivalences. "The Man with the Blue Guitar" first explored this logic: there Stevens let himself shift from figures defining the need for a "central man" to an emphasis on a continuous process of adjusting equivalences that constantly quicken our sense of the values residing in our manners of experiencing the world. This poem still seems bound to the figure of a hero in the person of the musician. But now the hero is overtly far less significant than the powers displayed by the music he creates.[11] And even the artist-hero's functions resist idealization to the degree that they successfully echo the dynamic space where clashes among perspectives constitute modernist reality.

Perspectivism had been increasingly important in late nineteenth-century fiction's concern for how the world emerges as we put ourselves into positions to grasp it. One need only reflect on Henry James's figure of the mansion with many windows. But the novelists tried to naturalize this process by simply incorporating it as a more subtle realism based primarily on adjustments of characters to each other rather than adjustments to large and comprehensive situations like the rendering of doubled identity in *Great Expectations*. The painters saw perspectivism in a much more theatrical manner. Cézanne made the clash of perspectives central to the structure of many of his paintings. And early Picasso added an expressive dimension to this clash, as if all the energies of fauvism could themselves take their place in the vivid perspectival interactions that would put painting on the path to cubism.[12]

Stevens wanted to see how far poetry could go in honoring the bravura inventiveness with which modernist painting treated perspective. He could not do this without utilizing the figure of the hero, but with a different tone, "in another tree" (*CPP* 262), with strong anti-idealist implications. "The Man with the Blue Guitar" tries to recuperate the strangeness and the violence of that painting by linking affirmation of the hero tightly to the work of negation. In effect he shows that both negation and affirmation can be more subtle and more "central" than seems possible in his idealist uses of the hero. But it would only be after World War II that Stevens could fully develop this direction of his thinking, ironically because only then did he have enough distance from modernist art to declare his commitment to treating "imagination as an aversion to the abnormal" (*CPP* 737). This aversion, he came to see, was the best way the poet could see "his imagination become the light in the minds of others" (*CPP* 660).

Stevens gave extended paraphrases of sections of this poem to both Hi Simons and Renato Poggioli. This matters for two reasons. His letters indicate how uneasy he was in paraphrasing his work. Such uneasiness is typical of poets forced to paraphrase, but the very fact of trying may be an index of a deeper anxiety about the project.[13] Second, Stevens established an interpretive atmosphere by his paraphrases that suggested the most important feature of the poem is its varieties of thematic statement. Yet the poem's power seems to be manifestly more evident in the varieties of its modes of utterance than in the largely repetitious versions of what can be said on the topic of imagination and reality.[14] This variety consists primarily in perspectives and overall tonal shifts among stanzas. But it extends to even the smallest modes of expression, like choices among pronouns and tenses, that he manages to bring into accord with the forcefulness of Picasso's art. So it should not be surprising that in one of his most unguarded moments in this correspondence, Stevens indicates how aware he is of the radical affective experiment constituted by the varieties of manner that the poem emphasizes over matter:

> I want to face nature in the way two lions face one another—the lion in the lute facing the lion locked in stone. I want, as a man of imagination, to write poetry with all the power of a monster equal in strength to that of the monster about whom I write. I want man's imagination to be completely adequate in the face of reality.
>
> (*LWS* 790)

I will approach the poem in the spirit of this statement, emphasizing how the poem's manners of speaking extend and transform the work negation performs in *Ideas of Order.* There is a constant shifting in modes of expression involving tone, direction of address, emotional timbre, and kind of speech act. These function as literary equivalents of the multiple perspectives providing tensions and exposing aspects of surfaces in protocubist painting. And there is constant shifting among four focal objects of attention—a musician who equates things as they are with what he can play on his blue guitar; an audience desperately in need of help in bringing the dynamics of imagination within its sense of things as they are; an "I" who seeks power and a sense of belonging within the world by identifying with the guitarist; and the powers of the expressive medium of poetry to adjust and to intensify a reality that affords opportunities for readerly participation, thereby to a large extent replacing the rhetorical effort to foster a particular belief.

Let me illustrate how these differences function by citing the openings of the first five sections of the poem:

1) Scene in a narrative plus metaphor, then speech by audience

The man bent over his guitar, A shearsman of sorts. The day was green.

They said, "You have a blue
    guitar,
You do not play things as they
    are."

2) First-person projection   I cannot bring a world quite
                                    round,
                                Although I patch it as I can.

3) Expressive effusion by   Ah! But to play man number one,
    guitarist or the "I"   To drive the dagger in his heart
4) Distanced reflection in   So that's life then: things as they
    casual speech   are?
                                It picks its way on the blue guitar.

5) Imperative in formal mode   Do not speak to us of the
                                    greatness of poetry,
                                Of the torches wisping in the
                                    underground . . .
                                Exceeding music must take the
                                    place
                                Of empty heaven and its hymns,
                                Ourselves in poetry must take
                                    their place,
                                Even in the chattering of your
                                    guitar.
                                                (CPP 135–37)

The closest analogue to this kind of movement in Stevens's previous work is "Sea Surface Full of Clouds," a suitable painterly analogue. But that poem is all impressionist landscape, with no distinct agents, and the variety of expressive states does not depend on a variety of styles as this does. It is as if the old plan in the Boston Museum of Fine Arts could be revived, with all the impressionist work culminating in Cézanne's *Madame Cézanne,* whose bent nose signified a new art because the painting requires the creation of an underlying armature to rebalance her body and so compensate for the nose. What impresses me most about Stevens's departure from his own versions of impressionist intensities is the range of manners of speech ("and all their manner in the thing" [*CPP* 137]), all contending and all making visible the multiple worlds the guitar makes possible. These stanzas sound as if the guitar were continually giving birth by treasuring differences in perspective and modes of action.

Even more important is the fact that these differences depend less on claims about content than on transformations in voicing. In one sense such transformations provide an obvious way to correlate the poet's work with the guitarist. But the variations in language also remind us of another feature of music and another feature of imagination: it does not just register a world of things as they are but also inhabits it and makes it intimate, makes it something that elicits emotion through speech. To be a part of the world is to participate in some manner of its unfolding for consciousness. And because of this stress on emergence, there is also a strong sense that the copula of description is simply shattered by the mutual dependency between the real and the imagination.

One could say these opening five sections fracture the copula into perspectives and the subject into roles and positions. Then the important question becomes, how can we think of this fracturing so that it is not simply a source of lamentation and lack? How can we provide an alternative to Eliot while granting the same sense of the broken world both poets see causing so much pain? Stevens's response is to get away from thinking epistemically—where perspectivism is problematic—and turn instead to thinking musically, where differences create adventures in attunement. These adventures build a distinctive space in which the world folds into the person and persons fold into possibilities for appreciating the power of the various guitars to compose our senses for the world and of the world:

> A tune beyond us as we are,
> Yet nothing changed by the blue guitar;
>
> Ourselves in the tune as if in space,
> Yet nothing changed, except the place
>
> Of things as they are and only the place
> As you play them on the blue guitar . . .
>
> . . . The blue guitar
> Becomes the place of things as they are,
> A composing of senses of the guitar.
>
> *(CPP 137)*

"The Man with the Blue Guitar" as a whole makes an interesting counterpart to Stevens's other major poem on music in the 1930s—"The Idea of Order at Key West." "Idea of Order" is an intensely dialectical poem that I wish I had time to read closely. But I will have to be content to point out how the poem uses negation to expand from the singer to the song, to Ramon Fernandez's views on the song that open it up to an expanded audience, to the song's power when read in terms of its social implications for "arranging, deepening, enchanting night." One might think this brilliant way of putting the mystery of the song within the social world is in itself a substantial achievement. But Stevens adds another twist where the social world expands into reminders of a common mortality that perhaps haunts all mystery:

> The maker's rage to order words of the sea,
> Words of the fragrant portals, dimly-starred,
> And of ourselves, and of our origins,
> In ghostlier demarcations, keener sounds.
>
> *(CPP 106)*

The woman's song never quite accommodates to the object world even though it intensifies the impact of that world. The poem goes through several stages tracing the way the spirit of the song first modifies substance, then reabsorbs substance into spirit.[15]

The danger of this rich dialectical movement is that this poem risks becoming another version of Williams's "El Hombre." It exhibits roots deep in romanticism. And it sublimates and makes sublime the work of negation by putting negation to the work of realizing deeper forces latent within the situation. To be truly modern, "The Man with the Blue Guitar" suggests in contrast, is to develop negative forces that do not give up their resistance to any form of positive meaning. In particular the poem offers an interpretation of Picasso's "destructions" stressing two fundamental kinds of violence.

First, the poem never quite realizes attunement with nature except under the guise of the will of the guitarist. The various voices and moods and levels of diction aggressively pursue their own powers. So the work has no choice but to stage modernist juxtaposition as its basic composing of the senses. Here Picasso's influence entails the destruction of any kind of fluidity or casual expansiveness of mind because those traits would appear as simply an effort to tie the imagination to an outdated rhetorical means of presenting artworks. Second, Stevens's version of Picasso's modernism seems to require the total suppression of the old gestures of understanding that might also be considered outdated rhetoric. Each scene is absolute for the imagination. There is no context for the perspective except the principle of contrast within a continual war of perspectives. And especially in the opening sections of the poem, the mind is reduced to paratactic functions.

The sentences are evocative in their simple directness. So there is no effort to bring into language explicit hypotactic efforts to plumb and gather the implications of the contrast in order also to make them explicit. Because moments contend, each seems to have its own uncompromising absoluteness that refuses to submit to argument or accept a place in continuous narrative or extended description.

X

The closing sections of the poem repeat the variety of syntactic and tonal forms of the beginning, but with an urgent desire to adapt the blue guitar to the figure of "central man" and the "hero" developed in other poems of the period. This conjunction between the "hoard of destructions" (*CPP* 141) and the heroic imperatives of the penultimate section makes for striking poetry, but the crown must sit uneasy on this head. Despite the poem's assertions, it is by no means evident that we can honor the negative presence of the "actual stone" and still believe that "the imagined pine, the imagined jay" will suffice for our coming to terms with the destructiveness of the modern world. Once we recognize the difficulties involved in reconciling Picasso with Stevensian versions of the hero, we will understand better why after World War II he will reject the figure of the hero and be much more wary about identifying with modernist projections onto the modern reality they made inescapable.[16] But he will also reject the demand for clashing perspectives in favor of much more subtle versions of perpetual inner contrast that comprises what I call aspectual thinking. When Stevens returned after World War II to exploring the powers of mind and of minding that "as" gives the mind, the violent clash of perspectives seemed less important to him than mining the resources of syntax that underlie ordinary language. It will suffice to imagine other ways of challenging the copula by honoring the intricacy that quickens the mind and fleshes out the promise of an affective life wedded to the simple movement of imagination as it comes to live in change.

Perhaps Stevens came to think that the world that matters is never diminished or always diminished. Perhaps it takes a mode of thinking so adapted to the elemental work of constituting and assessing values to enable audiences to see through all modes of heroism for the romanticism that the poet's abstraction almost successfully conceals. Perhaps the entire modernist dream of linking language to radical presentations through the senses was a confused, historically driven suppression of those resources within language that could put the blue guitar within the capacities of everyday thinking. These are the questions and the possibilities that would eventually emerge from the final imperative of "The Man with the Blue Guitar":

> Throw away the lights, the definitions,
> And say of what you see in the dark
>
> That it is this or that it is that,
> But do not use the rotted names.
> . . . Nothing must stand
> Between you and the shapes you take
> When the crust of shape has been destroyed.
>
> You as you are? You are yourself.
> The blue guitar surprises you.
>
> *(CPP 150)*

CHAPTER 4

How Stevens Uses the Grammar of *As*

> In the presence of the violent reality of war, consciousness takes
> the place of imagination. . . . If that is true, it follows that the
> poetry of war as a consciousness of the victories and the defeats
> of nations, is a consciousness of fact, but of heroic fact, a fact on
> such a scale that the mere consciousness of it affects the scale of
> one's thinking and constitutes a participating in the rhetoric.
>
> (*CPP* 251)

> The imagination loses vitality as it ceases to adhere to the real. . . .
> While we are moved by it [imagination], we are moved by it as
> observers. We recognize it perfectly. We do not realize it. We
> understand the feeling of it, the robust feeling, clearly and
> fluently communicated. Yet we understand it rather than
> participate in it. . . .
>   The reason why this particular figure has lost its vitality is that,
> in it, the imagination adheres to what is unreal.
>
> (*CPP* 645)[1]

Since theory has become ubiquitous, the critics of modern poetry have
developed powerful tools for elaborating conceptual backgrounds by which
we might flesh out the possible imaginative resonances developed by poets'
attention to the resources of language. However, because this critical work
tends to rely on philosophical and cultural themes, it often overlooks a very
important factor in how poems develop those resonances. For in addition to
the ideas poets bring to their constructive labors, they are likely to develop
the conceptual implications of their medium by relying on the affective properties latent in the linguistic building blocks constructing the poem. This kind
of attention includes aural and phanopoeic registers. But I will be focusing
on the intensities available within a domain close to the mode of inquiry
Wittgenstein called "philosophical grammar." Here, though, I do not borrow
from Wittgenstein directly. His philosophical grammar attends primarily to
implicit structures governing usage; instead, I emphasize how Stevens (like
other writers) activates philosophical implications within the elemental
building blocks afforded by our shared understanding of syntactic grammatical functions. For example, adverbial modes can bring an attention to

manner very different from adjectives, which articulate qualities of matter. "Of" is a marvelously intricate operator because it can set the subjective genitive against the objective: an expression of love can turn out also to express all the ways that love becomes a rhetorical stance reducing the person using it to a figure of pathos. And, as many critics have remarked, there are radically different implications when styles come to emphasize action terms over substance terms or to prefer paratactic to hypotactic relations.

It should be no surprise by now that my favorite grammatical resource in Stevens's poetry is his focus on the capacity of "as" to take on multiple, mutually reinforcing levels of meaning and to provide surprising and powerful senses of agency.[2] I love how "as" complicates actual situations by combining temporal, qualitative, and psychological registers for staging events so that there is simultaneity in events, parallelism in qualities, and opportunities for expressing the manner of one's interactions with objects. And I love how the grammar of "as" provides the basis for what I treat in my next chapter as a general aspectual thinking that extends well beyond specific grammatical forms. "As" produces a continuous capacity to blend observation with second-order reflection and so comes as close as any linguistic element to embodying the powers of imagination Stevens idealizes. So his use of this grammar goes a long way toward clarifying why he insisted that there could be a modern poetry that did not rely on the image but could extend the powers of discursive thinking by scrutinizing the affective energies it could elicit. More important, Stevens develops material for undermining the authority of the copulative verbs on which so much of empiricist thinking on values is based. Clearly, poetry is not likely to challenge that authority successfully where practical matters are at stake. But it can display how exclusive reliance on the copulative misses the qualitative dimension of experience and has to be reductive about the qualities of mind that can make a difference in how we live our lives.

On the broadest conceptual level "as" matters for Stevens because it provides a vehicle by which he can develop procedures for the work of imagination in the world that have significant parallels with Emerson, although I do not see enough evidence to claim he derived those procedures from Emerson.[3] These procedures have two basic aspects. Both come under the auspices of the concept of participation, and so derive from what Stevens recognizes is the Platonic ideal that "all things participate in the good" (*CPP* 855). First, "participation" provides a quite forceful way to formulate the modernist resistance to description and representation. As in modernist theories of expressive activity, writing does not provide a picture of the real but offers an intervention in the real by which one creates an event weaving feelings and facts into each other. But the ideal of participation helps to correct the subjectivist tendency of much expressionist theory, from *Der Blaue Reiter* to abstract expressionist painting. Participation is not self-expression. It is the energizing of self because of the shape one's feelings take as they interact with objective conditions. One need not let those feelings impose a shape on the world, like a blue guitar might. Rather, the poet can cast the work of connecting feelings to objects as a project of bringing the self to the object and allowing each a richer existence as each fulfills the other or, one could say, as each attunes to the other.

Imagine my feeling that *as* I focus on a bouquet of flowers, the flowers themselves welcome me and eventually create a sense that they complete me by filling out the scene: they allow my full involvement in the senses as these senses attach to the object. It is crucial to attend to my particular state *as* an intimate involvement in what the object offers. But that is not the end of the story. It is also crucial to imagine the possibility of the state of the object taking on a kind of completion in what happens because of my activity. Subject and object visibly bring each other to a state of satisfaction by turning metaphysical differences into correlated harmonic registers:

> The infinite of the actual perceived,
> A freedom revealed, a realization touched,
> The real made more acute by an unreal.
> *(CPP 386)*[4]

The term "realization" here is not chosen lightly. Stevens mentions Cézanne's use of that term, probably because it perfectly complements the ideal of participation *(CPP 671–72)*. Cézanne's fundamental concern is how he can integrate the visible energies of his making with what calls to him as an aspect of the world eliciting those painterly energies. So, rather than seeing those energies as displacing or interpreting or even expressing his state before the object, he imagines a mutual process in which subject and object live one another's lives.[5] Art can produce a world where subject and object each anchor the other as each resists the transformation of realization into mere understanding. It is only when realization is supplanted that we have to deal with the imagination as the maker of fictions that we force upon the world.[6]

Because that fall into mere understanding is always imminent, always a risk for any effort to have the unreal imagination participate in realization, the temporal attunement possible in the grammar of "as" becomes especially important. We might say that it adds a second level of participation where the focus is not on the mind in the world but on possible simultaneity between the two subjective presences of author and audience. When an artist or writer can see as one who shares a world with the emerging flowers, he or she can also make a world in which that moment of recognition is not only reported but also reenacted. This reenactment can be offered so as to emphasize who the reader can become as participant in the writer's activity. Modernist theory from Kant to Eliot attributes this possible identification with an audience to the objective nature of the work: the work provides the terms for shared conditions of experience.

Stevens's fascination with "as" provides a grammatical basis for this level of participation. An audience can align itself with the artist *as* the artist presents the conditions of experience so that there is an equivalence between the two in what can be one time and one space:

> There were ghosts that returned to earth to hear his phrases
> As he sat there reading, aloud, the great blue tabulae. . . .
>
> And laughed, as he sat there reading, from out of the purple tabulae,
> The outlines of being and its expressing, the syllables of its law:
> *Poesis, poesis*, the literal characters, the vatic lines
>
> Which in those ears and in those thin, those spended hearts,
> Took on color, took on shape and the size of things as they are
> And spoke the feeling for them, which was what they had lacked.
>
> (CPP 365)

By attending to these grammatical possibilities, we can track closely how Stevens changes his priorities at different phases of his career. But my interest in spelling out those differences requires a word of caution. When we construct clear conceptual boundaries among phases of a poet's career, we lose the quality of inchoateness that is a dynamic feature of the poems. And then at least this critic is tempted to project chronological differences onto what are typically more tentative poetic gestures that try out various ways of stabilizing feeling for the world. So I have to be careful to recognize how at times Stevens tries out stances that will not fit into my story or that attempt unique combinations of elements that I try to keep distinct. At best I can speak only about general patterns and emphases.

Finally, I hope this chapter puts us in a position to begin righting a serious imaginative wrong that has been perpetrated by how critics have construed the modernist heritage. From the time of the New Critics at least, discourse about poetry, not just about modern poetry, has been dominated by the figure of metaphor, with simile consigned to useless and distracting processes of unnecessary ornamentation. The first rule of creative writing classes was "Go in dread of simile because it is a sign that you lack either the courage or the talent to make direct presentations and pursue the condensation of metaphoric processes." Yet reflecting here on the powers of equivalence and analogy should provide a convincing framework for insisting on how the similes in classical epic establish substantial powers to intensify and modify feeling. So in an appendix to this chapter I outline a case for reversing modernist bias for metaphor by fleshing out what I think had been fundamental classical assumptions about the imaginative work simile can accomplish.

I

Much as I would like to continue in this speculative vein, I cannot secure my claims about the kind of collective agency grammar provides without paying careful attention to specifics. I begin with how linguists characterize this grammar of "as" and then I try to isolate concrete and distinctive powers that Stevens employs in sections of particular poems. After we become familiar with the range of effects elaborated by these poems, we can turn in the next chapter to what I call "aspectual thinking," by which Stevens after World War II makes the interplay of these grammatical features fundamental to his entire poetic project. Aspectual thinking proceeds by postulating equivalents rather than names. Therefore it is not quite argument and not quite association. Rather, it pursues the various semantic and affective implications that emerge when we characterize phenomena in terms of constant equivalences and resemblances. The authorial mind represents itself as attempting to contour itself to an environment that is constantly changing and offering opportunities for the intensities that can characterize successful participation—in a world of constant change and in a social space where we can identify with authorial projects. For Stevens this becomes a way of realizing how imagination as a force may reenchant the world without remystifying it.

My first obligation is to review what I can understand of how linguistics treats the ordinary grammar of "as." According to R. W. Zandvoort, "as" has two primary functions—*as* a preposition performing the task of a predicate adjunct and *as* a conjunction introducing six kinds of adverbial clauses that can often "shade off into one another" (643).[7] *As* preposition, "as" typically provides adjuncts clarifying the scope of nouns: "We chose him as leader," or "As a doctor, John is quite personable."[8]

The range of adverbial clauses is more complex, so we need a list.

1) Temporal simultaneity: "As I grow more tired, his energy increases."[9]
2) Clauses of proportionate agreement (220n2): "As I grow richer, I become more ambitious."
3) Clauses attributing reasons, where "as" can be substituted for "since." We could use the examples posited in the first two cases because equivalences in the dimensions of temporal relations and proportionate agreements also typically have a trace of causal force. One could say that it is "because I grow more tired, his energy increases." The same logic holds for the relation between increase in wealth and in ambition.
4) Clauses introducing concessions or restrictions: "The apology is good as far as it goes," or "Poor as I am, I am honest."
5) Clauses offering comparisons: "They behaved as well as could be expected." This kind of clause readily shades into predicate complements qualifying "the direct object of the main clause" (628), like "I found him as I left him."
6) Clauses defining manner: "I will do as you advise."

My citing the formal language of grammatical analysis is primarily to show I have done some homework and to establish the complexity of the appropriate grammatical resources. That homework will help us keep in mind the capacity of "as" to establish intricate equivalences among qualities of being and states of mind. As I have suggested, these equivalences take the form of attunements between subject and object making possible simultaneous states of mind by different agents. But for literary purposes it is even more important to show how these modes of expression interact than it is to identify them in the first place. So I am going to add to our grammatical repertoire for "as" the brilliant reflections on the topic in Lyn Hejinian's essay on the work of Leslie Scalapino.[10] Hejinian turns our attention from the properties of clauses to the qualities of action that occur when various uses of "as" create conditions of activity—for example, in stressing adverbial attributes of verbs, or establishing intensities, or serving as markers of both "causative" and "temporal" relativity. On the basis of that potential for multiple functions, she makes a series of claims for the effects that "as" can have in writing. "As" becomes "the site of relationship—neither one thing nor the other": "The 'as' effect is an 'occurrence structure' within whose realm everything is what it isn't and is not what it is." For Scalapino at least, the emphasis on "as" functions to reveal "the inseparability of everything."

Hejinian may be right about Scalapino. But to extend this work to Stevens (as well as to related poets from William Wordsworth to John Ashbery) I think we can put Hejinian's sense of complexity to somewhat different ends. Stevens, at least, does not seem interested in so ontological a claim about the inseparability of everything. However, he is very interested in how the mind handles particular grammatical possibilities for expressing particular aspects of relatedness. So for him the crucial feature of relatedness is the mind's capacity to override descriptions of things as they are by an insistence on specifying the manner by which the mind forms "resemblances" (*CPP* 687–90; cf. 862–67).[11] His interest after "The Man with the Blue Guitar" lies in the positive features introduced by equivalences rather than in the sense of "neither one thing nor the other." Only then can one concentrate on or "realize" what the powers of "as" can do to enhance our sense of continuous possibilities for extending and contextualizing perceptions. The activity made possible by grammar becomes the basic source of values as it establishes ways in which we come to inhabit what we see and what we can care about.

The most important feature of Hejinian's essay for me is her clear grasp of how "as" can undo the authority of copulative verbs.[12] Clauses stressing "as" shift our attention from a world of identity thinking, where minds describe and stabilize facts, to one in which the mind is continually working in relation to processes and forces that provoke efforts at alignment and attunement. The key question becomes not "is it true?" but "how fully can I participate in what is unfolding so that I do not blind myself to how the world beckons?" And now my homework comes into play again because the linguists provide clear and powerful contrasts between the copulative and the relational aspects of predication. They argue that copulative verbs are restricted to two basic functions—one most pronounced in the resources of "be" and one carried by "is." "Be" as an active verb designates specific force or transfer of energy—"Be all that you can be" is how the US Army interprets our grammar. This force is well represented by Heidegger's being as *phusis,* or "self-blossoming emergence." (In fact, Heidegger makes another significant grammatical remark when he observes that the infinitive "to be" most fully captures his force of emergence because it defines a state prior to an action becoming qualified by the declension of verb tenses.) The second use of the copula establishes a transfer of meaning. Here the emphasis is on asserting that the predicate is in fact included in our understanding of the subject—"the rock is igneous" or "this poem is difficult."

"As" makes major modifications of both kinds of predication. Copulative verbs attempt to articulate judgments about how percepts fit into one's

sense of the world one inherits. These judgments aim at stability of reference and so facilitate truth claims—with respect to events and with respect
to our understanding of recurrent features of experience. "As," on the other
hand, leads not toward completing judgments but toward appreciating possibilities of relation and resemblance (and perhaps declension). The positing
of equivalences takes us from the descriptive task of stabilizing predication
to the projective task of qualifying these descriptions by specifying temporal
and associative contexts limiting and complicating the role of reference.
These equivalences call attention to the present tense of the writing and rel-
egate descriptions to accounts of how phenomena take a place in the subject's
emerging world.

For Stevens this primary grammatical difference comes out most strongly
in a statement that offers a strong contrast with the biblical view of God as
"I am that I am":

> There is a month, a year, there is a time
> In which majesty is a mirror of the self
> I have not but I am and as I am I am.
>   *(CPP 350)*

The biblical evocation of God's power of self-predication has had major effects on how the West now constructs personal identity. For it suggests the
possibility of stable parallels between an inner and an outer life. In contrast,
the mode of thinking about personal identity I quote from Stevens does not
invoke any underlying substantial psychological traits. Instead, what can
stand *as* an assertion of personal identity requires only locating a specific
time and a set of qualitative equivalences—perceptual and affective—that
define the conditions of participation in an aspect of the world. In effect,
Stevens need no longer talk about a hero because the powers of imagination
to establish values stage themselves in these different ways of being "I." Ultimately "as" is only as valuable as the concrete work it can actually do to
quicken our senses of the world by virtue of the equivalences it sustains or
the moments in which it displays the vitality of our imaginations.

II

While Zandvoort's differentiating among kinds of clauses provides a useful
backdrop for our coming to appreciate the complex functions of "as" in
English grammar, I prefer to align with Hejinian in emphasizing the kinds

of actions that "as" is capable of performing. From this perspective I rely on how the use of "as" predicates different kinds of equivalences. I have already suggested dividing the roles of "as" into sponsoring two basic equivalences— temporal and participatory. Now I need a more refined model with four basic variants of the participatory. Participatory equivalences can stress either the role of the subject in bringing feelings to bear on how objects take on substance or the drawing of parallels between various states of objects. As evidence of the first, consider "But one looks at the sea / As one improvises on a piano" (*CPP* 213). And for the effects of one object seen in another Stevens offers, "Then the sea / And heaven rolled as one and from the two / Came freshest transfigurings of freshest blue" (*CPP* 85).

Then there are two modes of equivalence that actually position the subject in a self-conscious, second-order relationship to these states of observation. The first is the equivalence in time that I have already commented upon—most intricately realized in "I am as I am." Then we need a category for second-order states that involve the will or, minimally, a kind of assent or dissent to what emerges on the perceptual level. This can occur positively, as in Stevens's "And there he walks and does as he lives and likes" (*CPP* 449). The mode of assent can also take a negative form: "pears are not seen as the observer wills" (*CPP* 181). Notice, too, that these examples play more than one semantic role, although Zandvoort avoids that dimension. "But one looks at the sea / As one improvises on a piano" draws both modal and temporal parallels since joining the actions in time also suggests that there are shared qualities in looking and improvising. Similarly, "I am as I am" stresses temporal equivalence but also involves identification with a mode of being. And "there he walks and does as he lives and likes" works on a second-order level because it also joins temporal and modal equivalence to a sense of approval and even envy.[13] Living and liking become more than descriptions of the philosopher's state. They also record a sense of wanting to identify with the philosopher's enacting such states.

Now it is time to test the usefulness of these categories by turning to more elaborate and dense examples of the kinds of imaginative values brought to bear by "as" clauses in a poem's handling of concrete situations. The first two involve different emphases—on the subject and on the object. However, both make it clear how language can shift valence so that, rather than invite description and interpretation, it dramatizes how participation produces conditions of feeling.

In the first case, "Bouquet of Roses in Sunlight" challenges the subject to play a significant part within a scene whose rich objectivity threatens to expunge any role for the imagination:

Say that it is a crude effect, black reds,
Pink yellows, orange whites, too much as they are
To be anything else in the sunlight of the room.

Too much as they are to be changed by metaphor,
Too actual, things that in being real
Make any imaginings of them lesser things,

And yet this effect is a consequence of the way
We feel and, therefore, is not real, except
In our sense of it, our sense of the fertilest red . . .

Our sense of these things changes and they change,
Not as in metaphor, but in our sense
Of them, so sense exceeds all metaphor.

It exceeds the heavy changes of the light.
It is like the flow of meanings with no speech
And of as many meanings as of men.

We are two that use these roses as we are,
In seeing them. This is what makes them seem
So far beyond the rhetorician's touch.

                    (CPP 371)

Stevens can offer a counterforce to rhetoric (in talk about roses of all things) because he mines the capacity of *as* to create equivalences between the emergence of the roses as an event for the speaker and the attunement of consciousness possible when language need not make claims that go beyond that sense of emergence.

The poem is brilliantly structured. It begins with a quietly frightening, self-sufficient plenitude of the object that seems to render any imaginative complement by the subject mere unanchored imagination. This plenitude unnerves the speaker to the point that he has at least to imagine bringing the construction of metaphor to bear and so transforming impressions into objects. But here metaphor would be only displacement into a lesser object that in turn reveals a lesser subject eager to impose a self as a defense against the fullness of the immediate object. The only way out of this painful divide is to recast what the subject can bring. This complement to the bouquet becomes a mode of realizing it or participating in it without replacing it with a figure that sacrifices its plenitude for a form of human meaning. Recasting takes place here by mining the sense of "sense": "sense" does not become a metaphor but instead is treated as a word capable of bringing to bear significant capacities for reconciliation, especially when supplemented by the "as" clauses in the poem, which also emphasize the mind's working within the world rather than upon it.[14]

"Sense" imposes its own opening to infinite self-reflexivity. However, at the same time it composes the possibility that sense can take the form of equivalences posed by "as" so that a renewed sociality becomes possible. After the general statement "as many meanings as of men," the poem immediately turns to the plural as those multiple meanings converge in the last stanza. As long as the roses dwell linguistically in adverbial clauses shaped by "as," the speaker can himself be content to adjust a sensibility rather than impose a meaning. So the speaker proposes to connect to his audience not by asking the audience to test a proposition but by inviting it to explore its own powers to track how the equivalences exemplified make it possible to participate in the vitality of what the roses become. Then the utterance is beyond rhetoric because it is not primarily an exercise of subjective intensities creating interpretations. Rather, the speaker's effusion also offers a shareable imaginative power to develop lines of connection allowing the rose to address common imaginative needs. Participation replaces being overwhelmed by objects at one pole and seeking uneasy domination over them at the other.

In other words, getting beyond rhetoric requires creating a convincing immediacy for poetry. The old eloquence threatens to displace the world into figures of pure will manipulating others to do what the rhetor desires. In response to this threat, imagism established the hope that sharp presentation of particulars in intricate, juxtaposed conjunctions will provide a sufficient mode of reenchantment. Eloquence becomes the power of an immediacy rooted in how the present tense in the poem overwhelms all mere context. A plausible eloquence depends on specific properties of presentation. Stevens proposes a different and probably more defensible understanding of presentation, at least on the level of theory. A convincing eloquence depends on making the subjective component of the presentation so transparent as energy and as intelligence that the subject's passions fuse with the aspects of the object that become the focus of attention. Where "rhetoric" had become focused on persuasion, Stevens could emphasize what in the world given to us by perception seems capable of engaging and quickening imaginative states that can be shared with others in the form of immediate involvement. Presentation becomes a secular version of Emersonian participation. Poems can ground the forces of figuration and syntactic effulgence in energies that manifestly need not be traced primarily to the psychological dispositions of an individual authorial will. "As" opens us to equivalences that sharpen participation in what comes before consciousness. Moreover, it encourages a sense of participation in the forms of sociality possible because of attention to the grammars we share.

III

My second category provides a necessary means for tempering the enthusiasms of the first. Rather than working explicitly to provide alternatives to rhetoric that still stress subjective powers, Stevens in some poems makes "as" function to emphasize transformations in the perceptual order that force the ego into equivalences with objective conditions. , Such conditions seem to demand acts of sympathy with what are not at all standard modes of the ego's being in the world.

"Variations on a Summer Day" is particularly noteworthy in this regard because the poem shares with "Cy Est Pourtraicte . . ." a strangely generous refusal to pursue standard human desires because of the intricacy of its appeal to a different kind of presence. Hence the concluding stanza:

> You could almost see the brass on her gleaming,
> Not quite. The mist was to light what red
> Is to fire. And her mainmast tapered to nothing,
> Without teetering a millimeter's measure.
> The beads on her rails seemed to grasp at transparence.
> It was not yet the hour to be dauntlessly leaping.
>
> *(CPP 215).*

On the way to this stanza two others stand out for the ways they absorb and redirect subjectivity into other modes of sensibility that define what variations in imagination can entail. Here are sections VIII and X:

> An exercise in viewing the world.
> On the motive! But one looks at the sea
> As one improvises on the piano.
>
> *(CPP 213)*

> To change nature, not merely to change idea,
> To escape from the body, so to feel
> Those feelings that the body balks,

The feelings of the natures round us here:
As a boat feels when it cuts blue water.

(CPP 214)

We might notice first how "as" allows a smooth transition from looking at the sea to looking at the self. Rather than offer further descriptions of the sea, the poem tries to imagine what it might be like to modify the subject who is looking.[15] If we were to stop with this observation, however, we might be tempted to join the chorus of those criticizing Stevens for his muted but even more solipsistic version of Wordsworth's egotistical sublime. But this would be to ignore how what grammatically modifies the subject can migrate to include an equivalence born of the object. Here the focus on the subject's looking at the sea becomes caught up in feelings emphatically connected to the sea, as if the only way sufficiently to honor the immediacy and intricacy of the object were to read it through what it elicits in the subject. Then the second passage proposes a more radical demand to honor the object by attributing to it subjective powers to feel in relation to actions that subjects cannot quite perform. Rather than transpose feeling into an image that indicates the subject's powers to absorb the world into its ways of making sense, the poem uses the image to elaborate feelings that extend well beyond the image, indeed beyond the capacities of language to do anything but note what is happening.

Here it may not be a huge leap to suggest that these lines offer grounds for a comprehensive theory of feeling. Feeling depends on how the subject makes equivalences, yet those equivalences in turn suggest possible new aspects for connecting to what happens in perception. Feeling, like lyric itself, may have only analogues and no determinate referents. These passages offer a marvelous fusion defining a specific moment in time as inseparable from a particular sense of what occurs in space. The perceiver eventually merges completely with the figure of feeling because subjectivity stages itself as capable of giving itself up to its own inventions. Yet the invention marks the subject's capacities for having feeling immerse him further in the world. "As" here becomes more a matter of finding than of inventing. The poem attributes feelings to the boat because it then can revel in a pure eventfulness of equivalence with no defensive need to test to whom the feelings belong. The feelings are cut loose so that they occupy a space of possibility that subjects enter. And then identification takes place not just through observation but also through the sense of literally participating in the relation between boat and water.

This commentary brings me very close to Hejinian's great observation that when Pasternak compares a woman's song to a nightingale, Russian grammar allows him to suggest that she is not just *like* a nightingale because "in singing she becomes the nightingale." Hejinian is then led to her celebration of the freedom of poetic language because it can reveal "the inseparability of everything." There can be no greater recasting of the empiricist version of "it is." But while Stevens shares this critique of empiricism, his primary concern is far less abstract. He wants to explore the possibilities of feeling to flesh out these equivalence functions: How far can what lives in the subject find through its intensities a distinctive home in the relations emerging at the "object" pole of the perceptive process?

IV

Stevens could not have accepted Hejinian's ideal of "the inseparability of everything" because it would have seemed to him too indiscriminate. Various capacities of language matter to us for various reasons that employ distinctive mental powers. It matters whether one emphasizes the subject's position or the relations among objects, and it matters whether one is emphasizing first-order perceptual relations or second-order reflections on who the self becomes by virtue of certain stances toward the world. My third and fourth basic Stevensian uses of the grammar of "as" emphasize those second-order relations. We have already considered variants of the third use. These are cases where the poem projects an anticipation of readers entering the same time frame as the speaker so that they are invited to imagine directly sharing the speaker's experience as it unfolds. Poetry manages to share not just an idea about experience but also the very conditions motivating a particular process of speaking. Then there is a fourth use of equivalence that is more difficult to fix but also perhaps even more important. I refer to the way "as" allows intonations that indicate not just the recognition of an equivalence but also the speaker's alignment of something like the will with the situation. "I am as I am" can be a deliberate assertion of identity and not just a description. In such affirmations I believe it is possible to treat the will as something other than the specific psychological faculty posed by both Kant and William James. Will itself becomes inseparable from the possibility of a speech act taking actual responsibility within the poem for what one sees oneself becoming.[16]

The simplest use of second-order equivalence occurs in imaginative states that develop immediate parallels among sensibilities. The concluding section of "Credences of Summer," for example, presents a quiet discursive passage that the closing "as" tries to bring into a mode of lyrical celebration:

> The personae of summer play the characters
> Of an inhuman author, who meditates
> With the gold bugs in blue meadows, late at night.
> He does not hear his characters talk. He sees
> Them mottled, in the moodiest costumes . . .
>
> The huge decorum, the manner of the time,
> Part of the mottled mood of summer's whole,
>
> In which the characters speak because they want
> To speak, the fat, the roseate characters,
> Free for a moment, from malice and sudden cry,
> Completed in a completed scene,
> Speaking their parts as in a youthful happiness.
>
> *(CPP 326)*

I make this claim about lyrical celebration because I can see no other role for this final clause about happiness. Zandvoort would probably call this a comparison clause, but I think it also uses the resources of temporal equivalence and equivalence of manner. That clause is striking in part because the poem manages to hear and to characterize the speaking parts in summer's little drama even though we are twice told that "the inhuman author" cannot hear them. The only way I can explain the apparent contradiction is that as this author meditates, his mind gets so absorbed in the scene of summer that the scene takes on a life of its own. We hear even if the inhuman author cannot because the summer scene puts us in a position to appreciate what it means to want to speak, as another way of realizing the "mood of summer's whole." As the characters speak, they complete the scene. Then the poem can suggest by another strange gesture of using "completed" twice that the mind, in registering that completeness, repeats the term as its mode of expressing an awareness of its own sense of flourishing. That flourishing directs the mind back to the scene not just to hear the speaking but also to characterize it—not as "the expression of youthful happiness" (which is what I would have written) but as the eliciting of an equivalence to "youthful happiness."

I guess that the difference between expression of happiness and equivalent of happiness invites our postulating a contrast between what the speakers do and what the poem does as it reaches for a summary figure of how the activities might be included in "summer's whole." The "as" clause places speaking in a larger play that readers can flesh out if they are willing to envision their own capacity to draw equivalents from the imagining of the whole of summer. And in doing that they find themselves in a position to reflect on how the physical values summer brings expand into reflective social values: *as* we hear the speech of summer's personae we gather it into a single image of shared happiness. No other modern poet would risk such banality in the last phrase in order to extend the act of reading into the space of shared self-reflection.

Stevens is perhaps most explicit on the capacity of grammar to produce a shared, self-reflexive present tense in these concluding passages from "Looking across the Fields and Watching the Birds Fly":

> And what we think, a breathing like the wind,
> A moving part of a motion, a discovery,
> Part of a discovery, a change, part of a change . . .
>
> We think then, as the sun shines or does not.
> We think as wind skitters on a pond in a field . . .
>
> The spirit comes from the body of the world,
> Or so Mr. Homburg thought: the body of a world
> Whose blunt laws make an affectation of the mind,
>
> The mannerism of nature caught in a glass
> And there become a spirit's mannerism,
> A glass aswarm with things going as far as they can.
>
> *(CPP 440)*

This passage is remarkable for two features. First, it establishes a sense of actual spirit at work by finding in the glass, which reflects nature, something not quite reducible to its blunt laws. The mind may be only an affectation in relation to the blunt laws of nature. Nonetheless, it is still the necessary correlate of things, making it possible for them to go as far as they can, presumably, toward realizing their own potential to sustain relationships. So each phrase, like "think" or "discovery" or "body of the world" or "glass," gets repeated and unpacked. It is as if the poem had to examine what was involved in accepting the words used to represent the world, if only to establish what possible participatory role the mind could have within an "element . . . not planned for imagery or belief" (*CPP* 439).

It is crucial here that this mind does not think about the sun or the wind; it thinks as they enact their nature. This "as" is the "as" both of manner and of comparison. It unites thinking with these dynamic physical activities. It also suggests affinities in their nature *as* both the thinking and the physical activities come to share a present tense that also opens into the present tense of the reading. These repetitions enable the mind to rest in the first-person plural because they stage a scrutiny that seems destined for public form: these are not mere momentary impressions. The mind can be naturalized by analogy to the wind precisely because it has the same overarching yet discreet presence as the atmosphere. This thinking matters because it participates in what the wind does and because it then allows reflection on what it provides. Perhaps that reflection also allows participation in something grander than the elemental process, something that drives the effort at the first-person plural in the first place.

Second, this passage is remarkable because its way of extending participation to the first-person plural has something intimately to do with how the "as" clauses extend equivalences in time as well as in space. Thinking becomes a phenomenon rooted in the present. It need not explain experience by reaching back to past regularities or predict how covering laws will affect those phenomena. Thinking accompanies states of being as they take on appearances, and it accompanies how those states emerge in a way that invites attention from this plural "we." It may be only a slight exaggeration to suggest that this "we" is actually constituted by the possibility of such accompaniment since the communal seems a necessary complement to things in going as far as they can.

This sense of social bonding in a poet as patently individualist as Stevens is noteworthy in relation to our general understanding of modernist poetry. I think Stevens's two levels of participation—in the scene and in reflection on the scene—offer a theoretical alternative to the standard modernist model for representing how reading can be a social force. For Eliot the principles of establishing sociality were negative. If the poet could achieve impersonality and through that objectify expressive forces, then the object could provide a direct presentation of experience that had the same ontological status as any object. Any reader who learned to read poetry as a relation among objective forces could share in reassembling what the author had imaginatively constructed. But for Stevens this model gives neither a sufficient motive nor a sufficient reward for the effort to share the tracking of imaginative labor. Participation provides both an ontological and social goal for treating the text as something objective and shareable. It matters then that *as* we become aware of our pleasure in participating we also recognize how important the grammar of *as* can be to this enjoyment. For we then make less mystical the claims to sharing reflective experience. We can see that the poem itself utilizes the powers of grammar that we all share on a fundamental level. The poet's task is to make us appreciate powers we already possess.

V

The fourth category, in contrast, concentrates on individual self-consciousness. It cannot suffice ultimately if we limit our discussion of second-order states to an awareness of how we can enter into mutually reinforcing processes of engaging the flow of time. For that mode of activity gives us only an awareness of what we share without allowing discussion of how we regard such sharing. So we need to test the possibility that there is also a dimension of second-order states of consciousness that allow individuals to express states of affirmation and even the kind of will that commits one to responsibilities. Perhaps willing can become evident simply as a second-order quality of affirming a way of seeing or of thinking. There is no transcendental philosophy here. There need be only the capacity to see the artist's shifts in perspective as also a mode of orienting the self toward action. There need be only that and the willingness to trust in what emerges from close reading.

Let me track this volitional use of second-order reflection chronologically through three poems. Returning to "Evening without Angels" will allow us to see this work of will at its most elemental:

> Bare night is best. Bare earth is best. Bare, bare,
> Except for our own houses, huddled low
> Beneath the arches and their spangled air,
> Beneath the rhapsodies of fire and fire,
> Where the voice that is in us makes a true response,
> Where the voice that is great within us rises up,
> As we stand gazing at the rounded moon.
>
> *(CPP 112)*

We probably notice first the temporal use of an "as" clause: thinking about the voice takes place while we gaze at the rounded moon. But what are the equivalents established that give content to this moment and serve as articulate vehicles for the will? We have to correlate that temporal use with a clause that defines manner. The poem conjoins sight to voice, *as* if the diction could connect the greatness of the voice within to a kind of pregnancy for which the rounded moon stands. (And the pregnancy seems itself a transformation of the appeal of bare earth, but cast in a way that allows identification.) But the most striking aspect of these conjunctions is produced by the remarkable materializing force of the series of vowels that move from long *a* to long *o*. Parallels in manner run deep. Simple effects of voice end up performing the second-order task of self-consciously sustaining elaborate existential analogies between gazing and willing. What is real here has to be envisioned as no less than complete harmony between the voice within and the moon without—romanticism by aural effects sustained by grammar. The poem internalizes all the gathering powers of the image of the moon while externalizing the powers of voice to take into itself how that gathering allows access to the space of concrete objectivity. And that route to pictorial objectivity evokes the larger social implication that every reader can occupy this mode of affirming what the ear can shape in the world.

However, when Stevens tries to focus on those implications, he runs into trouble because he eventually succumbs to heroic images that fix and so limit identifications he seeks to abstract forms.. Therefore I have to take up two different problems with the work "as" is asked to do in the construction of community because these provides a powerful contrast to the concreteness of willing in "The Rock." Consider this stanza from "Yellow Afternoon" as it tries to take the imagination beyond the immediate presence of the equivalents that it first produces:

> He said I had this that I could love,
> As one loves visible and responsive peace,
> As one loves one's own being,
> As one loves that which is the end
> And must be loved, as one loves that
> Of which one is a part as in a unity,
> A unity that is the life one loves,
> So that one lives all the lives that comprise it
> As the life of the fatal unity of war.
>
> *(CPP 216)*

At first the "as" clauses perform sheer second-order reflection: I am one who can identify with various possibilities of loving. This obviously risks the emptying of equivalence into tautology, and so the gesture gets implicated in the basic danger inherent in his flirtation with idealism's "I am I." Stevens partially rescues the poem from tautology and makes it dialectical by the increasingly abstract objects on which that love is focused. Love moves from having as its object one's own being, to the sense that one is part of a unity, to loving that aspect of the unity because it bears love, to loving a unity that aligns with "the life of the fatal unity of war." War becomes the ultimate test of a dialectical expansion of love because it clearly involves the entire society and demands taking responsibility for one's own social being. But the deep irony here is that one cannot just take responsibility for social being in the abstract. One needs another "as." One has to take responsibility for one's social being in relation to some role or path of action beyond the possibility for general identifications.

On the basis of poetry like this it is not surprising that Stevens would see the limitations perhaps inherent in his idealizing strategies. Here the poem's considerable intelligence seems inseparable from the willful self-blinding that allows such generalized statements to stand as if they were true. So he turns to the very different version of second-order intensity built into the life of the senses. This is the triumphant conclusion of "Esthétique du Mal":

> And out of what one sees and hears and out
> Of what one feels, who could have thought to make
> So many selves, so many sensuous worlds,
> As if the air, the mid-day air, was swarming
> With the metaphysical changes that occur,
> Merely in living as and where we are.
>
> *(CPP 287)*

Here "what one see and hears" produces the space "where we are"—a space that one could not have thought to make because thought is bound to repetition of the worlds it contains. But this space is not quite bound by determinate thoughts. The poem's thinking enables the speaker's sense of full participation to become self-reflexive by means of the expanding syntax. And because the space is not bound by specifiable thought, it may also not be limited by the boundaries of the ego or of the first "as if." The movement from "one" to "many" to "we" is seamless, producing a feeling of community closely linked to the willing of the poet's relations to these sensuous worlds. "Merely" is terrific here for insisting on the simplicity of this "living" while also completing a contrast with the expanding rhetoric that is in my view the ultimate sign of self-aware will. The big claim about the air "swarming with metaphysical changes" sets the context for the particular adjustment that affirms the situation.

Yet the very power of this passage brings with it an obvious danger of falling into another version of the fundamentally aestheticized sense of self that proves so tempting in *Harmonium*. One can live a full life under the auspices of this version of selfhood. But one cannot produce a convincing version of sympathy with pain and loss since it gets subsumed under the eventfulness of the *I*'s various ways of coming into being. So the more Stevens feels the need to address pain, the more he needs a sense of limitation and of necessity as a feature of the equivalents the imagination brings to bear on sensation. The route to satisfaction for Stevens here lies in first developing the rhetorical elaboration of equivalences into a general style of thinking based on something close to the constant negotiation of resemblances. Then he can manage to incorporate the tragic sense within the constant threat of loss embodied in those intensities. That route is the subject of my next two chapters.

Appendix: An Attempt to Recuperate the Force of Simile

First, however, I want to develop what I feel is an important lesson about modernist criticism that I learned in preparing for this chapter. Among the many minor revolutions John Ashbery's poetry helped establish, one at least has gone relatively unnoticed. He is a master of "as." And when he began "Self-Portrait in a Convex Mirror" with "as Parmigianino did it," he made manifest the possibility of a sharp break with modernist theory and New Critical doctrine, to which we are still trying to adapt.[17] For those strange allies, it was crucial for aspiring writers to recognize the weakness of simile and learn to load every metaphoric rift with ore. But Ashbery did not shrink from drawing a very different conclusion, partially on the basis of his readings in Stevens. Perhaps writers could emphasize resistance to identity thinking by calling attention to the powers of constant comparison. Perhaps they could find in simile a way of envisioning poetry not as a sophisticated mode of naming but as a model for ways of thinking leery of the quest for this kind of authority.[18] Asness could be one means of establishing indeterminacy as a set of positive states.[19]

Ironically, as I was warming to the dynamics of comparison I taught a class in the Western epic. I want now to elaborate a strange conjunction between celebrating innovative contemporary work and honoring traditional ideals of literary power that have been lost to literary critics, primarily because they felt literature needed defending by showing that it, too, could provide a kind of empirical objectivity. To accomplish this I first show how the critique of the simile derives from conditions in which literary study had to establish itself through the fantasy that it could somehow find equal cultural standing with the sciences. That equal standing could occur only if literature had its own versions of objectivity in the form of non-discursive ways of offering names for existents. Then I examine a few magnificent pieces of writing for their display of what the work of equivalence can do when it is free to imagine alternatives to ideals of complex naming.

Let me begin with how critics conveyed this sense of the importance of naming in the practical teaching of writing and in theoretical poetics. All writers, not just poets, were taught to avoid simile because similes betrayed lazy writing; why say what something is like when you could with more effort contour your language exactly to the impression itself? Then writing could make the world present by what Pound called bearing "true witness" (LE 3–7; 42–44). Metaphor engages the world directly because it treats the figural properties as parts of the object of attention. It also establishes felt thought for the presentation: the figural is justified by the event presented so that it is not imposed by will. Rather, the immediacy of presentation brings the making and the perceiving together. There is no space for self-consciousness to bring doubts and qualify the presentation with signs of authorial weakness of mind or hesitation. On the other hand, simile seems incompatible with presentation since it reminds us of the separate state of the observer only partially committed to any new names that can become present through art. In addition, self-consciousness through simile can only be self-division because of this unwillingness to commit feeling to naming. These critics had to admit that the space of equivalence opens all sorts of possible ways to elaborate analogues. But this space is itself a sign of weakness, of refusing to devote one's art to the powers of naming and to becoming totally present in what is presented.

In this case practical advice followed theory closely and even elaborated some psychological dangers only implicit in the theory. Let me first take Cleanth Brooks as a model for New Critical thinking on metaphor, which I think provided the conceptual underpinnings not only for reading poetry for four decades (1940–1980) but also for the writing of poetry for an even longer period.[20] Brooks's arguments depend on an initial separation between illustrative metaphor and functional metaphor. Illustrative metaphor is essentially ornamental, much like simile, and can make no claims to any distinctive cognitive functions from literary experience. But functional metaphor provides a cognition that can rival the impoverished world that science produces in its quest for certainty: "Poetry is not merely emotive, therefore, but cognitive. It gives us truth, and characteristically gives its truth through its metaphors. . . . The metaphor is a symbol when it alone expresses or embodies our ideal meaning" (259–60).

Brooks rarely drops the mask of literary critic. To elaborate the full stakes of the New Critical arguments about metaphor one has to go to John Crowe Ransom. He makes two strangely linked arguments. The first is that because metaphors provide names for states that one can observe but not reduce to scientific language, literature has its own claims to the "truth." This claim to truth entails treating literary experience as not just emotive, not just a matter of audience pleasure and the dispositions that generates. Rather, literary experience is as necessary as scientific argument for living as an alert and responsible citizen of the world. In fact, literary experience is the more important because there is no incentive to reductive analysis that can satisfy disciplinary criteria.

Second, Ransom buttresses this relative hierarchy by arguing that ultimately the truth literature provides is a spiritual truth. Minimally this truth displays the capacity to create unity within complex experiences that science would have to divide into discrete segments. That division destroys the mystery that is their interconnectedness. More ambitiously, Ransom is fascinated by the way that this logic of metaphoric unity both reflects the logic of Incarnation and sustains the possibility of faith because we regularly acknowledge the principle of mystery embodied in flesh. Ransom even has a name for this mode of perception—"miraculism." No wonder he treats the secularizing movement of romantic poetry as often lapsing into mere simile:

> Clearly the seventeenth century had the courage of its metaphors and imposed them imperially on the nearest things, and, just as clearly, the nineteenth century lacked this courage, and was half-heartedly metaphorical, or content with similes. The difference between the literary qualities of the two periods is the difference between the metaphor and the simile. . . . [he admits there are exceptions] One period was pithy and original in its poetic utterance, the other was prolix and predictable.[21]

Unfortunately, making historical claims about how simile and metaphor cohere with other ideological features does not exhaust the topic. One also has to test the concrete effects of both figures. How can simile display substantial literary power when it cannot claim to secure cognition? Perhaps there are significant resources that become available just because simile has to stage a mind that cannot be content with any form of description or argument, however sublime. Perhaps it can matter that in the place of providing new names simile calls our attention to what the act of naming itself can involve. Simile invites us to turn away from cognitions to something like participation in complex attitudes that develop analogies and correspondences.

I look at *The Iliad* first for two reasons. One can imagine this text working on a relatively clean palette to invent the primary forces that simile brings to narration. It seems that from the beginning of Western writing storytelling has involved the construction of analogical spaces that expand the audience's capacities for placing the details within affective contexts. That is, the text works out why analogies and equivalences might matter in constructing a narrated world. And one can imagine becoming self-reflexive about this state so that there can be moments in the narrative that deliberately build on the space the analogies construct for intensity and for projecting the possible significance of the actions involved.[22]

Here I must be very selective because my examples have to stand for a substantial variety of instances. My first passage easily rises to this challenge:

> The two named Aias held the fighting Trojans
> and threw them back. Still they pressed on . . . As a cloud of starlings
> or jackdaws shrieking bloody murder flies
> on seeing a hawk about to strike; he brings
> a slaughter on small winged things: just so
> under pursuit by Hector and Aineas
> Athenian soldiers shrieked and fled, their joy
> In combat all forgotten.

(17: 854–60; 425)

On the most elemental level the simile works to bring a sense of precision and energy to the battle scene for those who may not have experienced such scenes or who revel in remembering them. It also matters ontologically that the readers be reminded of the similarities between men and animals—in part to ground the emotions in natural processes and in part to stress how distant these men are in battle from the lives of the gods. But to dwell only on such features is to ignore the dramatic effect of the similes. This passage functions less to describe the rout than to expand the space of the narrative to include what it must be like to be affectively present in such scenes. Simile affords contexts for sympathy, sympathy for an entire group of agents. Sympathy then establishes a reminder that even as we observe war, our imaginations reach out for associations that qualify the scenic dimension and bring memories only loosely associated with the relentlessness of the narrative. In fact, this passage in particular seems to celebrate this arena of relations by allowing the simile to work its way beyond fear to other affective states that further the work of identifying with the distribution of psychic energies in the scene.

My second simile is more insistently self-reflexive. It occurs as Achilles rejects Hector's bid for a pact about giving the loser's body back to his army:

> Hektor, I'll have no talk of pacts with you,
> forever unforgiven as you are.
> As between men and lions there are none,
> no concord between wolves and sheep, but all
> hold one another hateful through and through,
> so there can be no courtesy between us,
> no sworn truce, till one of us is down,
> and glutting with his blood the wargod Ares.

(22: 308–15; 517–18)

Here the primary role of the simile is to give us a glimpse of how Achilles thinks. Again we see the text's fascination with relations between humans and animals. Here, though, the simile is dramatically spoken rather than providing part of the narrative. So, rather than simply being invoked as context, this comparison lets the speaker clarify the nature of his situation without explicitly describing his own state. In fact, he could not describe his own state because that state is dynamically unfolding. Achilles is trying to identify with his own simile so that he can resolve for this moment the conflicting pulls upon him to recognize the heroism in his opponent and to destroy everything that reminds him of the mortality that made Patroclus no longer his companion.

We have to recognize three levels of action that the simile creates. There is the analogical description of Achilles's position; there is the exercise of will within the state that the simile affords, and finally there is the embodiment of a terrifying finality of judgment. In other words, the ability for simile to compound emotions we saw in our last passage modulates into the ability of simile to complicate the affective qualities within the scene by what it demonstrates about the speaking. Analogy becomes the site of actions that supplement the narrative but are not reducible to the scene.

The Odyssey brings a new force of simile appropriate to its focus on a single character's adventures. This force is the capacity of simile to establish an inwardness without establishing interior monologue. Simile simply draws analogies that explain the feelings as intensifications of ordinary practical desires. Homer even complicates this problem by having his hero so self-protective that, if he must weep, he wills to weep inwardly. How can we then within the constraints of narrative come to appreciate how and what

Odysseus feels? Homer's response is to convert twenty years of suffering into an analogical space where the lovers can recognize each other and will the significance for them of that recognition:

> Now from his breast into his eyes the ache
> of longing mounted, and he wept at last,
> his dear wife, clear and faithful, in his arms,
> longed for
>
>   as the sunwarmed earth is longed for by a swimmer
> spent in rough water where his ship went down
> under Poseidon's blows, gale winds and tons of sea.
> Few men can keep alive through a big surf
> to crawl, clotted with brine, on kindly beaches
>
>   in joy, in joy, knowing the abyss behind:
> and so she too rejoiced, her gaze upon her husband,
> her white arms round him pressed as though forever.
> The rose Dawn might have found them weeping still
> had not grey-eyed Athene slowed the night.
>
> (23: 232–44; 436–37)

Clearly naming will not do. One needs extended equivalences in order to get time and intensity into the naming that takes place. In particular, the swimmer analogue pulls in two directions at once. It seems to condense the entire narrative into one moment of completely liberated feeling while at the same time expanding that story by bringing to bear again the entire weight of narrative, this time literally embraced by her consciousness. For the moment, that weight makes even the gods their servants.

One cannot leave the topic of simile without elaborating two further features where its differences from metaphor are most strikingly visible and where, therefore, it can sponsor a kind of poetry very different from the metaphysical work idealized by the New Critics. The first is its capacity to compose transcendental spaces that gain in power to the degree that they can plausibly resist or defer the capacity to fix complex predicates by placing them in our actionable world. Here we have to distinguish transcendental religious projects from those projects that seek the modes of secular transcendence sought by the structures of correspondences much beloved by symbolist poets. Dante will have to do to illustrate both sets of possibilities. Second, there is the possibility of sponsoring self-reflexive conditions where similes and analogies not only comment on the world but also provide a site where the artist can specify what it feels like to will that state and seek an identity based on that power. When Emerson took up Jacob Boehme's correspondences, he saw also this possibility of seeking a place for the writerly will in his participation in that set of figural possibilities.

I suspect that few readers are surprised that the opening of Dante's *Paradiso* is replete with similes—how else signify trying actually to live in what the imagination produces? One might mention, for example, this great invocation to Apollo using the resources of imaginative identification: "Enter my breast and breathe in me / As when you drew out Marsyas" (1: 19–20; 5). However, I think what happens as Dante tries to locate the power necessary to adjust to Beatrice's gaze offers an even more articulate sense of simile's capacity to expand worlds rather than bring fresh modes of denotation:

> And, as a second ray will issue from the first
> and rise again up to its source,
> even as a pilgrim longs to go back home,
>
> so her gaze, pouring through my eyes
> on my imagination made itself my own, and I
> against our practice, set my eyes upon the sun.
>
> Much that our powers here cannot sustain is there
> allowed by the nature of the place
> created as the dwelling fit for man. . . .
>
> Suddenly it seemed a day was added to that day,
> as if the One who has the power
> had adorned the heavens with a second sun. . . .
>
> As I gazed on her, I was changed within,
> as Glaucus was on tasting of the grass
> that made him consort of the gods in the sea.
>
> To soar beyond the human cannot be described
> in words. Let the example be enough to one
> for whom grace holds this experience in store.
>
> (1: 49–72; 5–7)

Here the two uses of "as" that the translator deploys for the comparison of the pilgrim's state to that of Glaucus help immensely in recognizing how names have to give way to the elaboration of examples. Simile may be our best figure for transforming our sense of limits "here" into possibilities for dwelling imaginatively "there." "As I gazed on her" is an adverbial clause specifying a moment in time. But it also can introduce a qualitative condition: it is as I gaze, or deploy the powers of the gaze, that I am moved to sustain a comparison with Glaucus. The qualitative modifier and the temporal modifier are mutually supportive. Then as Dante gazes, he is transformed into someone who can fully appreciate what such gazing might involve. Glaucus is an ordinary fisherman blessed with the momentary gift not only to see God but also to participate in divine life. Participation in turn becomes the crucial model for both life in Paradise and the path for moving from seeing God's work in nature to seeing God. At the beginning of the *Paradiso* the poet can finally expand his self-consciousness to enter an active dialogue between human powers, always inadequate, and divine reality, always sufficiently generous to reward whatever level of understanding or vision those powers might accomplish. And, we are told, that dialogue will be in the form of a series of examples so that training the mind to enter the paradisical is inseparable from learning to trust the exemplary for what it can convey that words as descriptions cannot. (Incidentally, as Hollander and Hollander point out [27], Dante's turning to three major Ovidian myths in this first canto indicates how fully texts devoted to imaginative expansion of experience rather than intensive reference prove necessary for Dante's heroic task.)

There are many instances of comparisons that define how the poet at the climax of his journey can realize identification with the Divine even as he laments his lack of powers to report on this transformation. But for me the richest elaboration of what even a secular world might consider paradisical about the powers of simile occurs in the transition Canto 30 affords from the fixed stars to the empyrean, where the blessed actually dwell:

> and such was the new vision kindled within me
> that there exists no light so vivid that my eyes
> could not have borne its brightness.

> And I saw light that flowed as flows a river,
> pouring its golden splendor between two banks
> painted with the wondrous colors of spring.

> From that torrent issued living sparks
> and, on either bank, they settled on the flowers,
> like rubies ringed in gold.

Then, as though intoxicated by the odors,
they plunged once more into the marvelous flood,
and, as one submerged, another would come forth.

"The deep desire that now inflames and prods you
to understand all that you see
pleases me the more the more it surges.

But you must drink first of these waters
before your great thirst may be satisfied."
Thus the sun of my eyes spoke to me.

Then she continued: the river, the topazes
that enter and leave it, and the laughter of the meadows
are all shadowy prefaces of their truth,

not that these things are in themselves unripe
but because the failure lies with you,
your vision is not yet strong enough to soar."

No infant, waking up too late
for his accustomed feeding, will thrust his face
up to his milk with greater urgency.[23]

(30: 61–84; 817)

This is for Dante the anagogic level of writing, where the reality is the state
of the soul that determines the shape of the figures used to express it. The
light is not the vehicle of the simile but its tenor. The light appears as a river,
but the river is only the figure for fixing various metaphoric properties that
become literal when we learn to experience the fullness of light in itself.
Hence the sparks play a role that birds or insects might play if the river were
the primary reality. Having set up this anagogic river, Dante makes two
stunning developments of it. First, there is the utter simplicity of Beatrice's
speech amid this spectacular setting since in fact this is the domain that for
her now comprises normalcy. Then there is the intense physicality of Dante's
response. He wants the same normalcy Beatrice experiences for what remains partially figural for him. So he concentrates on realizing as his nature
what keeps emerging as the perfection of his most fundamental desires.
Similes here produce a world that encourages all sorts of levels of equivalence, marked especially by how utter physical need and utter spiritual need
join as an infant does with the maternal breast.

Emerson cannot top Dante for intensity or scope. But he adds what
was to be a characteristic modernist quest not quite necessary in Dante's

world—the issue of what relation secular self-consciousness can maintain with its own figures. Must figuration ironically mock the soul trapped in empirical realities that science knows how to describe without figures? Emerson's version of this problem is to ask in *Nature* how fully the transcendental principle can enter qualities of secular experience. To experience nature fully is for him to be able to trace "the radical correspondence between visible things and human thoughts" (*Norton* 1119), whereby "every natural fact is a symbol of some spiritual fact" and "every appearance in nature corresponds to some state of mind." Many of the experiences we most value can be presented only by invoking "the natural appearance as its picture": "light and darkness are our familiar expressions for knowledge and ignorance; and heat for love. Visible distance behind and before us is respectively our image of memory and hope" (1119). Being able to formulate these modes of participation matters psychologically because it makes possible correlating agents' attentiveness to the natural world with an ability to characterize their inner lives. And this matters philosophically because it affords a clear sense of what spirit is: "That spirit, that is, the Supreme Being, does not build up nature around us but puts it forth through us, as the life of the tree puts forth new branches and leaves through the pores of the old" (1133).

Yet naming what spirit is does not necessarily secure the capacity to participate in it. It is easy to mistake the nature of spirit because we have long traditions of believing it works outside of us so that our task becomes traversing that distance by faith. Emerson wants to deny that distance. His means is the concept of participation because then we have a model for identification with the divine and of reflecting on the implications of that identification *as* it takes place. Spirit is not something we observe but something we make real by participating in its powers to gather relationships among phenomena. Awareness of who we become through this activity then requires a mode of writing that can continually see our own relation to nature as also an identification with what makes nature and spirit corresponding forces:

> Spirit does not act upon us from without, that is, in space and time, but spiritually, or through ourselves. Therefore, that Spirit, that is, the Supreme Being, does not build up nature around us, but puts it forth through us, as the life of the tree puts forth new branches and leaves through the pores of the old. As a plant upon the earth, so a man rests upon the bosom of God; he is nourished by unfailing fountains, and draws, at his need, inexhaustible power? Who can set bounds to the possibilities of man.
>
> (*Norton* 1133)

Here this first "as" realizes two aspects of spirit—that it aligns consciousness in the present with the life within the tree and that it aligns the qualities of consciousness that attend to the tree with the life force underlying the tree's activity. The "as" of temporal equivalence gradually emerges as the "as" of moral equivalence. And the second "as" surpasses this in scope by performing the work of epic simile: it inaugurates an extended comparison that makes convincing the real existence of analogies. The proliferation of "as" relations becomes evidence of the unboundedness of humankind despite the need for concrete vehicles for its expression.[24]

CHAPTER 5

Aspectual Thinking

> [Poetry] is an illumination of a surface, the movement of a self in
> the rock. A force capable of bringing about fluctuations in reality
> in words free from mysticism is a force independent of one's desire
> to elevate it. It needs no elevation. It only has to be presented, as
> best one is able to present it.
>
> (*CPP* 639–40)

>   But a politics
> Of property is not an area
>
> For triumphals. These are hymns appropriate to
> The complexities of the world, when apprehended,
>
> The intricacies of appearance, when perceived.
> They become our gradual possession. The poet
>
> Increases the aspects of experience,
> As in an enchantment, analyzed and fixed
>
> And final, this is the center. The poet is
> The angry day-son clanging at its make:
>
> The satisfaction underneath the sense,
> The conception sparkling in still obstinate thought.
>
> (*CPP* 383–84)

At the core of Wallace Stevens's thinking there is a metaphysical morality
play. The good character bearing redemption is the imagination; the character bringing the threat of damnation is identified with "the pressure of
reality," "that pressure of an external event or events on the consciousness to
the exclusion of any power of contemplation" (*CPP* 654). Such pressure
takes two outward forms—the overwhelming events like war that make human consciousness seem small and irrelevant, and those discourses that gain
social power by accepting their incapacity to do anything but model themselves on the logic of force and compulsion. Then two more characters
enter, making the play more complicated. First there is the projected audience, unified by the fear of succumbing to the pressure of reality unless it
can find relief through how the poet makes imagination also a part of life.
And there is the poet, or the many moods and dispositions of the poet, all

trying to treat expression as something other than (but including) the presence of psychological states like personal worries or neediness or even joy.
The poet is often melancholic but unwilling to surrender to the Keatsian
pleasures of the states melancholy can bring. Or one might say that Stevens
knew a melancholy that was too deep for Keatsian pleasures. So the needs
of the audience actually help the poet avoid the melancholy. He has to extend his cares so that he can make the audience feel that those cares emerge
from their own struggles and possibilities. This imagination must become
abstract in order to bridge the poet's life with the audience's. At the same
time it must take pleasure in the concreteness of abstraction as it finds satisfactions and values within these new possibilities for identification.

The present chapter elaborates the primary forces this allegory organizes
in Stevens's poetry after World War II. It has been difficult for me to clarify
the particular achievement of many of these poems because they vacillate
between an intrusive rhetorical presence and a too successful merger with
something like sheer statement or sheer process of thought. I cannot be
comfortable producing an abstract language about how poems have their
own distinctive form of abstraction. Yet there seems to be no alternative to
such abstraction because by this point in his career Stevens saw virtually all
significant poetry not as isolated jewels but as embodiments of an ongoing
imaginative practice. So the poet can make visible the power of the poetry
only by exploring in theory the limitations and the possibilities poems afford as a means of making connections to practical life.

The basis for my abstractions is an account of how Stevens develops a
style that I call the embodiment of aspectual thinking. Aspectual thinking
provides an overall model for what his poetry performs as he becomes increasingly reliant on the grammar of equivalences established primarily by
"as" clauses. In effect Stevens moves from occasionally relying on the resources of the grammar affording "as" clauses to fostering an overall aspectual perspective. The poet extends the grammatical resources we have been
considering into ways of treating the values of participation as absolutely
fundamental to ordinary living. Then it seems as if participation were less a
state at which we arrived than a condition from which we departed. Hence
Stevens comes to rely less on elaborate figures based on structures of equivalence than on a constant sense of imaginative intensity based simply on the
steady flow of "resemblances" perceived or felt as aspects of the writing process. Participation is less the result of momentary exaltations than it is a vision
of steady alignment with what emerges as being. By developing this style I
think Stevens could imagine a substantial breakthrough that put considerable
distance between his later writing and the two primary modes of poetic

thinking basic to modernism. One mode relied on the values of presentation that make the image capable of forcefully resisting conceptual practices, while the other emphasized the modes of presentation developed by symbolist uses of analogy and symbolist understandings of the powers of the authorship making those analogies possible. Aspectual thinking seeks the same kind of presence as the image. But it is not a presence circulating around a totemic object by which feelings and thoughts are intensified. Rather, it is a presence derived from aligning the self-reflexive mind to the flow of experience as it emerges in the artifice that is writing. And aspectual thinking differs from symbolist thinking with respect to the status of the analogies developed by the poem. Stevens is not much interested in a constructivist *frisson* developed by the poem's power to gather multiple elements within a single complex analogical structure developing an interlocking set of correspondences. He is interested in making the constructivist force simply continuous with "increasing the aspects of experience." Writing becomes inseparable from rendering a process of thinking that is continually adapting analogies as it attunes itself to the objects soliciting the effort at participation. This mode of thinking requires a more process-based model of lyric value than is called for by the other two primary models of modernist lyric thinking. Stevens wants to bring the symbolist goal of producing secular "enchantment" within a fundamentally realist understanding of "experience."

This new style is at once obvious and difficult to characterize adequately. Given how many critics have tried to say what is distinctive about Stevens's later poetry, I am going to err on the side of caution and risk boring my audience. I first examine two essays in order to trace Stevens's own version of the constituents for this model of thinking. "The Irrational Element in Poetry" defines the poet's presence as the irrational element that develops imaginative relations to the world as a continual process of the mind's engagement with what it confronts. And "Effects of Analogy" makes clear his relationship to the imagist and symbolist traditions as he tries to develop new possibilities of analogy based on this ongoing self-reflection. Then I indulge in abstractions about abstraction to clarify the basic goals of this new style and to describe five of its central features. My basic example here is "Reply to Papini," the poem from which I take my epigraph. This poem struggles to combine the large rhetorical claims of the idealist Stevens with a subtle responsiveness to how the imagination quickens the ways we moment by moment inhabit the forms of practical life. So it provides a useful instance of the difficulties he had to overcome in developing a somewhat new style. Understanding these difficulties provides a useful backdrop for my final section, in which I treat part XII of "An Ordinary Evening in New Haven" as a fully articulate aspectual thinking capable of establishing processes of conferring immediate values distinctive in modernist American poetry. The poem's major achievement is finding ways to have self-consciousness diminish the sense of distance that can make our relation to the world a source of despondency. The achievement of that achievement is to provide a powerful realization of the kinds of values involved in straight-forward shifts of our imaginative relations with concrete situations.

I

I state this ideal of aspectual thinking as if it were a coherent theoretical position. And by the time Stevens was working on "An Ordinary Evening in New Haven" he had probably come to pretty much this level of connection between principle and practice. But I am as interested in the complications along the path as I am in the final result, in large part because we can appreciate then how difficult it was to transform a set of grammatical resources into a coherent and timely overall attitude capable of shaping significant stylistic commitments. By patiently examining the two essays I refer to we can track Stevens's attempting to work out the options that seemed available to him as a poet after *Harmonium* and after his sense of failure in developing a poetics attuned to specific social themes.[1] He found himself late enough in the century that he could survey the possibilities developed by modernism as if they all lay before him.[2] But at the same time this belatedness gave him a painful awareness of the limitations that seemed embedded in each source of permission. So he tried in the thirties to formulate abstract arguments about what one could imagine imagination to be and why that mattered for social life, while his essays in the forties grew increasingly personal as he developed claims for his own specific mode of writing.

"The Irrational Element in Poetry" (1936) offers an important example of this effort at self-definition in the thirties because he reflects there on his specific relation to a modernist heritage. In particular this essay concentrates on two concerns that he had to work out in order to correlate his desire for a version of personal expression in poetry with his hatred of the romantic. First, he tries to secure a unique and engaging route by which to elaborate the importance of personal expression in poetry: "What I have in mind when I speak of the irrational element in poetry is the transaction between reality and the sensibility of the poet from which poetry springs" (*CPP* 781). Who the person offering the expression is matters considerably less than the fact that this person manifests the irrational dimension of all imaginative activity—that "it takes place unaccountably" (*CPP* 722).

In 1936 Stevens still connected this ideal of manner closely to a manifest will to 'individuality" (*CPP* 783) since the Nietzschean aspect of *Harmonium* would prove difficult to expunge. But Stevens's idea of how individuality works was already undergoing a massive reconfiguration. In *Harmonium* subjectivity was the space of "excess continual" (*CPP* 48) or Hoon's descending in purple to find himself "more truly and more strange" (*CPP* 51). By the time he wrote "The Irrational Element" Stevens could present himself as performing for a more severe master who demanded philosophical language. For this master, subjectivity would have to be defined primarily in terms of what it takes to complete perception and constitute apprehension. Subjectivity was simply a power of agency by which a being could make the unreal play a role in establishing the space of attention and concern transforming a world of fact into a dwelling place for projections by the imagination. Such projections need not be fictions, in the sense of falsehoods. Rather, the projections simply occupied a different plane from the plane of fact, producing the feelings that are lacking within the empirical world. One task of poetry was to explore and test the ramifications of interrelationship between these planes. The position of author retained a version of personal presence sufficiently constructivist to blend within modernist poetics without at the same time being quite subject to its strictures.

Second, this interrelationship depends on not allowing the irrational element to afford an escape into transcendental claims, even about the powers of the ego: "I wanted to apply my own sensibility to something perfectly matter of fact" (*CPP* 783), and "I do not for a moment mean to indulge in mystical rhetoric, since for my part, I have no patience with that sort of thing" (*CPP* 791). Stevens had become in *Harmonium* too much the antirealist to grant power to empiricist thinking. However, he also had grown acutely aware of how history makes demands on writing—had history not recently imposed the lesson that playing on the harmonium did not provide tunes sufficiently attuned to social realities. So he also developed as a social and rhetorical imperative a commitment to the secular world based on the notion that "the imagination loses vitality as it ceases to adhere to what is real" (*CPP* 645) (as he was to put the case five years later). More important, he recognized by 1941 the horror of how we weaken our grasp on that real when we try to defend what has lost vitality: "Having created something unreal, it [the imagination] adheres to it and intensifies its unreality" (*CPP* 645).

The only way for poetry plausibly to reconcile the irrational subject with the real was to set itself the task of measuring the imaginations of makers by how fully they could engage other people's models of objectivity, which meant for the twentieth century their faith in science. Stevens would never deny the imagination the freedom "to tintinnabulate if" the poet likes (*CPP* 789). But the poets' audiences "are equally free to put their hands over their ears" (*CPP* 789). If poets were to participate in the real and become part of the world, they would have to combine intricate antitintinnabulating sounds with what could count as sense in a public secular marketplace.

II

I think Stevens did not quite know how he was going make good on these two emerging commitments—to a poetics willing to risk the discursiveness of rendering a person overtly thinking as his mode of inhabiting experience and to honoring the demand that this thinking adapt itself to what seemed the factual texture of that world. So he experimented with several styles and modes of engaging the world before pretty much settling on an apparently casual discursiveness in poetry that seemed a powerful means of wedding the theory of poetry and the theory of life. "The Effects of Analogy" (1948) strikes me as the best analysis of the possibilities for that discursiveness. There Stevens took responsibility for a distinctive mode of analogical poetry with which he had been experimenting for the past decade. He showed how the analogies might be transformed into a fully aspectual writing, primarily by treating analogy as a constant process often beyond the maker's will or sense of reason. Identifying both the enduring impulse to analogy and its problematic status within symbolist practice prepared the way for casting analogy as source for a constant sense of imaginative vitality.[3]

Stevens does a masterful job in this essay of analyzing how analogy played significant roles in what he once again projected as the two major traditions competing for the loyalties of the modern poet—the tradition stressing what could be made present by virtue of imagist "constatation" and the tradition stressing what could be kept mysterious by fostering a fluid sense of the correspondence between flesh and spirit basic in exemplary symbolist work. At its best the imagist spirit reminded audiences at every moment of the pressure of the real world on the imagination. It also defined the kind of poetic labor that would prove necessary if the imaginative responses to such pressure were not to lapse into romantic narcissism about the imagination's powers. But Stevens could not be content with the feeling of presence in the world without second-order reflection on how such presence can carry the ramifications of the mind's quest for meaning.[4] So his deeper affinities were with symbolism's deliberate confusions between the object as mysterious presence and the object as primarily evocative sign revealing its possible roles in the dynamic processes of the mind. Yet that tradition also would not offer a satisfactory figure for the capable imagination. "The Effects of Analogy" expresses Stevens's frustration with what he saw as the symbolist's ways of naturalizing rhetoric in order to get transcendental or mystical effects.[5]

Despite the evident power in each tradition, the limitations of each required testing a third possibility that combined the recuperation of ideals of rhetoric pilloried by Pound and Eliot in order to project a new purposiveness for how the symbolists displayed the imagination's flexibility within the world of fact. Acknowledging the powers of rhetoric would allow him to articulate a poetics suited to his temperament and his ambitions for poetry. At the same time, however, he had also to naturalize this rhetoric so that it would seem to come from the irrational element visibly attempting to orient itself to what the facts demanded. Rhetoric had to acknowledge the role of artifice in our perceptions and reflections. But the relevant sense of artifice for Stevens was not located in the well-structured and elegantly composed overall presentation. Rather, artifice was primarily a condition of living in a series of present moments without repressing impulses toward creativity. Artifice is a mode of participating in the real with one's full sensibility. That sensibility in turn had to struggle to overcome the temptation to fall in love with the finished product and so desire a stability in its own right incompatible with the reality of change and the pressure of the real.

Classical imagism cast the speaking energies in the poem as grounded in the effort to transpose perception into a dynamic and compelling present tense. In contrast, symbolism let the eloquence partially float so that it seemed in contact with secularized versions of a creativity coming from beyond the individual consciousness—typically in some mysterious aspect of the psyche attuned to deep forces producing correspondences between nature and spirit or in the dynamics of textuality. Stevens's essay announces his refusal to participate in this illusion. He wanted instead to find a means for treating the energies of rhetoric as aspects of a plain speaking imaginatively situated within the empirical world. Rhetorical intentions, too, could be a visible aspect of speech capable of changing as experience changed its tonalities. So Stevens developed a case for analogical thinking that could demystify symbolism by rooting it in specific needs and desires for ongoing relations to the practical world. He could then preserve symbolism's density of complex equivalences[6] while demystifying them and bringing them closer to an overt personal presence committed to how the mind continually manages to participate in the world beyond it by forming analogies.

"Effects of Analogy" begins with how "as we read Bunyan we . . . are rather less engaged by the symbols than we are by what is symbolized" (*CPP* 708). In effect, Stevens claims that John Bunyan is content with what Derrida would call used and usurious figures to ensure that audiences get his religious allegory. Rather than accept that binary between symbol and what is symbolized, Stevens posits "a third reader, one for whom the story and the other meaning should come together like two aspects that combine to form a third, or if they do not combine, interact" (*CPP* 708). Then he goes on to give a distinctive version of the common modernist fascination with the work of metaphor and juxtaposition: this interaction takes place because "one influences the other and produces an effect similar in kind to the prismatic formations that occur about us in nature in the case of reflections and refractions" (*CPP* 708). By refusing to emphasize the speaker's activity as situated in a clear dramatic context, Stevens lets the process of developing analogies become itself an expression of how nature elicits the imaginative acts that complete it.

The oppositions Bunyan establishes prove useful for reading symbolist poetry because there the symbol itself becomes more central to the authorial consciousness than whatever might be symbolized. Stevens is particularly respectful of Valéry because his work seems to capture the fundamental condition of symbolist speaking: Valéry treats the authorial imagination as "not wholly his own" but seeking to be "part of a much larger, more potent imagination" (*CPP* 712). For this reason Valéry tries to live "on the verge of consciousness" (*CPP* 712). The result is "a poetry that is marginal, subliminal" (*CPP* 712). In contrast, Stevens identifies with an alternative theory closer to imagism's sense of the task of modern poetry. This theory "relates to the imagination as a power within him [the poet] to have such insights into reality as will make it possible for him to be sufficient as a poet in the very center of consciousness" (*CPP* 712). It also entails removing the artifice by which imagination works from an exclusively aesthetic domain:

> The adherents of the imagination are mystics to begin with and pass from one mysticism to the other. The adherents of the central are also mystics to begin with. But all their desire and all their ambition is to press away from mysticism toward that ultimate good sense which we term civilization.
>
> (*CPP* 713)[7]

Thinking of poetry in rhetorical terms leads Stevens to recast the nature of image. It has to function as symbol in order to bring into play the full power of discursive thought. But it also has to retain sufficient concreteness to preserve a sense of opening into the mystical or participating in it, albeit in the very muted form good sense demands. Keeping this balance requires Stevens to emphasize two particular features of this rhetorical sense of poetry.[8] The image must also function as a sign because its role is both to serve as the "medium for communicating" (*CPP* 710) an emotional state and to establish an analogical force that enables it to "partake of the nature of the emotion" (*CPP* 710). Then the worldliness I have been speaking of has to produce a distinctive mode of appearance that preserves both facts and the irrational element that makes them important to a subject. What matters are the facts in the poet's "sense of our world" (*CPP* 715). Unlike both Mallarmé's and Valéry's symbol, analogy is fundamentally justified by how it puts us in the world rather than how it completes the poem:

> There is always an analogy between nature and the imagination, and possibly poetry is merely the strange rhetoric of that parallel: a rhetoric in which the feeling of one man is communicated to another in words of the exquisite appositeness that takes away all verbality.
>
> (*CPP* 714)

In essence analogy has the power to grant what symbols bring that images do not, but under a more practical mode of thinking than Mallarmé would have accepted.

I admire this statement for several reasons. It makes clear Stevens's commitment to a decidedly unmodernist sense of rhetoric—and so provides an anchor for his transformation of symbolist thinking into an explicitly analogical mode. But at the same time it displays his persistent symbolist fascination with the mystical, now not as a proclaimed relation to mystical states but as the commitment to a power impossible to conceive rationally. Rhetoric is naturalized not by its dramatic situation but by Stevens's sense that artifice is necessary if the mind is fully to participate in the real as it emerges. Now participation becomes simply the force that makes values possible within a world divided between absolute objectivity and aberrant subjectivity.[9] This route of naturalization treats rhetoric as inherent in the working of the unreal in the real—not only in the making of overt equivalences but also in the simple procedures by which we bring value to facts in a way that takes on a kind of objectivity because poetry makes it hold for others as a possible aspect within the real.[10]

The conclusion of this essay (from which I drew the quotation featured in my introduction to this book) offers an even richer statement precisely because it offers a magnificent simplifying of the role of analogy that will become the focus of aspectual thinking. Here analogy is distinguished from the image not because it sustains elaborate figures of relationship but instead because it evokes an order of elemental mystery in a life where memory and the present tense simply approximate fusing with one another even as they give one another almost allegorical significance:

> We have not been studying images but, however crudely, analogies, of which images are merely a part. Analogies are much the larger subject. And analogies are elusive. Take the case of the man for whom reality is enough, as, at the end of his life, he returns to it like a man return-ing from Nowhere to his village and to everything there that is tan-gible and visible, which he has come to cherish and wants to be near. He sees without images. But is he not seeing a clarified reality of his own? Does he not dwell in an analogy? His imageless world is, after all, of the same sort as a world full of the obvious analogies of happiness or unhappiness, innocence or tragedy, thoughtlessness or the heaviness of mind. In any case, these are the pictorializations of men for whom the world exists as a world and for whom life exists as life, the objects of their passions, the objects before which they come and speak, with intense choosing, words that we remember and make our own. Their words have made a world that transcends the world and a life livable in that transcendence. . . . It is the imaginative dynamism of all these analogies together. Thus poetry becomes and is a transcendent ana-logue composed of the particulars of reality, created by the poet's sense of the world, that is to say his attitude, as he intervenes and in-terposes the appearance of that sense.
>
> (*CPP* 722–23)

This statement celebrates the possibility of getting beyond the rhetorical use of analogy so that analogy becomes the literal state of certain conditions for dwelling in the actual world, in the sense that apprehension seems the destined fulfillment of appearance. The deployments of "as" become the pas-sage's central means of enabling the break from conventional rhetoric be-cause "as" demonstrates the practical ability of rhetoric to develop a dynamic sense of lived equivalence. The aspects of life established by one's manner become inseparable from how the will becomes aligned with the world when there is an experience of plenitude derived from limitation. The first "as," in line 4 of my quotation, offers a marvelous unwobbling pivot. This simple adverbial conjunction gives a syntactic place for not one but two extensive clauses bringing a whole life to bear for a definition of "enough." The next two "as" clauses come closely together to show how thinking and valuing can proceed without images and yet bear "intense choosing." Perhaps the will makes its appearance when analogy manages to sustain large-scale equivalences without surrendering the feel of things as they are. And the final "as" stands as one of Stevens's richest equations between modality and eventuality. The qualities brought by this intervention go beyond what can be shared as descriptive states because they allow the speaker an acute sense of participation in the present tense of his own reflections, like "rubies reddened by rubies reddening" (*CPP* 302).

III

We can extract from these essays five fundamental features of what would become Stevens's enactment of aspectual thinking as a fundamental style: 1) the embodiment of subjectivity as the irrational element, 2) the work of analogy by which this irrational element imposes a creative pressure on the world capable of pushing back against the pressure of reality, 3) the effort to reinterpret rhetoric so as to identify it with the role artifice plays at the very center of actual experience, 4) a new definition of the image that stresses not just the presence of analogy but also the subordination of image to a thinking involved in the play of aspects, and 5) the recasting of the reader's role so that it requires identifying with exemplary performances, especially those in which self-consciousness takes on exponential force.

1) The concept of the irrational elements allows Stevens a distinctive way of negotiating the relationship between the personal and impersonality, which is so basic to modernism. The personal is preserved, but only as an element that manifests as a kind of force, a working against the pressure of reality. The personal is not here something that can become an image for consciousness and so not something that can be a locus for staging "personality." Its presence is entirely in its effects. This has significant implications. Since the personal is within the processes that elicit its irrational element, Stevens can give the appearance of erasing almost all the deliberate artificiality of poetry that produces staged events and elaborate arguments.

Conversely, instead of having to stage a separate person, the personal element becomes continuous with a manner of thinking that presents artifice as a condition of living. That manner of thinking then becomes part of the object world to the extent that it makes itself visible within the event of the poem. This is why Stevens wants to treat imagination less as a mental category than as a metaphysical one: "To regard the imagination as metaphysics is to think of it as part of life, and to think of it as part of life is to realize the extent of artifice" (*CPP* 728). Rather than develop elaborate figures for the powers of mind, aspectual thinking has to offer direct manifestations of "the extent of artifice within us and, almost parenthetically, with the question of its value" (*CPP* 729).[11] And then poetry can make visible how imaginations actually inhabit the world: artifice as a mode of dwelling must be distinguished from artifice as a purely aesthetic value so that our notion of aesthetic experience can be extended beyond its circumscribed cultural sphere.

2) This distinction between artifice and the artificial generates two basic commitments to the real within aspectual thinking—an insistence on treating the domain of fact as always potentially compatible with imagination and an insistence on writing as the embodiment of the activity of the subject in the process of rendering how it can discover values. Poetry must enchant within the parameters of a disenchanted world.

As the text from which I have taken my epigraph puts it, the ideal poem addresses "a nature that must be perceived and not imagined" (*CPP* 383). But just fidelity to perception is manifestly not sufficient. The poet must show how the activity of engaging the "objective" world elicits also a feel for accompanying states that frame appearance as something apprehended. That means our engagements in finding an appropriate language for experience bring imaginative values to bear that might be taken seriously in public life.[12] Poetry is the art of elaborating analogies that emerge in the process of reflection. And the poet has to deploy all the possibilities of the present tense of the writing, *as* he thinks, if he is to make indubitably concrete what the poem offers to those attempting to participate in its processes.

In my concluding chapter I take up some important scholarship on the significance of Wittgenstein's work on "seeing as" for our understanding of aesthetic experience. Now I simply want to point out how aspectual thinking continues to rely on the grammatical features that my last chapter emphasizes, but in a less theatrical manner. Poems do not build to emphatic equivalences so much as they rely on a constant texture of resemblances based on a range of registers for participating in the world of fact—on grammar, on syntactic parallels, on cadence (which mixes syntax and rhythm) along with a variety of other aural effects. We can also put this observation in another way that to a large extent explains Stevens's surprising influence on contemporary writing. By emphasizing the limitations of viewing the lyric as primarily artifact, Stevens opened the poem to a constant ascetic discursiveness that provided a dynamic background for new modes of lyric intensity.[13] It seems possible to treat the lyric as continuous with the discursive, letting itself be disciplined by fact and argument at the same time as it makes manifest the work of artifice even within the task of giving a faithful impression of fidelity to the ordinary aspects of experience.

3) Already perhaps more than implicit in my presentation is my next fundamental feature of aspectual thinking—its effort to desublimate rhetoric by having it fuse with an affinity for the ordinary and the typical. Desublimating the stagey righteousness of rhetoric is a far cry from the calls for its elimination in the manifestos by Stevens's fellow modernists.[14] The intricate syntax rendering Stevens's praise of Matisse for his effort in his work on his chapel at Vence makes clear how he imagines rhetoric as potentially inseparable from the possibility of producing an art continuous with the prose of the world:

Final for him, the acceptance of such prose,
Time's given perceptions made to seem like less
Than the need for each generation to be itself,
The need to be actual and as it is.

(CPP 448–49)

Time's given perceptions here matter because they manage not just to capture the facts but also to present them in relation to the needs of the culture mediating our awareness.

Stevens still honors eloquence and intricacy, but he wants those attributes manifestly to serve an apparent immediacy of situated thought. This goal requires turning from extended lyrical meditation on a focal object to an emphasis on the mind's activity as the mind processes the sources of its intensities. The actual is not an object but a condition of equivalence. In Stevens's psychomythology this orientation expresses the desire to have the world of the mother replace that of the father while retaining the father's efforts to produce objectivity. When the mother grows old and the transparence she gives is destroyed, "The necklace is a carving not a kiss. / The soft hands are a motion not a touch" (*CPP* 357). Yet when she is in her full power she

stands for and stands as an imagination that takes all the verbality away
from the figures of plenitude she mediates:

As if the innocent mother sang in the dark
Of the room and on an accordion, half-heard,
Created the time and the place in which we breathed.

(CPP 361)

And this sense of innocence in turn requires that the poems open up
into short stanzas that can give the appearance of making notations for
thought rather than pursuing complex structural arrangements.

A major reason Stevens can recast rhetoric is that he imagines poetry
involving a very different status of discourse. Classical rhetoric focuses
on explaining the past and encouraging future outcomes. Stevens after
the war wants a poetry that can realize in the present tense what it is
asserting. As he developed his ability to accomplish this fusion of action and evocation, Stevens found that he did not need the fictive
world, where we narrate situations or project the lives of characters.
Instead, he could tie the satisfactions of making more directly to the
values of participation. We will eventually see several variants of this.
But now I want to stress the particular artifice of rhetoric that must
fully articulate the value of making participation our condition for
apprehending the real. I refer to the imagination's work in foregrounding cadence and other figures of sound as elements that can
honor the complexity of thinking while fully complementing a sense
that it has found its target in the real. The intricacy of sound embodies
artifice. But it can be an artifice separate from rhetorical efforts to
persuade or to display distinctive syntactic and thematic structures.
Cadence can be artifice naturalized.

Think of the three lines quoted above from "The Auroras of Autumn." The first line is a straightforward statement with no caesura.
Then the poem drifts into a casual chiasmus linking "room" to "place"
and "half-heard" to "time." The chiasmus in turn is enriched by the
emergence of two subtle caesurae in each of the next two lines—the
poem is after all about singing and hearing. These caesurae distribute
the directness of the opening line by slowing time and radically expanding the physical listening to correspond with the semantic reach
of the final line. The song may be only half heard, but the aural space
provided by the cadenced caesurae reinforces the sense of what it means

to breathe fully in this embrace of both space and time. Here sound play draws the imagination away from establishing points of view and binds one's "fated eccentricity" (*CPP* 380) to a more intimate sense of contributing to how moments can unfold. Attention to hearing what reflection can feel like allows the personalizing of experience to take place on levels not accessible to discursive thought or, indeed, to statements about the self. As an audience listens for the cadences, the play of sound and rhythm seems a naked means for the imagination to participate in the direct force of what one encounters.

4) I call this thinking "aspectual" because it builds on the poet's capacities to develop the grammar of *as* well beyond semantics, as if that grammar, too, were a fact in the world. The aspectual can be fully present only if we recast modernist expectations about the image. The image cannot be a picture of fact. More important, the image cannot be the primary evidence of the power of imagination in the world because even the fusion of imagination and fact that Pound idealized creates a fixity and self-congratulatory emphasis on the privileged moment that mistakes the potential force of an ideal of participation. One might say that the Poundian image celebrates the result of specific acts of participation. But that image also has to point to itself as the fulfilling of a chain of impressions and desires that produces an object now ultimately outside of ordinary time. Stevens cannot quite deny that there is a timeless dimension to art. But he can recast that dimension so that it is seen to result from an act of self-reflection on and within process. The goal is not to celebrate the image but to contextualize it within a constant push and pull of thought's efforts to produce a place for humans within time as it unfolds.

We might say that imagination in later Stevens becomes less a Shelleyean idealizing force because it gets more closely connected with elemental features of the manners by which individuals organize expressive energies over time. Manner is how images enter time and invite reflection. Only through the work of the most elemental forces of syntax, grammar, and cadence could Stevens feel he had reached the irreducible powers of imagination as it labored to distinguish itself from the discursiveness he imposed upon it. But then we have to be clear that "manner" is not a matter only of perspective and not *Harmonium*'s will to forge attitudes for handling the ever-present reminders of our mortality. Stevens puts the case clearly: "Manner is something that has not yet been disengaged adequately. It does not mean style; it means the attitude of the writer, his bearing rather than his point of view" (*CPP* 785).

"Manner" does not have the flexibility or contingency or adaptability of perspective. We cannot provisionally take up a manner, at least not without great obvious effort. For "manner" is a dimension of the irrational, of a force for the developing of resemblances that manifests itself within the very processes of apprehension—from the energies reflected in aural qualities of the speaking to the deliberate elements of style. Manner extends perspectivism beyond the epistemology of point of view by treating a person as a constitutive force over time and not just as an angle of vision. Manner is to perception what the logic of "as" is in relation to copulative verbs.

While we cannot quite share a manner of apprehension, we can have a public sense of the importance of individual manners and a sympathetic understanding of the work that manner does as a source of values for the individual. Aspectual thinking not only charges the world with feelings for how meanings occur but also offers the possibility of treating this thinking as embodied in expressions whose energies are open to being taken up by other agents in their own distinctive ways. One person can identify with another's way of thinking and entertain seeing with different eyes. And by abstracting that vision, by inviting the audience to treat the "I" as a "one," the audience might find all sorts of bridges among isolated selves. From this perspective, the measure of the poet's success is the degree to which an aspectual thinking manages to preserve and project into ordinary time what the audience might see as images expressing "the precious portents of our own powers." Aspects are the "asness" of participation that gives the "is" its force as realization.

5) I suspect no other modernist is as obsessed with the reading process as is Stevens. One could allude to his several poems where reading is an actual figure within the poem, like "The House Was Quiet and the World Was Calm." But here I am more interested in his sense of how the poem makes it possible for the reader to identify with it and take up the experience into the reader's own life. The crucial dimension of poetry in this regard is its power to exemplify what it asserts. There is available an extensive philosophical discussion of the subject of exemplification in the arts,[15] but here it suffices to note the distinctive characteristics asserted in this passage from "Imagination as Value":

Poetic value is an intrinsic value. It is not the value of knowledge. It is not the value of faith. It is the value of the imagination. The poet tries to exemplify it, in part as I have tried to exemplify it

here, by identifying it with an imaginative activity that diffuses itself throughout our lives. I say "exemplify" and not justify because
poetic value is an intuitional value and because intuitional values
cannot be justified.

(*CPP* 734–35)[16]

The value exemplified must be intrinsic because it cannot be derived from
argument. The utterance must actually possess the properties by which it
becomes metaphorically significant. But for Stevens it does not suffice
to possess these properties as an image or a dramatic event. The crucial form
of presence is what can take place as an imaginative activity, hence a process by which the imagination makes visible its own direct powers in the
world. Aspectual thinking realizes these powers in the most direct way
possible because it does not ask us to infer them. Rather, it directly stages
what can demonstrate the powers asserted. The role of intuition is to recognize how one might be implicated in the work that imaginative activity
performs.

For almost twenty years Stevens had sought to make good on a poetic
ideal whereby the work could be seen as the agent's participating in or realizing the world Stevens addresses. By the end of his career he could give
such states a more public form, so that the ego itself simply merges with the
condition of searching "a possible for its possibleness" (*CPP* 411). The
searching combines an abstracted desire with the satisfactions of complete
attunement to the prose world on a level that readily takes on transpersonal
force. The power of the poem is not its "truth" but its capacity to model
modes and intensities of participation in the real. Poems invite identifications with manners of engaging the prose world, like the actual demonstration of obstinate thought at work in "Reply to Papini." Those identifications
keep the mystical alive by locating it not in transcendence but simply in a
complexity of transpersonal presence that defies analysis.

But this model of the role of the reader has focused so far only on what
the poem can do. Stevens supplements that by suggesting that this exemplification of the imagination at work gives us the opportunity of expanding
reading beyond serving as a state of observation. Reading becomes a mode
of participation in which we become increasingly aware that the very conditions of thinking within the space of poetry present possible surrogates
defining how we might value what comes before the mind. I do not know
how much Stevens wants us to find significance in his using the figure of
the "exponent" several times (at least *CPP* 343, 938, 864). But I find it a
brilliant way to combine his commitment to the prosaic and his suspicion of
the artifice with all the intensities projected by his doublings of mind and

world. Now we see the full analogical power of the figure "rubies reddened by rubies reddening" (*CPP* 302).

"Exponent" is first of all a slightly overelaborate way of calling attention to acts of exposition by which "the peculiar speech" of poetry might bring sense within the prose world without losing its playfulness:

> The spokesman at our bluntest barriers,
> Exponent by a form of speech, the speaker
>
> Of a speech only a little of the tongue?
> It is the gibberish of the vulgate that he seeks.
> He tries by a peculiar speech to speak
>
> The peculiar potency of the general,
> To compound the imagination's Latin with
> The lingua franca et jocundissima.
>
> *(CPP 343)*

But there is also a mathematical aspect to this figure. The power of the speaking resides in how it itself magnifies "to their highest exponents" (*CPP* 864) the second-order activities that exposition organizes. Exponential magnification here consists in this fusing interplay among the peculiar, the general, and the strange compounding of the imagination's Latin with a playful actual Latin superlative. The exponential generates a feeling of expansiveness that occurs when one sees each step of understanding the intricacies of thought as intensifying one's sense of affinity with the proposed topic into whose proximity the intricacies bring us.

Consider, for example, the section of the "Notes toward a Supreme Fiction" after the one I have just quoted. There the heaping of apposition upon apposition, simile upon simile leads from passively sitting in the park to allying with a will to change in nature, to coming to a feeling of owning the entire process of thinking that is in the process of being intensified:

> A bench was his catalepsy. Theatre
> Of Trope. He sat in the park. The water of
> The lake was full of artificial things,
>
> Like a page of music, like an upper air,
> Like a momentary color, in which swans
> Were seraphs, were saints, were changing essences.
>
> The west wind was the music, the motion, the force
> To which the swans curveted, a will to change,
> A will to make iris frettings on the blank.

There was a will to change, a necessitous
And present way, a presentation . . .

. . . The casual is not
Enough. The freshness of transformation is

The freshness of a world. It is our own,
It is ourselves, the freshness of ourselves,
And that necessity and that presentation

Are rubbings in a glass in which we peer.
Of these beginnings, gray and green, propose
The suitable amours. Time will write them down.

(CPP 343–44)

Three features here stand out. Where there had been rhetorical elegance there are in its place simply surprising word substitutions or enjambments that complicate the present tense of reading. "Frettings on the blank" is a marvelous metaphysical transposition of what I expected to be "frettings on the bank" of the lake. And the two consecutive enjambments (very rare in Stevens) perhaps offer a response to this demand of making experience present. Lusciously varied diction gives way to a constant repetition of phrase, as if transformation could make itself visible by the repeated term taking on new angles of incidence that produced new turns for self-reflection. Finally, where the previous section employed intricate syntax, this section relies largely on parataxis. But the repeated "ands" are by no means Whitmanian expressions of horizontal continuity in many dimensions. The repetition produces changes in the levels of apprehension—from "the freshness of a world" to "the freshness of ourselves" to the possibility of linking freshness with the combination of necessity and presentation. It should be no surprise that the ending here speaks of beginnings. The aim is still to make artifice visible but at the same moment to deflect the energy of artifice into appearing primarily as an aspect of what is becoming present in the exponential process.

IV

Stevens in 1948 casts reading poetry as the activity of learning to seek out what can remain mysterious within the ordinary, so that it can model paths to significance that are not paths to conventional meaningfulness. To follow those paths he has to deal quite gingerly with two features of imaginative activity that he thought had a necessary place in poetry despite their being subject to severe modernist critiques. As we have seen, rhetoric must be naturalized as the artifice within living. And allegory must be preserved as an instinct, although the poet must also recognize that the instinct meets at best incomplete satisfactions. The life of the mind within poetry must be continually frustrated in its efforts to thematize meaning even as it is continually rewarded by the sense of the mind's influence in transforming what otherwise would be mere fact.[17]

I want in the concluding two sections of this chapter to draw out a contrast that promises to make clear how Stevens came to develop these two aspects of imaginative activity.

"Reply to Papini" seems to me a poem devoted to finding in high Stevensian rhetoric the power of allegory while also resisting allegory by specifying how the mind can produce a sense of realizing effective values within the flux of actual experience. Section XII of "An Ordinary Evening in New Haven," in contrast, concentrates on simple, elemental statements. These statements take on rhetorical power because of how they call upon the expansive energies possible for ordinary language when it can self-reflexively display our capacities to appreciate the manner by which the poem strings assertions together. I like to see the first poem as struggling with contradictions resolved by the later work. But it is equally possible that Stevens is simply exploring contrasting possibilities of what language can bring to experience and experience to language.

"Effects of Analogy" is especially important to our reading of "Reply to Papini" because the poem seems to struggle with a tension between the desire to naturalize rhetoric and the pleasures of tracing rhetoric's capacities to create elaborate analogies just for their evidence of what imagination can do. His analogies pull toward treating elements as signs participating in an eloquent presentation of a sense of mystery while also projecting signs as figures of participation in the elemental sense of artifice that might allow a real to stand out against a background of fact.

The second part of the poem cited as my epigraph gives sufficient evidence of what Stevens makes of these tensions, but we will also have to invoke a little of the first part to appreciate the pressures creating the pain out of which the poem speaks.

For a long time I regarded the lines I quote for an epigraph as consisting only of rather theatrical assertions that I could use to demonstrate the abstract shape of Stevens's concerns. I did not think there was much playfulness or concrete experience taking place. Now I consider the poem a remarkable effort to blend high rhetoric with powers of imagination that are so close to being absorbed within the prosaic that they run the risk of going unnoticed. "Reply to Papini" presents Stevens's contemporary reactions to a letter attributed to an invented pope, Celestin VI, by Giovanni Papini, a nineteenth-century Italian writer and philosopher. The pope challenges poets to give up their "calligraphies of concealed daydreams" and take up the work of singing "the hymn of Victory" or the "psalm of supplication." Stevens never directly contradicts Celestin VI, but the space for idealization that the pope opens provides both a temptation and a challenge. The temptation is to attempt producing a public counterrhetoric adequate to humanism's most self-exalting flights. The challenge is to find a means through which the rhetorical impulse can take on the capacity not only to state but also to embody the way aspectual thinking can provide an alternative to traditional humanism. For Stevens there is no escaping this challenge because writing must begin with the recognition that spiritual conditions have changed so that now in a world where mortality is final, "the way through the world / is more difficult to find than the way beyond" (*CPP* 382). Noble sentiments will not help us discover the appropriate way. All we have are our perceptions and our attitudes toward those perceptions. But we can find our answer about the values available to poetry in the visible difference between the effort at eloquent statement and the sense of vital imaginative habitation within a world inhabited rather than constructed.

Therefore, the poem's second section focuses on understanding "what it is to understand":

But a politics
Of property is not an area

For triumphals. These are hymns appropriate to
The complexities of the world, when apprehended,
The intricacies of appearance, when perceived.
They become our gradual possession. The poet

Increases the aspects of experience,
As in an enchantment, analyzed and fixed

And final, this is the center . The poet is
The angry day-son clanging at its make:

The satisfaction underneath the sense,
The conception sparkling in still obstinate thought.

(CPP 383–84)

This seems to be a passage about aspectual thinking but far from a realization of it. How will this conclusion connect abstractions like "perception" and "apprehension" with actual conditions of experience when it is so insistent on comparing the "aspects of experience" to an "enchantment"? How is this "enchantment" compatible with valuing "a nature that must be perceived / and not imagined"? And why, in what I claim is an instance of a poet concerning himself with a critique of identity thinking, do we find the poem so confident that it can fix the center of how the poet "increases the aspects of experience"? How can this finality be a necessary supplement for the process of intensifying or expanding perception into apprehension?

Perhaps Stevens is still seduced by the idea of enchantment even as he tries to discover what difference that sense of enchantment makes in an imagined real-world context. How, without some possibility of enchantment, can we retain a faint echo of heroic language about the poet within the constant self-diminishing of the post-romantic imagination? One answer to this question begins with recognizing how the final couplet syntactically and aurally makes present a set of intricate balances whereby the poem proves how the theory of poetry takes on substance as a dramatic theory of life. "Satisfaction" and "sense" on one level make very different demands—the one a multisyllabic abstraction stressing what subjectivities seek, the other a monosyllabic term (with multiple semantic registers) stressing here the union of perception and significance apart from subjectivity. Yet the two terms are linked by alliteration, by cadence, and, ultimately, by the mind's realization that these two separate states are really fulfilled only in each other. Perhaps then the heroic task of the modern poet is to give idealizing terms like "mind" and indeed like "poet" a home within the domain of process and the momentary construction of aspects. Poets can write so that the experience of the poem serves as a demonstration of the claims it is making and so a direct absorbing of the abstract into the concrete.

The ideal of "satisfaction" initially seems a dangerously bourgeois principle, better suited to an ironic moment in Gustave Flaubert than to a poet trying to put the imagination within the real. But the ending of "Reply to Papini" challenges such preconceptions because it dramatizes the role satisfactions play in mental life. The reader is asked to flesh out the many levels that are engaged by this "still obstinate thought" "underneath the sense."[18] The expression recalls what is involved in an imagined sense of the world perceived within "the intricacies of appearance." Perception and apprehension gesture toward different dimensions of the worlds made present by poetry.

We have to add a second aspect of "sense" created by the poem's hearing its own idealizing rhetoric. The projected hearing treats that mode of fleshing out the figure of "conception" as an aspect of being to which the mind can attune as it sparkles in still obstinate thought. Finally, there is the dark sense of "sense" contained by the poem's pushing against a pressure of mortality from which Pope Celestin is protected by his faith in eternal life. Such pressure seems to me the major source of the frustration making the poet the "angry day-son clanging at its make." This anger is an inevitable consequence of how the first section of the poem defines the ultimate task of the poet:

This pastoral of endurance and of death
Is of a nature that must be perceived

And not imagined. The removes must give,
Including the removes toward poetry.
                              (CPP 383)

No wonder there is much unsaid within the public rhetoric required by the imagined situation.[19]

But the "unsaid" is not the unheard or the unseen. This is why it is so important to hear everything that is suggested by the present participle in the line "the conception sparkling in still obstinate thought." Thought has the resources not to surrender to mortality but to produce an unreal that makes us care about what we can attend to in the real. And thought has a sheer present tense, a sparkling of aspects within conception that simply and powerfully provides this center in the constant possibility of decentering.

This sparkling is especially compelling in how this last metrically longer line deploys two significant syntactic features—the strange placement of "still" to stress its adjectival powers rather than the adverbial ones that would occur if it modified "sparkling," and the apposition with the previous line, which requires correlating what is underneath the sense with the "obstinate thought" that apparently is not content with satisfaction. More important, we have to realize how this density of syntactic connection just is the work of imagination inhabiting the real rather than displacing it or commenting on it. Syntax itself grounds but does not exhaust the correlation of "sense" and "conception."

Most of the work in this passage is accomplished by how "still" manages to adapt the force of "sparkling" to both perception and apprehension. "Sparkling" is put into time—no longer a condition of the moment but a constant bringing over of obstinate thought into the completion of sense. And "still" thickens the sense of completeness because its multiple uses operate almost as a definition of what habitation involves. First, "still" insists on its power to play its monosyllabic concreteness against the Latinate abstractions that characterize thinking in the closing lines. Then "still" backs up its claim to its own weight by having its functions unfold as both adverb and adjective. Adverbially there is still obstinate thought available, and the obstinate thought is somehow still going on (probably because contained within the present tense of a poem and therefore given an opportunity to "sparkle"). Adjectivally "still" functions as a qualitative term eliciting a sense of quiet that ultimately characterizes the obstinate thought as satisfying and not disruptive.

In short, syntax provides a home for a complex chain of semantic equivalences that mark what imagination can add to perception in order to provide a challenging state of apprehension. The apposition in the last two lines develops this same sense of "sense," while adding an even richer mode of staying within the boundaries of prosaic statement. What the poem mentions it also enacts: thinking and feeling come to life as in fact parts of the world functioning "as in an enchantment." The obstinacy proves inseparable from the "satisfaction underneath the sense" because the satisfaction is ultimately in the building of a perspective that makes this obstinacy visible as something that can be resisted. The apprehension is not primarily the arriving at truth. Rather, it constitutes the coming into awareness of the various equivalences brought together in these lines as contributions to our sense of sense. This is where the demand for stillness arises. Both senses of "sense" eventually promise to address a human need to feel a constant counterpressure exerted on the world as a perennial conative process of turning perceptions and the rhetoric they elicit into states in which values seem embedded.

V

Yet while one can explicate the intricacy of "Papini," one cannot quite love it. If there can be a case of too much effective artifice, this would be a good candidate. The one sense of "sense" not present in the poem is the actual world of the senses. So I turn to an example of a richer embedding of sense in sense congruent with aspectual thinking in part because that will also be a better test of how Stevens brings feelings and actual values into play. However, it is impossible now to offer a thorough analysis of the sensual movement of aspectual thinking because it is most in evidence when Stevens develops the modes of habitation allowed by his late, long poems like

"Auroras of Autumn" and "An Ordinary Evening in New Haven." The best I can do here is to attend carefully to one section within the second long poem as it self-consciously turns to the realization of values within the phenomenological processes the poem stages.

"An Ordinary Evening in New Haven" begins brilliantly with the eye's, and the *I*'s, version of the real caught in a flat objectification that cannot satisfy the questioning mind as it meditates on its situation. This space of thinking affords self-consciousness a distinctive role in the world, as self-reflection. How, though, will that self-consciousness partake of the world's objectness and in the process have that objectness compounded with what might fulfill it in the end? This is the question that drives the opening five sections to explore various resources of the mind as it seeks relief from its sense of isolation. But at this point the poem can only focus on the cause of the problem and, by appreciating the difficulty involved, imagine possible reconciliation between mind and world:

> Who has divided the world, what entrepreneur?
> No man. The self, the chrysalis of all men
>
> Became divided in the leisure of blue day
> And more, in branchings after day.[20] One part
> Held fast tenaciously in common earth
>
> And one from central earth to central sky
> And in moonlight extensions of them in the mind
> Searched out such majesty as it could find.
>
> *(CPP 399–400)*

The second loose collocation of five sections begins in just the opposite mode from the first. It is as if the text were modifying its quest, switching from issues of the incapacities of imagination to issues of scale and degree as the poem searches for imaginings that may suffice. Notice how the sixth section begins in an authoritative, almost pompous voice, only to generate a corresponding sense of reduced world where people have to come to terms with "having lost, as things, / that power to conceal they had as men" (*CPP* 401). As I read the poem, compassion for this reduced scale produces an emphatic "we" of sections VIII to XI. But this compassion is largely produced by a need for consolation. The closest the poem can come to resolving the distances it worries about is in attempting to reconcile itself to the "permanence composed of impermanence," which can "make gay the hallucination in surfaces" (*CPP* 403).

It seems that by its tenth section the poem has explored a wide variety of tones all predicated on the notion that the mind needs some kind of metaphysics capable of reconciling itself to the real. Section XII seems then a major break because it makes the Wittgensteinian move of raising the possibility that the problem underlying the poem is not so much finding a principle as finding release from the need for principle. Perhaps aligning the mind with appearances and practices can suffice, so the poem proposes to take responsibility for a specific manner of articulating that alignment:

The poem is the cry of its occasion,
Part of the res itself and not about it.
The poet speaks the poem as it is,

Not as it was; part of the reverberation
Of a windy night as it is, when the marble statues
Are like newspapers blown by the wind. He speaks

By sight and insight as they are. There is no
Tomorrow for him. The wind will have passed by,
The statues will have gone back to being things about.

The mobile and the immobile flickering
In the area between is and was are leaves,
Leaves burnished in autumnal burnished trees

And leaves in whirlings in the gutters, whirlings
Around and away, resembling the presence of thought,
Resembling the presences of thoughts, as if,

In the end, in the whole psychology, the self,
The town, the weather, in a casual litter,
Together said words of the world are the life of the world.

(CPP 404)

Here aspectual thinking is closely connected to Mallarméan analogies between the leaves and their "reverberations." But the analogies are given a distinctive cast because of the poem's emphasis on the present tense. Satisfaction will not come from deep meaning but from identifying with the poem's expansiveness. Analogy here becomes a principle of action—not just the apprehension of a set of relationships but also the emergence of a sense of relatedness as an explicit power to change how one imagines the mind's access to the world. The poem's contrast between aboutness and participation works on many levels to foreground reflection not just on what the analogies offer but also on the felt power that comes from generating them. And the fact that the analogies are ultimately analogies to words secures a second-order dimension to that process. We do not so much read into or interpret the analogies as participate in imaginative forces that ultimately allow the town and weather to speak.

That strange source of speaking, in fact, comes to seem a simple corollary of the emergence of "sight and insight as they are." So it would not be implausible to feel that the process here dramatizes the capacity of the speaking to lose all verbality as it absorbs itself in the unfolding of apparently actual equivalences inseparable from the prose world. Yet this is not the syntax of prose. Nor will prose be able to establish what is gained by the building of an intensity ultimately requiring that sight and insight be explained by themselves ("as they are"), through how the speaking develops responsiveness to these analogies.

Let me be more concrete. Here we might say value resides within the processes of how the world comes to resemble "the presence of thought." Certainly the poem spells out how the imagination works in relation to the statue and the windy night. But its task is not just to "realize" how those figures take on new life. The poem also tries to embody the force of such imagining as it dramatizes thinking's power to find a home in the world and to appreciate the value of this home.

The first three stanzas render a particular occasion from which the poem emerges as a cry. Stevens does not say what kind of cry—pain or ecstasy are both possible—because he wants to call attention to it as a sheer condition of being, not as a response to something that can be described independently of the poem. He also somewhat strangely begins with a complex situating of the poet's act before he describes the scene. Probably he thought he had to characterize the quasi-disembodied or constantly changing stance of this poem as the basic grounding context for the "reverberations" of the windy night that the poem eventually releases. Then the poem can be a part of and fully participate in the windy night's transforming the weight of statues into a striking mobility. The statue oddly matters more for its mobility as part of the scene than for any reference the images might have to nobility or authority. This mobility also can provide a source of value without any lamentation about lost nobilities that the statues as images might now signify. What the statues might mean is far less important than what they become for the imagination in the precise moment in which they seem transformed. That is how sight seems to blend with insight, "as they are" in time and in their capacity to elicit imaginative response.

It is as if this absorption in reflective processes manages to naturalize the being of the statues while actively forgetting that the usual task of statues is to mean something by offering signs of virtues a culture should value. So poetry is no longer an act of rhetorical persuasion. It seeks so much more than that of its audience. It does not want to evoke belief but to elicit self-reflection on what is involved in participating in this scene of metamorphosis. Participation offers an alternative to resting content with description that in turn stands for meaning. Participation is activity; it involves opening oneself to all the equivalences that can occur when there emerges a cry as response to an occasion. In fact, now he realizes that participation may be definable simply as replacing a concern for aboutness with a concern for focusing all of one's capacities for feeling on the "reverberations" established by equivalences. "Sight and insight" then cannot be measured by the objects they bring into view. "Sight and insight" here become variable elements depending entirely on how one comes to participate in the reverberations they allow.[21]

When I teach Stevens I love to expound on the first three stanzas of this passage. Now, though, I am beginning to realize what I miss when I stop there. I see Stevens asking us to imagine a mental state that can exist "between is and was" and so between Pound's constatation and lack of melancholy. Notice how the fourth stanza shifts the focus from the wind to the leaves themselves. Stevens probably does that for two reasons. First, the leaves as simple phenomena prove the perfect inhabitants of the space between "is and was." They bear the marks of time, and they carry all the expansiveness of an entire autumnal season that in many ways also exists between "is and was." Simply the expansion from one evening to "Autumn" provides another context for that cry and shows how *as* the poem participates in the evening it also takes on possible metaphoric registers that develop the shift to a more melancholic tone. More important, the shift to leaves begins a series of resemblances that reinforces this sense of expansion—from leaves to thoughts to words. It is as if the occasion were moving from the scenic to the philosophical and hence from watching to speaking in a new way.

Yet the occasion does not quite yield directly to this expansiveness. For "words" seem a restriction or at least a condensation after the two references to "thought." Perhaps Stevens wants momentarily to make his situation more concrete by returning to a more specifiable present situation. Now the lyric situation includes awareness of the relation between "is" and "was" as well as resemblances of all kinds, all in a "litter" (not letter) that Stevens insists is "casual." I think this "litter" is casual because the leaves are not remarks and not formulated statements. They are the elements of statements, given an expansive possibility just because the poem arrives at this sense of capacity only after it has so expanded what an "occasion" can be. The words can eventually speak because they do not utter any particular judgment. They are content to affirm their coexistence with the world, and so they take on the capacity to modify how we become parts participating in all the expansiveness that the resemblances generate. Here words lose their rhetoricity and hence their verbality because they are only parts of the scene, almost parallel to the detritus. Freed from serving only as anchors in the physical world, they all, "together," say (not cry) that they are free to adapt themselves to serving as aspects of "the life of the world"—as it can become with their participation. Value itself depends not on fact but on a responsiveness to the world that remakes how words can dramatize a will to honoring experience without moralizing it.

CHAPTER 6

Stevens's Tragic Mode

Why the Angel Must Disappear in "Angel Surrounded by Paysans"

> The pressure of the contemporaneous from the time of the beginning of the World War to the present time has been constant and extreme. No one could have lived apart in a happy oblivion. . . . We are preoccupied with events, even when we do not observe them closely. We have a sense of upheaval. We feel threatened. We look from an uncertain present toward a more uncertain future. . . . Resistance to the pressure of ominous and destructive circumstance consists of its conversion, so far as possible, into a different, an explicable, an amenable circumstance.
>
> (*CPP* 788–89)

Aspectual thinking establishes a sense of value by eliciting feelings that emerge as real events of participation within the imagined features of the world invoked by particular poems. Stevens heightens these events in *Auroras of Autumns* by means of two linked emphases that are the focus of this chapter. He has the major poems confront the split between subject and object as an actual experience of distance, at times eliciting a sense of sudden fit that occurs as the mind tries to achieve a vantage from which the feeling of participation can become active. The poem need not do the work of negation; it begins in the negative and tries to become a means for feeling those realizations that occur when this distance is reduced or overcome. Second, Stevens elaborates a thematic framework for understanding this struggle with distance by returning throughout the volume to the motifs of evil and tragedy first elaborately broached in "Esthétique du Mal." Tragedy seems to comprise our vulnerability to natural disaster (*CPP* 285) at one pole and, at the other, a sense "in the self , from which / In desperate hallow, rugged gesture, fault / Falls out on everything" (*CPP* 279).[1]

These lines, from "Esthétique du Mal," are not exactly pellucid. In fact, they seem themselves in part defensive gestures "intended" to protect the self from human complicity in the tragic. Ironically, that sense of fault might be illustrated by the poem that most overtly faces the problem of tragedy. I think Stevens came to regard "Esthétique du Mal" as succeeding all too easily in converting what it addresses into "an amenable circumstance." This poem's elaborate rhetoric sustains an essentially aestheticist naturalism that Stevens came to realize could no longer suffice for his ambitions. As James Longenbach put it, Stevens's rhetorical brilliance here seems to justify surrendering to "a narrow version of what the world 'as it is' might be" when it is reduced to "the sensual pleasures his income afforded him and the aesthetic pleasures his accumulated capital of poetry could sustain."[2]

I argue that there is manifest evidence in Stevens's next volume, *Auroras of Autumn,* to support my contention that Stevens became uneasy with the mode of thinking in "Esthétique," especially with its ways of maintaining the distance from the evils that it nominally confronts. The challenge for *Auroras,* and for aspectual thinking, is to make visible that there is a lot more to "living as and where we live" (*CPP* 287) than meditating on the metaphysics of change. In this volume Stevens recognizes that such aestheticist values are less solutions to the problem of tragedy than aspects of its persistence in human life. So in *Auroras of Autumn* he takes up the challenge of casting evil and tragedy as constantly impinging on the life of the mind, posing imminent threats that have to be internalized and dealt with as aspects of the psyche. For "Esthétique" evil consisted in the kind of pain that could be handled by embracing the life of the senses. *Auroras* in contrast sought ways of accepting pain as an inevitable condition of participating in what life made available.

I focus my argument for what proved problematic about "Esthétique" through three simple concrete questions (which, of course, will only delay my abstractions). Why did Stevens choose to end *Auroras of Autumn* with the apparently slight poem "Angels Surrounded by Paysans"?[3] Why does this bare little adventure establish a fitting and even imaginatively provocative summary and farewell to the themes of one of the darkest and least playful of Stevens's books? And how can a brief lyric provide a climax for the forces set in motion by the volume's two long poems, "Auroras of Autumn" and "An Ordinary Evening in New Haven"? My answers require my asking how aspectual thinking can be extended to address questions of tragedy and simple exhaustion that recur frequently in *Auroras.*

Before I begin this inquiry, though, I have to address a metaquestion about speaking about tragedy at all. I imagine that most of those who concentrate on Stevens's participation, or lack thereof, in the political milieu will not be satisfied by this chapter. Dwelling on the tragic can seem an indulgent evasion that substitutes generalized reflection for particular worries about and practical strategies for how we might abate actual suffering in the

· real world. This point is important. Yet I do not think it can be the last word on the topic. We have to be aware that there are many ways of avoiding reality but also many ways of using realism as a means of escaping necessary complications in what we confront. Realism can present imposing instances of injustice. But how do we assess what our actions can be in relation to what we come to know? What kind of evil seems most oppressive and most compelling of our resistance And which must we learn to live with if we are to find any peace in our lives?

It seems inescapable that an adult consciousness at least ask itself what difference it makes for one's own life that suffering will continue to exist in ways that have no connection to justice. And for those with philosophical bents like Stevens, that question becomes, how can I affirm my own life, given that disconnect between suffering and justice? His answer is to dwell on small-scale but pervasive aspects of such suffering that take place at the core of intimate life. *Auroras* continually confronts the ways in which the tragic permeates our experience of time and space: time in the form of loss and space in terms of perceived difference between feelings that do and do not participate in the energies of the world beyond the self. Contemplating these conditions gives the self an opportunity to test the degree to which one can affirm such recurrent pains as conditions of whatever pleasures the psyche can will. It therefore allows one to confront tragic conditions without any of the self-ennobling rhetoric sustaining the myth of the tragic hero. Aspectual thinking in *Auroras* becomes the vehicle for a second-order challenge that persons affirm what they come to feel as they reflect on suffering, loss, and obtrusive distances. For Stevens all personal values ultimately depend on establishing a sense of individual identity that one can inhabit without self-alienation.[4]

I

"Angel Surrounded by Paysans" poses several practical difficulties that are necessary to address before we can answer the three questions I posed. Why did Stevens decide to recast into a dramatic scene a still-life painting by Pierre Tal-Coat that he purchased in 1949? Why did he not just produce another poem engaging the still life as still life, a genre in which he was quite accomplished? And why would he have thought that this poem's engagement with "an angel of reality" (*CPP* 423) could sufficiently engage the other poems so that it could be seen as an effective conclusion for the volume?

Because the contextual issues are so fascinating, critics have been insufficiently attentive to how the poem works and why that working might matter. The most interesting writing on the poem takes two related tacks—one concerning Stevens's interest in producing poems that evoke still-life painting and one concerning what Stevens does with the Tal-Coat painting.[5] Representing the first tack, Bonnie Costello concentrates on how the still lifes in *Parts of a World* establish a profound "reconciling of often violent historical formlessness" with "the human need for intimate arrangements" that can have "the force of epiphany" (454). Even "Angel Surrounded by Paysans," in a much more abstract volume often criticized for its aestheticism, uses the associations of still life as a low genre to retain "the mood if not the substance of still life" (454). The angel, "numen of Tal-Coat's simple pots and bowls," "is a figure both of the center and the periphery, the heroic and the common, megalography and rhopography."[6]

But Costello does not concentrate on "Angel Surrounded by Paysans," so we have to ask why this particular abstracting away from still life is the poem's route to common life. The poem opens with a strange way of staging the angel since "he" is introduced by his not being visible:

> One of the countrymen:
> There is
> A welcome at the door to which no one comes?
> The angel:
> I am the angel of reality,
> Seen for a moment standing in the door.
>
> I have neither ashen wing nor wear of ore
> And live without a tepid aureole,
>
> Or stars that follow me, not to attend,
> But, of my being and its knowing, part.
>
> *(CPP 423)*

Then the angel turns to defining his own identity in positive terms. Being "one of you" also involves "being and knowing what I am and know." And what he knows is at once comprehensive and enabling:

> Yet I am the necessary angel of earth,
> Since, in my sight, you see the earth again,
>
> Cleared of its stiff and stubborn, man-locked set,
> And, in my hearing, you hear its tragic drone
>
> Rise liquidly in liquid lingerings,
> Like watery words awash; like meanings said

By repetitions of half-meanings. Am I not,
Myself, only half a figure of a sort,

A figure half-seen, or seen for a moment, a man
Of the mind, an apparition apparelled in

Apparels of such lightest look that a turn
Of my shoulder and quickly, too quickly, I am gone?

(CPP 423)

Alan Filreis begins to answer these questions by reconstructing from Stevens's published and unpublished letters the details of his purchasing the painting and then Stevens's understanding of what was involved in transposing the still life into an allegorical scene.[7] For Filreis the point of the poem is to highlight this abstracting process as an experiment in placing "relations before substance as the basis of similarity" (345–46). Rather than portray what a painting is about, the poem replicates the painting only "through resemblances of relations" (346). Rather than have poetry imitate what a painter does, Stevens would have poetry celebrate its powers to define how paintings become valuable for us. He would abstract painting into part/whole relationships and then produce significance for those relations.

The pertinent historical details are in three of Stevens's letters that address both the painting and the poem. In the first, he playfully sets up the painting as a quasi allegory requiring the poem's abstractness: "The angel is the Venetian glass bowl on the left with the little spray of leaves in it. The peasants are the terrines, bottles, and the glasses that surround it. This title alone tames it as a lump of sugar might tame a lion" (LWS 650). The second letter makes sense of this language of "taming" because it presents Stevens praising Tal-Coat for his "display of imaginative force: an effort to attain reality purely by way of the artist's own vitality" (LWS 655–56). Here Stevens suggests a level of attention to authorial activity that can be transferred to other modes of expression. Then the third letter interprets the poem interpreting the painting:

> In "Angel Surrounded by Paysans" the angel is the angel of reality. This is clear only if the reader is of the idea that we live in a world of the imagination, in which reality and contact with it are the great blessings. For nine readers out of ten, the necessary angel will appear to be the angel of the imagination and for nine days out of ten that is true, although it is the tenth day that counts. . . . I have been fitted into too many philosophic frames. As a philosopher one is expected to achieve and express one's center. For my own part, I think that the

philosophic *permissible* [italics in the original] (to use an insurance term) is a great deal different today than it was a generation or two ago.

(LWS 753)

Our task now is to see what Stevens makes in poetry of Tal-Coat's attaining "reality primarily by way of the artist's own vitality." Filreis is right that vitality has to be understood as a relational feature of the painting and of the poem. But I think we cannot isolate relations from the substances that make them visible. After all, the angel for Stevens is a figure for reality, not for abstract relatedness. In what can that sense of reality abide, and how does it differ from what an angel of imagination might bring to the scene?

There are two basic aspects of content in the poem's transfiguration of the still life—the images of paysans and angel, and the activities of the angel, which provide for the poem what Tal-Coat's brushwork does for the vitality of the painting. I have very little to say about the first since Costello seems to me correct in proposing that transforming the still life into a scenic allegory makes explicit the painter's rejection of adornment so that the angel can be allied with the paysans' ways of being and of knowing. However, this description entirely avoids the issue of what the angel adds to the poem, especially by the poet's choice to risk the awkwardness of developing a first-person perspective for this character.

The first thing the angel adds is the necessity of introducing into our sense of the real a complex relation between first- and second-order states. The angel expresses the possibility of "being what I am and know." Therefore, it sharply repudiates equating reality with any sense of fact or description. Instead, the sense of reality depends on the active relation between being, knowing, and willing what one knows. Here Filreis reminds us that the angel can only represent such second-order states because he offers no specific substance. But that observation is itself not specific enough because even without specific substance the angel performs concrete actions and creates particular problems for the paysans, who cannot see anyone at the door. Probably they cannot see the angel because they are looking for something physical at the door rather than exploring what might change in their awareness of the relation to the scene if they could take seriously what might be seen when the door opens. One might say that the angel is the spirit of Tal-Coat's vitality in the brushwork—a spirit not to be found in the specific details but in the capacity to embrace the relations among the details that address a specific historical situation.

In order to help the paysans see the earth again, the angel must clear away the detritus that the imagination has imposed upon it. And in order to enable the paysans to feel their world as "reality," the angel must give access not only to the content of the earth but also to the framing of that content. Two lines devoted to sight are followed by five lines devoted to hearing the tragic drone that accompanies all our efforts to give these sights meaning. There is an angel of reality, but it seems inseparable from awareness that our attributions of meaning are always ultimately to be consigned to the dump. The metaphors allowing us to unite being and knowing are also the source of our necessarily tragic awareness that we are the very source of the destruction that we lament.

I have still to address what is probably the most intriguing feature of the poem and certainly its most surprising modification of still life. Why is the poem in the first person, after the introduction by the paysan who opens the door? Perhaps Stevens wanted to personify not quite the work of art but the kind of invitation it offers as a "welcome at the door," although no visible person emerges. Perhaps only the first person can create a second-order effect of substance even though the poem deals with fleeting feelings—the first person may be that mode of being that gives a home to the insubstantial. And perhaps only the first person can naturalize the question with which the poem concludes since there the angel worries about what kind of existence it can have, given what it knows. This kind of self-consciousness may be inseparable from the fear that it exists primarily as an "apparition." The repudiation of the earth it inherits under the auspices of standard aestheticist accounts of art seems to entail this internal instability, as if here the angel felt most forcefully the tragic forces that isolate consciousness from what it would embrace.

Notice how the angel's self-consciousness here occupies a strange future-perfect temporality where the present tense "I am gone?" is itself knowable only after the departure. The poem refuses the simpler expressions "I will be gone" and "I will have gone." This enables "I am gone" to be strangely cast as a first-person expression within a third-person point of view since the angel is probably "gone" only from the perspective of the paysans, although there is a sense that its disappearance is also felt as subjective reality. So it seems that the angel not only knows the effects of tragedy but also participates in them: its making reality visible and active depends on its knowing also the sense of mortality that has to frame any possible celebration—otherwise, that celebration would collapse into the imaginary. The angel of reality appears inseparable not just from the spirit of tragedy but also from the self-knowledge that has to recognize the limitations of any human power.

The poem's concluding question may be its finest gesture. This angel of reality turns out to need allegory in order to become visible and then perhaps only as an "apparition." Allegorically, this angel of reality has to recognize how fleeting a sense of reality is. Facts are stable, stable enough to invite angels of imagination. But "reality" is not fact; reality is the accommodation of imagination to those facts. The process of realization brings facts alive for the imagination without submitting to the imagination *as* it wills (see *CPP* 181). Such realization depends on combining the intensity of presence with a sense of the lag produced by a self-consciousness that is always afraid that the intensity is caused only by an apparition. No wonder the poem turns to repeated doublings like "liquidly in liquid lingerings," "an apparition appareled in / Apparels," and "quickly, too quickly, I am gone?" Beverly Maeder remarks that "quickly, too quickly" creates an odd slowing down or "pause" at the threshold of appearance.[8] But she does not recognize how the poem labors here to have the angel take on something like substance at the very point of its disappearance, as if accepting that transience were fundamental to the very conditions of its existence.

II

There remains a huge problem with my interpretation. Why is it so lugubrious in relation to so playful a poem? How can we integrate the playfulness into the reading and perhaps make the lugubriousness of my allegorizing about the allegory a little more dynamic? "Quickly, too quickly, I am gone?" comes with its own quickness, surprising the reader with its abrupt finality crossed with a delicate ruefulness—an intriguing combination difficult for criticism to address. Dramatically, this assertion matters because it acknowledges that there can be only momentary satisfaction of our investments in knowing reality.

In this poem there can be no mistaking the "real" for a substantial state that persists through time. All of the references to tragedy and to loss in the poem indicate that a sense of reality as presence is inseparable from a sense that the nature of realization is entwined with the nature of loss. Then, metadramatically, the poem adds two further considerations—the more telling because they are so playful. First, we are invited to notice that this departure is not only a figurative assertion within the poem. It is also a literal assertion about the volume since this is the concluding poem, so all of the angelic presences have to depart after their all-too-brief presence. This poem about the angel of reality as apparition turns out to be completely adequate as description, at least on one level. For it embodies the virtual condition of our possible identification with the angel. The medium in which the angel can appear now disappears. And we are left with this instance of the same tragic sense that the angel sees as the precondition of its providing an emblem of realization.

But if we are left with this sense of realization because of the lightness by which the angel handles its disappearance, then perhaps tragedy does not have the last word. This is the second consideration the ending invites. We cannot stop with how the poem realizes loss. In the angel's disappearance there may be the appearance of the very knowledge that the angel is to mediate—the knowledge of the relation between what we can see if we destroy the shape of meanings and what we can hear because we recognize the tragic dimension which this shape has come to constitute. Perhaps then at the ending the poem itself actually functions as an angel—both referring to and becoming a real instance of what can be realized as present when one is prepared to break from one's defenses and recognize how transient the realization of our values has to be. The lugubrious themes can be treated lightly because there remains a path to the angel based on how it stages its own disappearance. Poetry can lead us to understand tragedy while converting it "into a different, an explicable, an amenable circumstance" (*CPP* 789). It can take in the very mechanism of tragedy while incorporating that into an attitude that takes account of the satisfactions of so thoroughly acknowledging our condition.

This path invites the reader to accept that transience so fully that all of the reader's efforts to make the world real can be framed within it. The encounter with loss itself becomes a partially positive condition because it is manifest as the precondition for appreciating how the angel of reality can speak as first person—indeed has to speak as first person because the speaking itself becomes a dance where being, appearing, and disappearing are inseparable from one another. As Stevens put it in a slightly different context, "the physical never seems newer than when it is emerging from the metaphysical" (*LWS* 595). The lightness of being in this poem celebrates its metaphysical capacity to recuperate the tragic sense and make it a condition for understanding how reality is a matter of subtlety and not substance (*CPP* 750).

Now the back story of the painting that became a poem can alter the affective investments in the poem for those familiar with it. Stevens has transformed a still life into a dramatic scene in order to bring out two aspects of how this poem manifests an angel of reality rather than of the imagination. The first is the poem's staging of the importance of the maker as manifesting the power to adapt to the world of fact even as it transforms our sense of what contexts are necessary for this sense of realization. The second aspect is the poem's capacity to articulate how the painting can be the instrument for eliciting an interpretive language that stresses circulation and transformation. Even though the poet has transfigured the image, the inspiration it provides offers a means of absorbing the worldliness of still life, so dear to Costello, into figures of the sociality that must provide the frame for such worldliness. The poem offers the angel as the boundary condition of that sociality. The angel expresses the force of what cannot be seen as substance, yet proves the precondition for recognizing how a society might be constituted by this fusion of the sense of the tragic, as well as the sense of presence that this awareness of tragedy makes possible.

What better figure for acknowledging tragedy than this French painting—from a culture encountering after the war "something much more tragic than a literary panorama" (*LWS* 492).[9] Stevens has in effect realized that what this French still life shows about the passion for life in a time still riddled by the sense of death could itself not be articulated in a literary version attempting only to picture a still life. That conjunction of being and knowing requires dramatic allegory, and it teaches this poet, himself comfortable in his bourgeois accoutrements, how the tragic can be transfigured into the expressiveness of art.

III

So much for this poem as a source of concrete aesthetic experience. We now have to ask why Stevens might think it could provide a satisfying conclusion to *Auroras of Autumn*. One answer is that any other placement would cancel the effect of the angel's departure coinciding with the closing of the book. But that departure would only produce a gimmicky effect unless the poem could on its own merits stage a force of realization central to the volume's basic concerns. So I propose that this force derives from the poem's capacity to gather and sharpen the features of the volume that respond to the pressure put on it by "Esthétique du Mal," a profoundly unsatisfying but also profoundly generative poem where Stevens clearly stretched himself beyond his lyrical comfort zone. (It might be better to say that Stevens stretched himself so that he had to see the limits of his lyricism.) This poem stands at the opposite end of the pole from "Notes toward a Supreme Fiction," which concludes the volume *Transport to Summer* with triumphant but familiar figures of heroic fluency. "Esthétique" is far more troubling in its uneasy engagement with the difficulty endemic to modernity of telling one's desire from one's despair. For a typical critical response to the poem,

I cite Helen Vendler: "Esthétique" lapses from the general top
more lyric examination of the evil most tempting for Stevens—
nostalgia and self-pity, the appetite for sleek ensolacings—or worse a ....
arly' interest in his own pain."[10] But rather than add my own voice to the
chorus of interpreters, I suggest that we imagine Stevens himself worrying
that the poem settles far too easily for lyrical resolutions to the tragic conditions it projects as necessary responses to a world at war.[11]

"Esthétique du Mal" offers an eloquent intensity, combined at times with
a terrific precision about the sense of poverty in a world where "the death
of Satan was a tragedy / for the imagination" (CPP 281). The poem begins
almost self-mockingly with the speaker sitting at Naples "writing letters
home." This beginning shows the poet trying to create a protective shell
that might insulate him from the pain his observation of historical events
elicits. But at the same time, his mind wants to address a wide of range of
evils. That mind is trying to understand how one can most responsively feel
the evil of conditions ranging from harbingers of fatality, to the temptations
to self-pity, to experiences of distance from what one desires, to the red
wound of the soldier. These efforts constitute a brave attempt to be a realist—
not quite *by* distancing the self from these evils but *by* recognizing that they
play a necessary part in the physical world in which we must work out our
attitudes. So there is an underlying tension between the catalogue of evils
that pushes us toward sympathy and the possibility of a distance from such
sympathy, which will be the ultimate stance of the realist, now capable of
fully appreciating what is given by that physical world.

For me the most problematic passage is the poem's conclusion, with
what Vendler calls its "sleek ensolacings" made appealing by the urgencies
of phrasing and cadence:

> One might have thought of sight, but who could think
> Of what it sees, for all the ill it sees? . . .
> And out of what one sees and hears and out
> Of what one feels, who could have thought to make
> So many selves, so many sensuous worlds,
> As if the air, the mid-day air, was swarming
> With the metaphysical changes that occur
> Merely in living as and where we live.
>
> *(CPP 287)*

This turning to the mind's pleasures must replace attributions of evil to Satan
and provide the source of attachment to desires that are possible to distinguish

from despair. But this metaphysical path to the physical creates several problems. The quest for this lucid realism may force the poem to become an instance of the very problem of distance that brings it into being. The greatest sympathy the poem can imagine resides in the hope that this sensualist metaphysics can trump history so that the mind could be satisfied just in understanding why "necessity" drives it to this meditative praise of sensuous worlds. This reflective dimension allows turning one's back on "force of nature in action," which is "the major tragedy" (*CPP* 285). However then the poem's sensualism has to be muted and composed—a distanced means of containing tragedy rather than participating in it.

IV

I emphasize these features of "Esthétique" because the opening poems of the next volume, *Auroras of Autumn,* return to that poem's efforts to find attitudes by which to contemplate the tragic in modern life. But there is a big difference. These poems do not rely on the lyrical effusiveness Stevens called upon toward the conclusion of the earlier poem. Instead, he seems to be avoiding the temptation to draw thematic conclusions. A sense of what might suffice had to be located more intimately within the very processes of how imagination took its stances toward the world. Stevens could not be satisfied with a position that begins with distanced observing of evil as a kind of sublime and ends with the simplicities of living, as if this level of immediacy could now justify almost the same distance from other people's lives. Now the poet presents himself in a different, more elemental contemplative situation, observing the auroras of autumn and reading the auroras for the analogies that they might suggest for the extraordinary violence of the war years. Yet Stevens does not want to turn the auroras into romantic symbols. Instead, he seeks directly to recuperate the meditative space that symbols provide by indulging in the temptation to draw affective analogues from what he sees. Coming to terms with evil is coming to terms, among other things, with the processes it elicits in the mind. And coming to terms with evil requires more than using it as a background to frame what still warrants the status of desirable pleasures. It requires at least recognizing how we participate in the evil and suffer from it even as we turn to those pleasures.

The difference from "Esthétique" is clear if we attend to how the poem "Auroras of Autumn," which introduces the volume, calls attention to its own efforts to create a bridge from seeing to interpreting. For the evil resides there, not in what the poem explicitly discovers so much as in what it suffers in trying to develop any interpretation at all. At first the poem tries to be content with sheer seeing or accepting a roughly realist attitude toward the scene. Six of the eight stanzas in the first canto begin with "this," the beloved empiricist expression, because it promises the sufficiency of what can be observed in detail, with no irritable reaching after meaning or edification. But this feeling of distance, of resisting affective connection, also invites the very symbolic echoes that it seeks to repudiate. These are the last three stanzas of this canto:

In another nest, the master of the maze
Of body and air and forms and images,
Relentlessly in possession of happiness.

This is his poison: that we should disbelieve
Even that. His meditations in the ferns,
When he moved so slightly to make sure of sun,

Made us no less as sure. We saw in his head,
Black-beaded on the rock, the flecked animal,
The moving grass, the Indian in the glade.
(CPP 355)

The serpent is not Satan. Yet the poet cannot refrain from developing analogies for the fall even as he tries to maintain the distance enabling sheer fascination with the objects of attention. And once the analogies start, the last stanza turns them into a rush of standard metaphors for serpentine being. One could treat this situation as a process of description flowering into metaphor, as in "Study of Two Pears." But there seems to be an uneasiness here, a sense that the metaphors are being asked to supplement a dissatisfaction with the effort to stabilize the night scene by selective description. In almost a parody of Hegel, "this" turns out to undo the very empirical certainty it tries to secure. And the mind is left with the distance from its own desires, which is also a distance between the facts of observation and any sense that they embody a reality capable of making the observer's stance into a participant's.

The next four cantos involve elaborate elegies to what were the poet's trusted ideas and perhaps an elegy to the faith in forming ideas of any kind.[12] I will have to pass them over in order to concentrate on how the poem's effort to separate itself from romantic treatments of landscape produces significant problems. Sheer observation simply cannot satisfy the mind's needs as it finds itself also being fascinated by violent and sublime eruptions in the night sky. So after the elegiac spirit forces the poet to a somewhat sentimental fantasy for restoring what imaginative force he can to maternal and paternal roles, the fifth and sixth cantos turn from the effort at sheer observation to treating the auroras in grand theatrical terms. However, this ironically brings the sublimity of the auroras too close to certain horrors that in recent historical events have challenged reason all too successfully. So the speaking voice turns to a self-abnegating figure for the fear the speaker now feels. Perhaps the mind's allowing itself to enter this theatricality risks surrendering all boundaries providing "the frame / Of everything he is."

There must be another possible path. In that spirit Canto VII proposes a shift from unwieldy theatrics to the sleek consolations of the gay ironist. Now the auroras can be given their innocence, their pure naturalness not sullied by the demands of human observers. Yet this produces the poem's most disturbing social position because the price of pursuing this innocence is to deny the modes of consciousness that distinguish human being from natural being. The claim to innocence cannot but stir memories of what the serpent once did. It destroyed paradise, but it also created the possibility of deep compassion sponsoring a renewed dedication to labor on what had become an entirely historical stage. There might be a paradise within greater far.

The ninth canto of the poem desires both innocence and the social compassion that in Christian mythology (and Hegelian phenomenology) comes only after the Fall. I cite the first and last stanzas of this section in order to help us hear the complex lyricism of wanting to use the sensuality of language as an instrument for securing a belief to which the analytic mind will not yield:

> And of each other thought—in the idiom
> Of the work, in the idiom of the innocent earth,
> Not of the enigma of the guilty dream. . . .
>
> It may come tomorrow in the simplest word,
> Almost as part of innocence, almost,
> Almost as the tenderest and the truest part.
>
> *(CPP 362)*

Only when one hears the hesitations informing these lines will one fully appreciate the abrupt yet fairly quiet transition to a much more abstract mode of thinking in the final section:

> An unhappy people in a happy world—
> Read, rabbi, the phrases of this difference.
> An unhappy people in an unhappy world—

Here thinking becomes theatrical by calling for the rabbi to take the stage and perform something that can compensate for the loss of the Christian mythology in the background of this poem. The result is a striking gulf between the imperative "Now, solemnize the secret syllables . . . to contrive a whole" and the reality of this particular imagined rabbi's individual meditation:

> In these unhappy he meditates a whole,
> The full of fortune and the full of fate,
> As if he lived all lives, that he might know,
>
> In hall harridan, not hushful paradise,
> To a haggling of winter and weather, by these lights
> Like a blaze of summer straw in winter's nick.
>
> *(CPP 363)*

Stevens wants a stance that can adapt to this late autumn reality without feeling trapped by the demands to rest content with languages of observation. So he extends the domain of perception in order to project its possible social implications or, less abstractly, to project how it can at least be responsive to this unhappiness within a happy world without replacing "hall harridan" by a fantasized "hushful paradise." But to accomplish that here he has to rely on a quite romantic image, not unlike Eliot's "midwinter spring." The scene for meditation tries to make up in intricacy of sound for what it abstracts away from any actual sense of contact with the sources of unhappiness. More important, and more devastating, "know" is hauntingly intransitive, and "whole" is disturbingly vague. Whatever release there is here from the serpent's poison, it is at best tenuously poised on the cusp of becoming another idea to which one must say farewell. This rabbi cannot do much for an unhappy people in any kind of world.

V

This elaborate introductory poem imposes several burdens on the volume. We have seen the most important: "Auroras" has to explore a range of attitudes (rather than kinds of subject matter) so that the poet can hear what might be problematic in his ways of imagining. He has to recognize how what once provided lyric satisfaction can pose a temptation to avoid various challenges.

Yet a major step has been taken just by virtue of the fact that Stevens showed himself willing to begin a volume with a long poem, as if the imagination could not rest until it took responsibility for ways it might evade its own sense of obligation to address these experiences of a disturbing distance between thought and its objects.

Of course, Stevens might have decided to begin with this poem simply to balance the volume by providing separation from its other longer poem, "An Ordinary Evening in New Haven." But I think Stevens also wanted the initial shock of refusing any of the satisfactions of the short lyric because he wants to raise concerns about the lyric's inadequacy in dealing with the recurrent motif of tragedy and the tragic. Opening with a long poem helps cast the short lyrics that follow as aspects of continuing meditations rather than isolated gems offered for the reader's delectation. That decision makes it seem that aesthetic criteria simply will not suffice for such texts: these poems must be difficult, in large part because they can be only "parts" of an endless effort to restore the satisfactions afforded by traditional lyricism in somewhat different terms. The poems cannot rest in the fiction of a happy world or in the gestures by which the rabbi manages to find contentment in the unhappy one.

I use two of these lyrics to illustrate how the volume takes up the feeling of demand on the imagination to deal with the fact and the ramifications of the tragic. "The Novel" measures the adequacy of prose fiction "in a bad time." Here identification with the characters produces only "a knowledge cold within as one's own":

And one trembles to be understood and, at last,
To understand, as if to know became
The fatality of seeing things too well.

(CPP 392)

"Bouquet" provides an even more devastating summary of what still life can become under the new dispensation, where seeing simply cannot overcome the distance that is both the source and the result of our awareness of a pervasive unhappiness. Just the length of the poem suggests how difficult it is to create the illusion that poetry can bring a sense of the real to what the eye registers. Then the poem's final section attempts to perform in actual time and space what Costello claims the previous still lifes have asserted: imagination can inhabit the actual world. But neither still life nor the lyric has the necessary resources:

A car drives up. A soldier, an officer,
Steps out. He rings and knocks. The door is not locked.
He enters the room and calls. No one is there.

He bumps the table. The bouquet falls on its side.
He walks through the house, looks round him and then leaves.
The bouquet has slopped over the edge and lies on the floor.

(CPP 387)

Each short indicative sentence could be what Eliot treats as "the last twist of the knife," eloquent in its refusal to be absorbed within the lyrical imagination. There is only the serpent's poison of description without analogy. Poetry does not interpret tragedy; it invites the reader to participate in a tragic sensibility—on the level of imagined content and on the level of manner that is cut off from any celebratory energies.

VI

It is one thing to notice a pervasive uneasiness in the volume, another to explain it. Here I can only propose to account for one feature of that uneasiness. I think Stevens realizes that there is a dangerous conjunction between the distance demanded by the culture's ideals of description and the capacity of art to compose a present tense isolated from past and future (or from felt history and possibility). He had thought he could build the aesthetic order on the possibility of replacing matter by manner and description by imaginative participation in the flux of experience. But while the contrast between description and participation does establish a distinctive value for "the edgings and inchings of final form" (*CPP* 417), the usefulness of this contrast ultimately has to rely on what the imagination can make of it. There is a substantial difference between an epistemological awareness that description brings all the limitations of empiricism to the forefront and the felt recognition of the muted but persistent pain occurring when the imagination can do nothing with the world but describe it. Yet Stevens had blurred that difference by treating self-consciousness as an adequate instrument for registering not only the facts of suffering but also its moral and social import. Now he had to make explicit the fear that the imagination might offer only quite limited responses to the suffering of others because of its tendencies to rest within its own comfort zones without opening itself to the full conditions of human suffering. However simply asserting profuse sympathy for what after all were simply facts about the world seemed repugnant to him. So he had to find more subtle instruments for imagination's recognizing its complicities in evading pain while maintaining his focus on the meditative individual.

When Stevens asserts "The death of Satan was a tragedy / For the imagination," he refers to the fact that, once people stop believing in Satan, the imagination is no longer free to attribute tragic results to the machinations of a metaphysical personage. The imagination must face the possibility that evil is not caused by an outward agency: evil is simply an aspect of the secular world that neither needs nor invites the poet's supplements. Perhaps certain levels of evil are even caused by certain deployments of imagination, so that the poet has to learn to inhabit his creative power to take account of this kind of participation. Imagination, for example, can share empiricism's modes of distancing the mind from participation in what it contemplates. One need look no further than the modes of observation and commentary basic to "Esthétique." And the entire constructivist orientation of imagination may be too insistently positive, too capable of building worlds to recognize how such construction evades fundamental tragic realities about the place necessity occupies in our lives. The death of Satan may also be a tragedy for imagination because it exposes how the imagination tends to theatricalize evil and ignores the ways that evil is embedded in quotidian practices. Once we believe Satan is dead, classical tragedy seems almost as much a product of the rhetorician's imagination as it is a condition to which the writer is trying to respond.

I think Stevens eventually sees how an aspectual poetics can better align imagination with the facts of suffering because it resists such theatrical constructions. Instead, it treats self-consciousness as an aspect of a person's relation to imaginative processes that are more continuous with quotidian features of our lives. Even though this poetics obviously does not help us address all of the kinds of evil facing human beings, it can treat various forces connected to tragedy as intimate factors that affect immediate conditions of thinking and of feeling. It also provides a perfect vehicle for a poet as bashful as Stevens because it does not bind the imagination to stories of heroes and victims, which are always tempted to the twin poles of lapsing into self-aggrandizing pity or calling upon powers of moral judgment to change conditions it rarely fully understands.

In order to locate the domains in our experience of suffering where aspectual thinking can play significant roles I beg the reader's indulgence as I make a somewhat pompous distinction among three basic kinds of evil in relation to basic human interests. The first two inflict the greatest harm, but that magnitude dwarfs any effort by writers to do anything but register and mourn the sufferings created. First, we can isolate gross collective suffering that cannot be attributed to particular human agents as its cause. Ultimately, this class comprises all the factors that we attribute to the sheer facts of mortality and contingency—to what Satan cost humanity in provoking the expulsion from Paradise. The second category consists of evil that is clearly attributable to weaknesses or excesses in specific human agents and associations of agents. This class extends from cases of particular persons who will to wreak havoc to cases where agency is more diffuse but no less active, for example, in places where people persecute others for reasons of race, class, and gender.

Classical writing could feel itself waging significant battles against such circumstances because it could identify with the suffering and intensify it by emphasizing the social costs for all of the participants. But with the shift to romantic values and the centrality of first-person narratives of self-development, it became increasingly difficult to find writerly attitudes that could convincingly engage these modes of suffering: Tolstoy would have to yield to Dostoyevsky. When self-conscious subjectivity is foregrounded, writers often become uncomfortable in identifying with victims, however heroic or pathetic the victimization. It becomes difficult for the writer to avoid the two unfortunate alternatives I just mentioned in speculating about Stevens—lapsing into self-aggrandizing pity or calling upon powers of moral judgment to change conditions even though one cannot be sure what use these moral judgments might have. In both cases it seems that the writer and the writing stand apart from the evils represented in the text and that the writer's role becomes an imaginary substitute for impotence. If only one could believe that Satan exists, figuratively if not literally, then the author could postulate agency behind the evil. Once we believe Satan is dead, tragedy can seem almost as much a product of the rhetorician's imagination as it is a condition to which the writer is trying to respond.

This is why it is important for writers such as Stevens to postulate a third kind of evil, where writers can imagine their presentations making a difference in how an audience might respond and behave. In these cases, one must begin by admitting that such audiences are for the most part not responsible for the major evils in the world. However, they are responsible for how they develop or fail to develop modes of attention and of recognition that affect the quality of personal and social life. Here the writers do have significant power to affect how self-consciousness gets deployed. For Stevens at least, the poet could try to model or demonstrate ways of resisting the temptation to treat self-consciousness as a mode of protective distance from both the weaknesses of the agent and the reality of the suffering experienced by others. He could show how debilitating this sense of distance is, in part because it negates the range of intimate ways one is complicit in producing tragic circumstances. Phenomenologically, Stevens imagines evil as inseparable from inversions of our most fundamental sources of joy in experience—the experience of time as growth or development and the experience of space as affording various feelings of connection and belonging. These inversions were central to Stevens since at least his critique of description in "The Latest Freed Man." Yet it took a while for him to recognize that the domain of the aesthetic can often be in deep collusion with the empiricist orientations those invoking the aesthetic are trying to resist. "Esthétique du Mal" sees the problem and tries to recast the aesthetic so that it is less a matter of the construction of objects than of the assuming of attitudes that directly engage the world of sensations. But even this move does not successfully grapple with the source of this collusion, at least if one takes seriously Stanley Cavell's magisterial analysis of how skepticism can be located as the deep cause of much of this distance and especially of modern thought's comfort with this distance.[13] For Cavell skepticism is particularly dangerous because it enmeshes those who try to oppose it in the narrow confines that it establishes. The form of total doubt that skepticism cultivates forces most of its opponents into stark empiricist claims that jettison all trust in what seems incapable of direct proof. So even when thinkers develop principles purportedly able to resist skepticism, they end up buying into a destructive distance between observation and other psychological states or social relations. And there is then a tendency to want to take revenge on the world for not being in accord with our fantasies.

Consider the case of G. E. Moore, which Wittgenstein takes up in *On Certainty*. Moore thinks he has refuted skepticism by asserting as philosophically self-evident the fact that he has two hands. But Wittgenstein takes great pains to point out all that this assertion misses about the kind of action it establishes. "I have two hands" is not a fact but a condition. Since no one would doubt I have two hands, this statement does not give significant information. What it manages to do is position the self in the world so that other statements become intelligible: "I have two hands, so I can carry the groceries," or "my awareness of my hands suggests that I have the necessary powers to reflect on aspects of human interchange with the world." More important, statements like these simply open the world to fundamental interchanges that ultimately provide a social foundation within which structures of doubt and refutation take pride of place. And, more dangerous yet, the way Moore brooks no disagreement leads Wittgenstein to imply that his assertions betray an ontological uneasiness that Derrida's remarks on empiricist ideals of presence will elaborate. The need for fact becomes imperious, and it takes its revenge by weakening any faith in the complex webs of relation that tie us to the world.

Even though its audiences might plausibly deny responsibility for large-scale suffering, *Auroras* might lead them to be concerned about how they develop or fail to develop modes of attention and of recognition that affect the quality of personal and social life. Stevens could show how debilitating this sense of distance is by making an art whose primary concern is to participate in the possible feelings that might be inseparable from direct yet subtle engagements with loss and with distance. This might be the great permission established by modernity's converting the world from substance to subtlety (*CPP* 750).

VII

Not surprisingly, it is "An Ordinary Evening in New Haven" that most fully articulates the outlines of a new attitude toward the various modes of distancing that the volume has presented. Helen Vendler makes my job considerably easier because she offers extended commentary on how the poem works variations on its first line, "The eye's plain version is a thing apart" (*CPP* 397).[14] All I need to point out is how part of this meditation on the eye involves Stevens's struggle to resolve a basic tension in his other long poems written in the 1940s. There he seems torn between developing an argumentative sequence where the poem arrives at some discovery, stated in the form of an organizing image, and developing a mode where the resolution consists simply in coming to accept the poem's ways of circulating. "An Ordinary Evening in New Haven" goes a long way toward resting within the processes of constant transformation as the mind attunes itself to the emerging possibilities of what it encounters. For the mind, there simply is never "the eye's plain version": "The eye does not beget in resemblance. It sees. But the mind begets in resemblance as the painter begets in representation; that is to say as the painter makes his world within a world" (*CPP* 689). Where there is a mind working, there is an "as," more or less visible. Even plainness is not a condition of the object but primarily an attribute of the seeing. Objects are necessarily related to needs or desires that both contextualize the seeing and afford it various possibilities of further realization.[15]

Stevens's first essay in "Three Academic Pieces" emphasizes how poetry's work with resemblance "enhances the sense of reality, heightens it, intensifies it" (*CPP* 691). He is not explicit about how that intensified sense of reality might be inseparable from a tragic awareness of the instability of such satisfactions. But I think the connection is not difficult to make. Where there is constant resemblance and so constant transformation, there is also always a playing out of the drama of mortality. If it is the case that "there is not grim / Reality but reality grimly seen" (*CPP* 405), then the noun "tragedy" has to become the adverb "tragically." And the adverb has to be in constant interaction with other attitudinal modifiers. A lesser thinker than Stevens might conclude that modern thinking has therefore reduced tragedy to one disposition among many. But the shift to seeing things "grimly" does not at all banish thinking that is shaped by considerations of a constant tragic dimension to life. It only entails presenting tragedy as also fundamentally a part of the world, always potentially fused with other frameworks, just as resemblance is always a mix between deconstruction and construction. Reality as a force becomes inseparable from the shade it traverses:

> And something of death's poverty is heard.
> This should be tragedy's most moving face.
>
> It is a bough in the electric light
> And exhalations in the eaves, so little
> To indicate the total leaflessness.
>
> *(CPP 407)*

Even this total leaflessness frames the light and a sense of the exhalation it gives. The reminder of mortality can also involve coming to terms with the world of facts: here the light functions both as a symbol of the mind and as an aspect of the physical world helping to make specific particulars vivid for consciousness. Stevens cannot completely repress his penchant for generalization. But he can temper it by an often-surprising return to details of the world and the sense of the equivalences they define as the life this world shares with poetry. I cite in two parts the complete canto XXVII of "Ordinary Evening":

> If it should be true that reality exists
> In the mind: the tin plate, the loaf of bread on it,
> The long-bladed knife, the little to drink and her
>
> Misericordia, it follows that
> Unreal and real are two in one. New Haven
> Before and after one arrives or, say,
>
> Bergamo on a postcard, Rome after dark,
> Sweden described, Salzburg with shaded eyes
> Or Paris in conversation at a café.
>
> *(CPP 414)*

The realities that exist in the mind are insistently humble objects, modulating into figures of poverty. The relations among these objects, however, tell another story. This passage modulates from a series of objects, to affects implied by those objects, to little evocative details whose incompleteness as objects allows a rich suggestiveness for the subjects attending to them. *As the images get transformed into sites of mystery and possibility, aspectual thinking can become aware of itself as a distinctive power for transforming conventional objects into an irreducible promise of meaningfulness that will not resolve into determinate conditions. Meanings here are not indeterminate, but they are open to further development by the continued fleshing out of implicit contexts. The references to European place names here function to indicate how much of our elemental lives can be lived in a realm of constantly shifting possibilities. Incompleteness as loss becomes inseparable from the actual experience of incompleteness as resource.

Now the poem can generalize without worrying that the generalization will be taken as theory. Instead, generalization becomes another instrument by which to deploy our capacity to build upon evocative possibilities as means of attaching ourselves to an expanding present tense:

> This endlessly elaborating poem
> Displays the theory of poetry
> As the life of poetry. A more severe,
>
> More harassing master would extemporize
> Subtler, more urgent proof that the theory
> Of poetry is the theory of life,
>
> As it is, in the intricate evasions of as,
> In things seen and unseen, created from nothingness,
> The heavens, the hells, the worlds, the longed-for lands.
>
> *(CPP 415)*

These deployments of "as" are simply brilliant. Stevens typically uses "as" to compare states of mind rather than to specify relations between abstractions. But here the equivalences invite the sense that, although each concept has the same extension as the other, they do not resolve into the same entity. The theory of life manifests itself in a distinctive manner when it is bound to the life of poetry (as "A Collect of Philosophy" argues) because theory then is sustained by the imaginative life available in how the particulars modulate from objects to the evocation of moods. Because we see how the theory of poetry consists largely in the life of poetry, some of us, at least, might be ready to agree that the play of equivalences offers a unique contribution to the theory of life. The actual life lived within these lines readily extends into our sense of vital experience. We are invited to recognize the words as events making true what they demonstrate *as* these intricate evasions reconfigure the forces involved in supplementing the work of description.

The final lines summarize these forces by attributing to them the capacity to make the seen and the unseen live one another's lives and die one another's deaths (as Yeats would put it). This play of seen and unseen registers in generalized form the movement of the canto from tin plate and loaf of bread to "Salzburg with shaded eyes" and "Paris in conversation at a café." Yet this play does not quite explain why there is this particular sequence of appositions in the last line. I think the point of the sequence is to set another level of intricate evasions upon that of the play between "seen" and "unseen." Now the fundamental relation is between the world where literal reference is called for and the world where imaginative forces strive to take on a similar sense of indubitable presence. If we read the details from left to right they seem to become increasingly less fanciful and more psychologically explicable. To put it crudely, "the longed-for lands" provides concrete evidence for unsatisfied desires that get displaced into fantasies of heaven and hell.[16]

But that is to put a binary condition on the psyche. Either the psyche binds itself to what can be unpacked into references to empirical experience, or it must be interpreted symptomatically as surrendering to evasive tactics. If, however, we stress the equivalence between these terms rather than allowing the most empirically salient to interpret the activity of invoking the others, we get a very different view of "the intricate evasions of as." From this perspective we would emphasize the metaphoric qualities of the plural "heavens" and "hells" *as* parallels to the relation between "world" and "longed-for lands." Now desire and not fact governs the appositions. And if we can maintain the priority of desire, we experience once again the competing pulls of the seen and the unseen. I think these competing pulls define the force of those intricate "evasions of as" *as* they make it possible for a completely secular thinking to resist the demands of a traditional empiricist perspective.[17]

VIII

The better we appreciate "Ordinary Evening," the more puzzling it becomes that Stevens chose not to end the volume with this poem. Had he done so, he would have produced a satisfying symmetry, with the two longest poems holding the introductory and closing positions. So what is it about the two poems following "Ordinary Evening" that led him to prefer those as the volume's final gestures?

I can only speculate here, but that decision seems in keeping with the idea of equivalences between things seen and unseen. "Things of August" begins by concentrating on time rather than on thinking in relation to a particular place:

> These locusts by day, these crickets by night
> Are the instruments on which to play
> Of an old and disused ambit of the soul
> Or a new aspect, bright in discovery—
>
> *(CPP 417)*

Stevens replaces the speculative intensity of the previous poem by this binding to specific details, which, as details, present a problem for the very nature of the poet's claims about poetry as theory. Can the poet make the details once again a "new aspect, bright in discovery," or are they reminders of how often the poet in fact plays "old song" while convincing himself that he provides fresh news? The possibilities of a vital poetry become now the "longed-for lands." Stevens intensifies the challenge here by rendering it in a manner that echoes the diction and even the rhythm of "The Man with the Blue Guitar," arguably the least exhausted poem Stevens ever wrote. But what was not at all exhausted then seems very different when it is repeated almost fifteen years and three large volumes later.

So I suspect Stevens put "Things of August" after "Ordinary Evening" because the triumphant abstractions concluding the longer poem simply did not match his persistent feelings of despondency. Perhaps the ultimate pressure of time, unlike the pressure of space, is the feeling that even "the intricate evasions of as" are used and usurious coinage marking the poet's failures to provide yet one more invention that might prove capable of linking the theory of poetry and the theory of life. At the least, adding this poem could challenge the more ebullient sense of evasion by a much more personal and tired flatness of soul, all evasions spent. The concluding canto keeps its sense of wonder and possibility, but almost at a distance, in another tree:

> The mornings grow silent, the never-tiring wonder,
> The trees are reappearing in poverty.

> . . . The rex Impolitor
> Will come stamping here, the ruler of less than men,
>
> In less than nature. He is not here yet.
> Here the adult one is still banded with fulgor,
>
> Is still warm with the love with which she came,
> Still touches solemnly with what she was
>
> And willed. She has given too much, but not enough.
> She is exhausted and a little old.
>
> *(CPP 422)*

However, this, too, is not the volume's final word. The exhaustion of "Things of August" brings out by contrast three remarkable features of "Angel Surrounded by Paysans." The first is the poem's playfulness, its capacity to insist on a metaphysical dimension to the earth's becoming while treating the natural world as an extension of the imagination's irreducible capacity to escape the lugubrious and the pious. This playfulness need not allude to the role of equivalences because it can dramatically occupy an imaginative site so carefully poised between exhaustion and exaltation.

Second, this poem claims authority to conclude the volume because it offers a subtle integration of time and space—time in the form of change and loss, and space in the form of the angel's helping us "see the earth again." Now this seeing again does not depend on any kind of theoretical abstraction, even theorizing against abstraction. Rather, and this is my third point, the seeing overcomes exhaustion by in effect succumbing to time, but not in an expected way. Now time is not primarily sequential and the cause of aging. Rather, time becomes part of what gives power to the possibility of a full present tense, however fleeting. In fact, this present tense is characterized by a striking transformation that metamorphoses change into a series of immediate states. The painting reconfigures a still life into poetry, and the poetry manages to make Tal-Coat's vitality intensely visible by metamorphosing still life into dramatic scene presenting a brief and enigmatic narrative. Perhaps it takes the abstracting of narrative to return to a level of the concrete that can be at home within the lyric—not the representation of concrete transformations but the concrete embodiment of a figure for the very logic of transformation.

Time and exhaustion and loss are necessary aspects of experience, but they do not exhaust its possibilities. While the angel leaves all too quickly, and we must shut this volume of poetry, the book remains as fact and as possibility. Indeed, the book is the most perfect emblem we have of how the unseen and the seen continually interpenetrate, especially once we have encountered the angel who probably played a part in its construction. Continual transformation manages both to embrace exhaustion and to provide through that embrace a sense of what a perennial present might be.

CHAPTER 7

Aspect-Seeing and Its Implications in *The Rock*

Certainly a sense of the infinity of the world is a sense of something cosmic. It is a cosmic poetry because it makes us realize . . . that we are creatures, not of a part, which is our everyday limitation, but of a whole for which, for the most part, we have as yet no language. It is true that philosophy is poetic in conception and doctrine to the extent that the ideas of philosophy might be described as poetic concepts. . . . A realization of the infinity of the world is equally a perception of philosophy and a typical metamorphosis of poetry.

　　Essentially what I intend is that it shall be as if the philosophers had no knowledge of poetry and suddenly discovered it in their search for whatever it is that they are searching for and gave the name of poetry to that which they discovered.

(Stevens, "A Collect of Philosophy")

Here it occurs to me that in conversation on aesthetic matters we use the words: "You have to see it like *this*, this is how it is "meant""; "When you see it like *this*, you see where it goes wrong"; "You have to hear this bar as an introduction"; . . . "You must phrase it like *this*" (which can refer to hearing as well as to playing). . . .

　　Seeing an aspect and imagining are subject to the will. There is such an order as "Imagine *this*", and also: "Now see the figure like *this*", but not "Now see this leaf green!".

(*PI*)

I so enjoyed beginning my previous chapter with a concrete poem that I am going to do something similar here, but this time I will begin with a comparison. Recall the state of exhaustion presented by the final lines in "Things of August." Many critics attribute variants of this flat exhaustion to the poems of the next volume, *The Rock,* while admitting that somehow Stevens offers a magisterial coming to terms with the disappointments of the body and even the spirit.[1] I want to pay careful attention to the first poem in the volume, "An Old Man Asleep," in order to demonstrate how, while the content shares a great deal with "Things of August," the mode of writing and so the mode of thinking are quite different. I also think the differences are remarkable for creating a distinctive site within English poetry for how the unseen takes on visible power. Here it is as if the spirit of artifice could make itself as elemental as the necessities of aging and the diminution of physical powers. An abstracted personal force proves inseparable from the burdens of impersonality to create in every register strange qualities of doubling that pervade the volume:

> The two worlds are asleep, are sleeping now.
> A dumb sense possesses them in a kind of solemnity.
>
> The self and the earth—your thoughts, your feelings,
> Your beliefs and disbeliefs, your whole peculiar plot;
> The redness of your reddish chestnut trees,
> The river motion, the drowsy motion of the river R.
>
> *(CPP 427)*

This is *not* a simple poem of reconciliation to old age. But to appreciate the full resonance of that simplicity we have to engage some difficult questions that do not arise in dealing with the flatness of "Things of August." Why does the poem switch from the passive "are asleep" to the more active "are sleeping"? Why represent this sleep by referring immediately not to persons but to the two worlds of self and earth? Why make repetition so dominant in the poem, as if the river R were really the river of Nietzsche's Eternal Return? Why connect the density of sound so closely to the motif of repetition? Why switch almost at the center of the poem from third-person description to second-person address? And why does the poem so confidently identify with what apparently remains another person's peculiar plot, only to conclude with an overwhelmingly general and abstract description?

All these questions are elicited by the poem's effort to develop a transparent directness of description compatible with intimacy, a very difficult task because we usually equate intimacy with the kinds of identification that require a text to leap into the mysteries of an inner life. The poet does give the sleeping person a psychology, but it is a psychology so elemental that it manages to correlate completely with the bare facts of the situation. That is why the poem moves from "asleep" to "are sleeping"; why the sleeping is attributed to an elemental relation between self and earth; and why there is such a smooth transition between that general condition and the terms of direct address, "your thoughts, your feelings." It is as if the poem found a level of being where the condition of address and the condition of description were almost identical. But to realize this identity we need to open ourselves to an order of being different from the practical one to which we are accustomed.

We have to produce an imagined world in which we can honor "your peculiar plot" while recognizing that this plot consists largely of simply sleeping. But it is *his* sleeping, as all of the markers of address in the poem insist. Because of the shift in point of view in line three, all of these general terms do not preclude address but solicit it, as if agency could be fully recognized and invoked by accepting the minimal yet completely expansive shift that occurs when something compels us to move from description to address.

Ultimately, it will be this self-consciousness about the force of address that establishes *The Rock* as a significant departure from the reflective action characterizing its predecessors. In "An Old Man Asleep," the movement into address seems to me to constitute a two-fold affirmation—of the power that the individual still has to take responsibility for his or her meanings and of the sleeping itself as an acceptance of continuity with the rest of being— without complaint and without regret. The ease with which the poem combines levels of being has to be attributed to the person sleeping, if only because that ease is so carefully interwoven with a repetitiousness that itself becomes an affective feature of the old man's world. But even in this repetition there is evidence of the peculiar plot. How otherwise can we explain the resonance of "drowsy" here? The addition of "drowsy" to the repetition of "river motion" provides a little climax in relation to the poem's use of address because even when the self is reduced almost to an object it can elicit something excessive and distinctive.[2]

I have to admit that the distinction is mostly on the level of sound since "drowsy" so exaggerates the *o* sounds in the line that it takes the line itself beyond description to an affirmation of peculiar presence. But that seems to me an utterly brilliant means of expressing how pervasive the sense of human presence can become as the unreal takes up active residence within the real at its most elemental—as if "being there together is enough" (*CPP* 444). Once the sleeping person is regarded as having a point of view, the return to sheer objectivity has to include something of the freedom of that point of view, some moment of playfulness that runs counter to the bleakness of the elemental and objective picture. The pathos of aging trumps the expressivist dimension embodied in address, but not without a struggle or trace of what the objectivity cannot quite enclose.

I

All the critics recognize the elemental character of being embraced by the poems that *The Rock* comprises.[3] And most of them speak in some way of two basic sets of elements at work—call them the seen and the unseen or the real and the unreal. But no reading of the poems that I know sufficiently accounts for what Stevens accomplishes by means of the interplay between these two elements. My attempt to provide that story begins with my returning to his essay "A Collect of Philosophy," where Stevens wants to "identify a few philosophic ideas that are inherently poetic and to comment on them" (*CPP* 857). That poetic quality does not derive either from philosophers commenting on poetry or from what poets do with philosophy. Rather, the idea is simultaneously "a perception of philosophy and a typical metamorphosis of poetry" (*CPP* 856).

Against this backdrop, Stevens's primary example seems surprisingly banal—a commentary on George Berkeley's argument that "we never the see the world except the moment after, in reflection rather than in perception":

> Here is an idea, not the result of poetic thinking and entirely without poetic intention, which instantly changes the face of the world. . . . The material world, for all the assurances of the eye, has become immaterial. It has become an image in the mind. The solid earth disappears and the whole atmosphere is subtlized, not by the arrival of some venerable beam of light from an almost hypothetical star but by a breach of reality. What we see is not an external world but an image of it and hence an internal world.
>
> (*CPP* 857)

Yet if we appreciate why this idea of an internal world attracts Stevens, we will see the significant role it can play in shaping *The Rock*. Stevens does not stress any kind of perspectivism resulting from this doubling of the world into an internal and external world. For him the prospect of an inner life does not involve each person having his or her own distinctive meanings for experience. Rather, it involves only each person having the capacity to invest different degrees of significance in what everyone can see in common. This feeling of investment lies behind Stevens's sense of artifice. Stevens does not turn to perspectivism in relation to Berkeley is simply because he is more interested in what is shared by each having a perspective than by what differs because of how perspective gets enacted. What we share is a doubled world—a world perceived and a world internalized as an image. This doubling in turn makes for a reality that cannot be reduced to fact but bears the marks of human artifice—as manifestations of power and of need.

This is why the motif of address in "An Old Man Asleep" proves so powerful a figure for the old man's affirmation of his bare existence. Address doubles the scene and calls attention to the forces that give sleeping itself an internal component. Address assumes the old man's capacity of self-reflection, which can affirm his situation and so forge a will that binds the psyche to the necessities of mortality. For Stevens, will is that "principle of the mind's being" that seeks satisfaction in "knowing itself" (*CPP* 648).[4]

II

I will show how this fascination with the inner image as a prime instance of the poetry of philosophy helps us appreciate the conceptual precision and imaginative depth of three innovations that make *The Rock* a different lyric enterprise from what has gone before. I can be brief on the first two innovations because they simply elaborate the implications of what I have been claiming about "An Old Man Asleep." First, Stevens alters his idea of what the image can do in poetry. In his earlier writing, Stevens had been suspicious of the magical thinking involved in the concept of image when poets claimed for it a special capacity to make present the relation between feeling and object. For Stevens, subjective feeling cannot be fully contained in objects because the life of the mind is always in process within and around objects. One can feel participation in the life of objects but not full identification with them. But his thinking about Berkeley showed him that he could talk about the internal image and place all the subject's energies within the object doubled by that internalization. As "An Old Man Asleep" indicates, the internalized sleeping leads us in a very different direction from the ideas of doubling that ground the ironic displacements of self-reflexive fiction. Instead, Stevensian doubling becomes a lyric celebration of the full constructive energies of mind while still securing a claim on the world *as* the mind remembers it. Addressing the old man asleep can involve honoring the exact mirror image of what he and the reader see as a life completely absorbed in fact. Moreover, Penelope's meditating on her image of the sun returning each morning gives it the capacity almost to replace her longed-for Odysseus.

Internalization is also the place of artifice and so the place for registering all the feeling that the art responsible for the sounds of "drowsy" can muster. This means that we can tweak my first claim about innovation to disclose a second. The first involves the doubling of the world so that it can bear the value concerns of specific characters. The second involves the place of artifice in that doubling. Stevens wants a form of objectivity that includes the mind's labor on what it perceives. So he tries on repeated occasions in

The Rock to heal the breach he had developed between copulative verbs establishing stable predicates and verbs elaborating momentary equivalences produced by particular states of mind. The ideal of participation had been one way Stevens could elaborate such states. In *The Rock* Stevens wants not to celebrate participation per se but to imagine elemental forms of life as themselves always already implicated in mind's search for its own center of gravity. He wants in this last work to create lyric situations in which "is" and "as" prove necessary to each other, as if developing resemblances led consciousness back to a version of copulative stability. Stevens imagines that the site of the poem allows a thinking in which the production of resemblances continually reveals an underlying "cure of the ground." By participating in this cure we can see how it is the very productivity of resemblances that allows us to eventually identify with a productive source underlying those resemblances. The poem can explore what is involved in inhabiting a world by virtue of constructing an image for it—think again of what Penelope accomplishes with the sun and what "a rat come out to see" manages to recognize in "The Plain Sense of Things." That stability in turn composes a grander staging of what can be at stake for the mind's confronting and accepting the sense of necessity that lies at the center of the volume's idea of tragic vision.

Finally, there is a larger issue related to how "is" and "as" are treated in a new way. I think *The Rock* alters two of the five fundamental features of aspectual thinking to create a shift in sensibility for which I have to invoke Wittgenstein's treatment of aspect-seeing. For my second feature I emphasized the constant attention to the shifts in sensibility established as the thinking shifted analogical contexts. And for my fifth feature I called attention to how Stevens relies on the performance of such thinking as the exemplary presence with which the reader is invited to share a present-tense engagement in experience. We can combine the two by returning to a passage we discussed from "Notes toward a Supreme Fiction":

> The casual is not
> Enough. The freshness of transformation is
>
> The freshness of a world. It is our own.
> It is ourselves. The freshness of ourselves,
> And that necessity and that presentation
>
> Are rubbings in a glass in which we peer.
> Of these beginnings, gay and green, propose
> The suitable amours. Time will write them down.
>
> *(CPP 344)*

Notice how the mind is always looking at itself as it uses repetitions and analogies to keep modifying its own path. Every shift in direction becomes an opportunity to reflect on the space in which the mind enters. And every reflection becomes the possibility of engaging the forms of release afforded by "these beginnings" in order to identify with the momentary "amours" that they make "suitable."

Then compare "An Old Man Asleep" or "the little by little" through which "the poverty / of autumnal space" expands into "the stale grandeur of annihilation" (*CPP* 430). The focus now is on one extended and elaborated analogy, as if the mind did not need always to begin again but could be fulfilled by reflecting for some time on what one angle on the real could produce. The poems in *The Rock* are less process oriented. They prefer extended analogies that derive from the speaker's seizing on a particular aspect of the scene and developing its possible implications. By taking this stance the sense of someone thinking gives way to a different kind of exemplarity—not the exemplarity of an action but that of an impersonal condition on which the mind is invited to dwell.

I find it useful to invoke Wittgenstein's "seeing as" in order to clarify Stevens's change in his use of analogy. It is highly unlikely that Stevens read Wittgenstein or that he even knew about the philosopher's later writings. Yet I think *The Rock* brings out the poetry in this later philosophical work. For Stevens concentrates on the modes of self-reflection that arise when one meditates on what is involved in seeing one thing as another. Think of Henri Matisse at Vence offering "a new account of everything old" (*CPP* 448) or George Santayana in Rome speaking to his "pillow as if it was yourself. / . . . so that we feel, in this illumined large, / the veritable small" (*CPP* 433). The crucial feature in this new orientation is the replacing of the thinking process with the opportunity to let a single analogy take hold. It turns out that an analogy, like Santayana in his room or Penelope greeting the sun, can itself serve as an exemplar gathering the equivalences in time and quality and mode to which we have been attending.

Because the speaker also becomes a figure for an audience, there is a strong impulse to bring second-order willing and assessing into play differently and more fully than in the play of equivalences. In developing the aspect, the mind gains a position by which it can observe itself appreciating what is involved in producing a new way of seeing. And appreciation need not rest in quasi-passive admiration. Appreciation can become itself an aspect of various second-order acts in which reflection takes on an attitude toward the first-order seeing. Imagine the difference between appreciating what is seen in a situation and actively identifying oneself as a creature committed to this kind of seeing even when the aspects bring out dire aspects of mortality. I hope that by dwelling on the affirming of one's seeing I can show how Stevens comes quite close to Wittgenstein's own contemporaneous efforts to establish a role for personal affirmations about value that have no place in the world available for description. And in Stevens's version of these affirmations he can ultimately turn back to Nietzsche—a master for both thinkers. In *The Rock* Stevens develops a lyrical model by which the Nietzschean dream of the hero affirming necessity becomes an elemental possibility for any consciousness willing to face its own mortality.

III

I imagine that Stevens's late interest in Catholicism derived from the doctrine of incarnation, the belief that the world of grace can be correlated with the world of flesh. But his poems do not promise salvation: they promise only metaphysical reconciliation between necessity and spontaneity and psychological reconciliation between exhaustion of the body and the possibility of self-delight in a mind that can use artifice to establish accord with that body. The sleeping man is completely a part of the scene of exhaustion, while the poem celebrates what poetry can reveal as the value possible in seeing that exhaustion a certain way.

How can I not begin elaborating doubleness in *The Rock* without attending to a two-part poem, in this case a quite bleak one that I imagine poses a challenge for the use of doubling in the other poems? The first part of "Two Illustrations That the World Is What You Make of It" is titled "The Constant Disquisition of the Wind":

The sky seemed so small that winter day,
A dirty light on a lifeless world,
Contracted like a withered stick.

It was not the shadow of cloud and cold,
But a sense of the distance of the sun—
The shadow of a sense of his own,

A knowledge that the actual day
Was so much less. Only the wind
Seemed large and loud and high and strong.

And as he thought within the thought
Of the wind, not knowing that that thought
Was not his thought, nor anyone's,

The appropriate image of himself,
So formed, became himself and he breathed
The breath of another nature as his own,

But only its momentary breath,
Outside of and beyond the dirty light,
That never could be animal,

A nature still without a shape,
Except his own—perhaps, his own
In a Sunday's violent idleness.

                    (CPP 435–36)

This is profoundly the space of art. The sequence of images here begins with particular details but soon modulates, through negation of the force of shadow, into the controlling affective key imposed by "the sense of the distance of the sun." The sun is doubly distant—in space and in the remoteness of this abstract "sense" by which the person finds himself in the world or even as the world. This mode of identity, however, proves only momentary and provisional because it involves only the presence of a thinker. To have a more stable self the poet has to turn to a second-order identification with the violence of the thought's relation to the scene. One gains a stable self here by aligning the self with a constant possibility of the agent's destroying the object world in order to establish the individual's image of that world.

If he is unwilling to accept that uneasy solipsism, Stevens's speaker will have to find some way in which this second-order reflection leads beyond the self to something that can stabilize its permutations without exacting fantasies of destruction. Second-order reflection will have to find substance in the capacity of "seeing as" to get beyond the confines of the needy empirical self. The second section of the poem, "The World Is Larger in Summer," provides a response to that need, but it only deepens the irony. If the thinker ends up caught in an unstable and frustrated sense of inescapable isolation, perhaps a corresponding focus on the artist rather than the thinker will place the powers of making more firmly within the actual world:

He left half a shoulder and half a head
To recognize him in after time.

These marbles lay weathering in the grass . . .

He had said that everything possessed
The power to transform itself, or else,

And what meant more, to be transformed.
He discovered the colors of the moon,

In a single spruce, when, suddenly,
The tree stood dazzling in the air

And blue broke on him from the sun,
A bullioned blue, a blue abulge,

Like daylight, with time's bellishings,
And sensuous summer stood full-height.

The master of the spruce, himself,
Became transformed, but his mastery

Left only the fragments found in the grass,
From his project, as finally magnified.

(CPP 436–37)

Now there is no violence on the part of the ego because it gets absorbed into its own artistic work. The artist escapes solipsism: he composes a reality. But this accomplishment proves no less ironic than the thinker's. This artist begins by discovering the colors of the moon in single spruce, presumably because the darkness of the spruce initially counters the force of the sun. Then the sun's power emerges fully in the blue it confers on the spruce. The contrast between dark and light that the mind composes as one scene comes to constitute the full height of sensuous summer, earning the artist the title of "master of the spruce." Yet the poem wants more than this achieved objectivity. It wants a historical second-order perspective by which one can appreciate one's own achievement. But from the point of view of history, not even the object remains. There are only fragments for this modern Oxymandias.

The ironic force of this second section is concentrated into the question of what is involved in this final line—"his project, as finally magnified." "Project" can refer to either the specific work of art or the overall ambition to be master of the spruce. The "as" phrase nicely picks up this ambiguity. "As finally magnified" can be a narrative judgment, probably proposing an image of personal failure. The historical story is one where art makes no difference in the world except for the loss of the artist's sense of a personal life. But "finally" need not be primarily a narrative operator indicating the last element in a story. The grammar of "as" allows "finally" to serve also as a logical operator indicating that something has at least revealed its true or its elemental form. All the artist's labors can only make survive the realization of how art itself may be able to provide only such fragments of selves and worlds. The alternative to the thinker's violence may be the artist's submission to the violence of history, which leaves only a sense of self reduced to the same fragmentation that the artwork suffers. Yet how do we not wish for what undoes us since the magnifying process may be inseparable from how the mind provides doubles of the world in the first place?

Can there be alternative ways of making investments in an individual's life that are not evasions of this fate? Perhaps it is possible for poetry to show how doubling need not depend on idealizing the role of master—either as thinker or as artist. Perhaps one can treat consciousness as a means of bracketing the self so that it becomes a vehicle for a more generalized human condition of caring for what takes its place as the agent's inner image of the doubled world. Then magnification comes from the reflective process in its quest for the "normal" rather than from the position of an objective observer. This possibility is beautifully presented in how thoroughly "A Quiet Normal Life" seems to be a response to the divisive doubling of "Two Illustrations." Even the title makes a quiet rejoinder to the dark ironies of "Two Illustrations" by playfully accommodating two adjectives that seem somewhat redundant. Then syntax takes over the job of celebrating this quality of expansiveness within a very narrow focus:

> His place, as he sat and as he thought, was not
> In anything that he constructed, so frail,
> So barely lit, so shadowed over and naught,
>
> As, for example, a world in which, like snow,
> He became an inhabitant, obedient
> To gallant notions on the part of cold.
>
> It was here. This was the setting and the time
> Of year. Here in his house and his room,
> In his chair, the most tranquil thought grew peaked
>
> And the oldest and the warmest heart was cut
> By gallant notions on the part of night—
> Both late and alone, above the crickets' chords

Babbling, each one, the uniqueness of its sound.
There was no fury in transcendent forms.
But his actual candle blazed with artifice.

(CPP 443–44)

I do not think there is any better example of a poem able to defend the claim that making and finding can be coextensive (nor any better example of how Stevens now can correlate the image with the presence of active imagination). Moreover, that coextensiveness affords self-consciousness a version of will that exists simply as the inhabiting of the possessive pronoun in the poem's repetition of "his." The basis of this assertion is the work "here" does to define how one can respond to possessing an inner image of a scene. Rather than the divided modes of doubling in "Two Illustrations," Stevens uses the contrast between the first two stanzas to let "here" range over all the capacities of the mind to double what is seen so that the doubling can serve also as a quiet surrogate for the activity of will.

Gallantry comes to fill the scene and require all the force "here" can establish. "Here" in this instance makes present a doubling of the scene within an inner life. Then the agent can feel itself fulfilled in how it comes to dwell in the situation composed by the imagination.[5] Stevens apparently realizes that fleshing out "here" by providing a string of concrete images would be the wrong way to proceed. Such images would only specify the details in the perceived world. It is more important in this poem to see what "here" leads to than to see what it depends on. In that regard, the only relevant particular is how the repetition of "his" incarnates the possessive as continuous with the actual candle.[6] This repetition offers a marvelous way of projecting the potential acts of will that are implicit in the mind's fully fleshing out the feeling of "here." The poem's syntax is the "artifice"; the expansion of the possessive gives the artifice its home. And the compression of the poem stabilizes the "here" by providing a viable habitation for the syntax. The stage for magnification becomes phenomenology and not history.

IV

Doubling emphatically brings out the psychological implications of the imagination's "here." Now it is time to turn to what might be called the ontological implications of this indexical operator. In *The Rock,* Stevens recognizes that so long as he holds to the opposition between "is" and "as" he cannot develop a sufficiently full sense of what it means to engage an actuality that blazes with artifice. Resemblances place that actuality in time and in the psyche. But they do not allow us any general judgments about the nature of the world as given to experience. And that cannot suffice for the aging Stevens. He wants to develop attitudes that engage something like totality for the subject so that it might test what states of will it could inhabit.

Stevens had to challenge the copulative verb in order to show how the perceiver modified the conditions of perception. But the great virtue of resemblances—the freedom they give the agent and the varieties of temporal and spatial relations poetry can engage—was haunted by a perplexing problem. So long as there is the freedom of constant variation, poetry might not have to confront the full pressure of repetition and limitation that refuses to yield to this freedom. (In fact, repetition and limitation often make claims to freedom seem evasive and arbitrary, as in part one of "Two Illustrations.") So Stevens turned instead to the possibility that poetry could treat resemblance as needing an ontological ground, while at the same time it could render that ontological ground as fully significant only as it continually generated resemblances.

Many of the poems in *The Rock* exhibit this effort at reconciliation. I have chosen two that display distinctive ways of handling this effort while offering contrasts in tone and mood. Consider first "Looking across the Fields and Watching the Birds Fly," a celebration of sheer assertion in which figuration explores its own ground. The poem begins as a reporting on one of Mr. Homburg's "irritating minor ideas" (*CPP* 439), but it soon becomes absorbed in its own sequence, so what begins as a "we" claimed by Mr. Homburg eventually assumes the full collective presence in the quoted passage. This transparency then takes on a content simply by virtue of the rhetorical intensity it sustains.

The climax of the poem shifts from the urgencies of thinking about what resists thought to imagining what happens in thinking itself. As we have seen, thinking about thinking in later Stevens tends to take the form of working through resemblances. But now the analogies offer a strange naturalism that reminds us of the effort of the beginning to think away our thinking. So the sheer process of thinking almost literally becomes an aspect of that ground that now manages to find itself inseparable from the process of drawing equivalences:

We think then, as the sun shines or does not.
We think as wind skitters on a pond in a field

Or we put mantles on our words because
The same wind, rising and rising, makes a sound
Like the last muting of winter as it ends. . . .

The spirit comes from the body of the world,
Or so Mr. Homburg thought: the body of a world
Whose blunt laws make an affectation of mind,

The mannerism of nature caught in a glass
And there become a spirit's mannerism,
A glass aswarm with things going as far as they can.

(CPP 440)

I am not sure there can be a richer use of "as" than in this last line. The poem seems to be so successful in its naturalizing the mind that it confidently asserts the power of "blunt laws" to make the mind seem mere affectation. Yet the figure for the figure the mind produces wrests from that conflict a startling image of cooperation. "Things going as far as they can" picks up the "as" in the "glass aswarm." So the poem can suggest that the mirror that doubles the world of things turns out not to be a mere rhetorical mannerism that traps the mind in its own structures. Instead, the mirror brings the mannerism within the life of things "going as far as they can." This is an indefinable limit since the range of things depends on the mirror's capacities at any moment. The mirror remains bound to resemblances and hence to images. But that site of resemblances now has to acknowledge a limit condition. Going as far as they can allows things their maximum potential. Yet the syntax here also captures an indefinable but felt necessity. The poem's final gesture invites us to treat syntax itself as capable of providing a sense of necessity: the limitation of things going as far as they can becomes also the permission for them to take their place in the glass. The giving of permissions and the seizing of advantages can be one.

One might say that the cure of the ground in "Looking across the Fields" is contained primarily in the scope of this ending, with its combination of expansiveness and limitation. "Lebensweisheitspielerei" offers a resolution that is both quieter and darker, but these tonal properties offer an even grander scope and sense of necessity:[7]

Weaker and weaker the sunlight falls
In the afternoon. The proud and the strong
Have departed.

Those that are left are the unaccomplished,
The finally human,
Natives of a dwindled sphere.
Their indigence is an indigence
That is an indigence of the light,
A stellar pallor that hangs on the threads.

Little by little, the poverty
Of autumnal space becomes
A look, a few words spoken.

Each person completely touches us
With what he is and as he is,
In the stale grandeur of annihilation.

(CPP 429–30)

In fifteen lines this poem moves from the collapse of any traditional notion of heroism to what seems the idealism of the total realist finding in "as" a reason to respect and revere the possibilities of sheer description. The total autumn scene requires an audience willing to accept so limited a humanity that its members can adapt entirely to a "dwindled sphere" almost without desire. But by their adapting to that space, gradually a minor miracle occurs. The scene itself comes to speak, so well suited is it to its inhabitants. Finally, each person completely touches us, not through the person's speech but by the sheer condition of existence become articulate through the poem. Here "what he is" requires for that articulation all the mobility in time and space of this marvelous "as." Now no voice says, "I am as I am." There is no first-person presence. But "as" does not need the first person; in this poem it needs only a description to adapt to. In this case "as" provides the adaptability to keep the person and the scene infinitely matched, and infinitely capable of a present tense in which to adjust that matching.

That copresence of existence and adaption, that doubling in space and in time, cannot ultimately stop with description. The most impressive achievement of this poem is its capacity to turn complete adaptability to poverty into a cause for lyrical celebration. But the celebration cannot be a matter of eloquence in syntax or in diction because traditional eloquence would belie the poverty. So Stevens finds a source of lyricism by which to celebrate artifice without imposing sensuous images that might sustain such eloquence. He achieves this with one of his finest sonic effects (that almost goes too far in its celebration of itself). The assonance in "stale grandeur" in itself would make the point. But making the point is not quite the point. The point is to exceed the semantic statement while finding an equivalence in artifice that can coexist as a measure of satisfaction with the entire vision of necessity. So the poem adds "annihilation." This word not only extends the assonance of long *a* sound of its penultimate syllable but also picks up the "in" and develops an intricate alliteration with three of the main consonants in "stale grandeur." Sound itself here provides an intricate asness that is completely capable of fleshing out how poverty can be inhabited without denying the facts that justify the description.

V

This compression also establishes the most visible manifestation of what has changed in Stevens's understanding of aspectual thinking. The phenomenon I have been calling aspectual thinking does not, for Stevens, depend on the actual developing of aspects. It is not Wittgensteinian. Rather, it is based primarily on the grammar of "as" and the opportunities that grammar offers for the lyric to turn from envy of the copulative to an embrace of resemblance as its constitutive stance toward the world. The situation changes when Stevens decides to return to a more dramatic lyric style that can force the mind to face bare simplicities—in this case the pressure to adapt oneself to the limitations imposed by age. *Auroras* required coming to terms with suffering and loss. *The Rock* requires a more personal and abstract sense of how to handle the sense of necessity that drives those tragic feelings. This demand elicits something different from a poetry of constant process elaborating equivalences *as* they arise. It requires finding the minimal degree of artifice possible to celebrate a stripped-down sense of personal powers nonetheless sufficiently compelling to make affirming one's entire state a plausible imaginative condition. Where aspectual thinking calls for the developing of resemblances, aspect-seeing calls for an extended elaboration of one mode of comparison.

Stevens finds this minimal degree of artifice in modes of action that parallel Wittgenstein's brilliant meditation on aspect-seeing. One need only recall the power of the shift to address in "An Old Man Asleep" or the shift in "Lebensweisheitspielerei" to the man "as he sat and as he thought" to indicate the promise of elaborating this connection. Aspect-seeing puts the mind actively in the world and allows it indirect access to its own powers and needs. And that in turn provides a means for interpreting how Stevens raises concerns for will and affirmation in his last volume. Aspects depend on equivalence. But they are parts of the world, not evasions of "as," and so they invite staging second-order relationships toward this world.

Even most philosophers (with the exception of John Verdi) treat aspect-seeing simply as a kind of pragmatic awareness of how changes in context involve changes in what counts as description and possible evaluations. But I think there is a rich and perspicuous model of human values and their place in a phenomenology of experience suggested in part II of Wittgenstein's *Philosophical Investigations,* his most extended reflection on the topic.[8] Let us therefore pursue a series of questions raised by Wittgenstein's analyses. Why is it philosophically interesting that we can say of a certain object that we see it as a duck or as a rabbit? More pertinent to poetry, why might it matter to see kindness in a face or irritation in a stance or a sudden sense that one sees in one face traces of another? Finally, how can literary criticism adapt Wittgenstein's question—what would one be missing if one were "aspect blind" and so could not recognize at all the possibility of seeing something as something else? What else could the person not do or not be aware of? What human practices would make no sense and have no appeal? Could there be any practice like the writing and reading of poetry for the aspect blind?

It is helpful here to begin with the clearest instance of how seeing an aspect of an object might be different from our typical models of perception (including Stevens's problematic idea of an inner image for outer perception). Seeing a duck or a rabbit in the same image is not quite a matter of interpretation. In fact, this case suggests the limitations of that standard model for making inferences from objects of perception. Neither the "choice" of alternatives in the duck-rabbit case nor the alternatives posed by the Necker cube involve adding an interpretation to an object that exists independently of what we come to see. The aspect is not something added to the world by the mind so much as a particular point of access that realizes a feature of the world otherwise doomed to go unnoticed.[9] When we see a figure as a duck or as a rabbit, we are not projecting meanings on it but engaging particular features of what is available to everyone's sight. Aspect-seeing opens a path of possible expectations aligned with what arises for perception.

The case of "seeing in" by "seeing as"—for example by seeing kindness in a face—is more problematic because one cannot simply deny that this is a case of seeing the face and interpreting it. But buoyed by the duck-rabbit model, we can suggest that the interpretation model is only one possibility, only one way of making a double of the world by the mind. In the interpretation model there is an object or a situation to which we give meaning and so allow it to play a role in our lives. The alternative is that there is here not a speculative interpretation but a change in affect that parallels what becomes a change in one's world. By this account we propose to others that we can find our affective expectations justified by how the face comes to appear. The interpretation model assumes that there is one real face and a set of inferences or constructions. It seems more ontologically generous to imagine all the variations of the face that are available to public vision are equally real, in part because then our response is also to something not of our own making. We do not interpret the face as friendly but respond to friendliness and judge whether that way of acting seems appropriate. And then our response need not be primarily in the domain of ideas. It can be an expression of feeling, or what Wittgenstein scholars call an avowal drawing out the affective implications of an encounter.

For me the deciding factor is that one who is aspect blind can still interpret faces. But that person cannot see the face as suddenly changing expression. Therefore he or she cannot offer a different mode of relation by which immediately to align with and pursue that connection. So we best make sense of aspect-seeing when we shift from the nature of the object to the expectations subjects display when they respond as if the expression were an actual mode of being in the world. By this shift we also come to a richer interpretation of why Stevens in *The Rock* pursues the combination of elemental situations he does. It is as if seeing so elementally allows one to offer direct assessments of what in those situations demands conditions of active responsiveness. He wants situations that elicit emotional states and create a stage for reflecting on what can be involved in those states *as* they become self-conscious.

Consider an exclamation as a condensed version of what Wittgenstein calls "the dawning of an aspect": "If I let my gaze wander round a room and suddenly it lights on an object of striking red colour, and I say 'Red!'—that is not a description" (*PI* 187). (One could develop a parallel explanation in relation to my last paragraph by substituting "Friend!" for "Red!") We could offer a Heideggerean reading of this contrast between description and recognition of the emergence of the liveliness of the color. But then we would be stuck with an inflated language about the object in terms of "self-blossoming emergence." And we would gain no access for talking about either agency or language. So it seems preferable to follow Wittgenstein's speculative practicality on what exclamation involves.

From this perspective we would have to ask how such actions complicate our ideas of what is involved in carrying out a range of human practices. Minimally, such attention enables us to ward off reductive languages about how humans experience the world. We gain the possibility of not interpreting exclamation in light of some theory of behavior but rather of simply treating exclamation seriously as one of the acts human beings perform or, better, as one of the language games for which they recognize the values involved, especially when poetry calls our attention to them.[10] That capacity to resist reductionism is one basic reason the dawning of aspects is of considerable interest to poets: these aspects manage to embed expressive energies in the actual world in such ways as to invite our continually modifying our modes both of reflecting and of feeling. The subject of the exclamation is not just seeing red but also ready to act upon that seeing.

Then there is a second, even stronger capacity Wittgenstein's analysis affords for resisting reductionism. When subjects make investments in caring that the world has appeared in a certain way, they cease to be mere observers because they are ready to provide some kind of account of that investment. A person might just love that shade of red, or the red reminds the person of certain situations or elicits attention for more complex visual links in the scene. Aspect-seeing offers the minimal model of artifice at work—so minimal that it need not be attributed to will at all unless there is a second-order dimension where one reflects on where the presence of artifice positions the self.

This way of calling attention to a person's stakes in the dawning of aspects takes on its full significance (at least for me) if we follow Wittgenstein for one more step. The step is a philosophically crucial one because it is one of his clearest formulations of why he is unsatisfied by empiricist and positivist ways of dealing with human experience. I think of the following passage in Wittgenstein's *Investigations* as a minimalist poem about what cannot be captured by description and so needs the language of expression and hence of at least a minimal inner life:

> I say "Do *this,* and you'll get it." Can't there be a doubt here? Mustn't there be one, if it is a feeling that is meant?
> *This* looks *so;* this tastes so, *this* feels *so.* "This" and "so" must be differently explained."

> (*PI* 186)

The different explanation is required because "so" here has important affinities with the dawning of an aspect: "do this and you'll get it" is comparable to "find a way of looking at the object of attention in a particular way."

The source of the difference between explaining "this" and explaining "so" is a grammatical one. "Feels" in the sense the sentence gives it involves a language game different from the apparent form of description the sen-

tence seems to take at first. Initially we have to interpret "this" as a demonstrative referring to some observable particular. But the phrase as a whole
gives immense force to "so" as the complement of "feels." Therefore the
sentence requires recasting the force of "this." Only a "this" specified inten-
sionally by the subject's rendering of his act of seeing can flesh out "so"
because that task calls not for description but for illustrating how the situation becomes important for the agent. And once the agent takes on this
degree of importance for determining the sense of "so," there must be doubt
that one agent can understand what the other feels. At the least, there can be
no argument that could show the way for them to reach agreement. Instead,
what agreement is possible depends on each trying to display what "feels so"
involves. One could say that the exchange now is not of descriptions but of
efforts to make sense of what human beings are doing in specific situations.

Were we to make a theoretical argument, we could use this moment in
Wittgenstein's text to show why particularity is crucial to art and indeed to
life. There is simply nothing to be explained in general terms: the individual
act is all that can be fleshed out if we want to elaborate what "so" means in
relation to the dawning of this aspect. And we could use this account of
"feels so" to show how the building of models that display rather than explain such dawnings proves a crucial alternative to the role of argument in
social life. The arts matter because expression is central in life as well as in
art, and the practices it involves do not invite argumentative generalizations.
Stevens does not use this language, but I think his model of expressive activity warrants our going farther with Wittgenstein before we try to draw
consequences from the parallels.

In the quotation we are considering, there are two crucial differences
from any account of perception followed by interpretation in discursive
terms. First, there is the sense that the dawning of an aspect is best conceived
as an event in the domain of feeling—that is why "so" cannot be explained
as if it could be treated as an object. Then there is the question of what can
serve as an explanation for "so." This will involve the concepts of building
a model, confession, and style—all matters of how expressions take on a
worldly content while resisting argument as the means for sustaining the
importance of that content.

For Wittgenstein, when I say "I am in pain," I am typically not showing
where it hurts but am avowing that pain and asking you to recognize that
my life is altered by it. I want your sympathy or help, not just your agreeing
or disagreeing with the hypothesis that pain is present in a particular place.
Similarly, if I say "I hope he will come," I am not referring to an inner hope

but simply letting you know my state as one of expectation. Then once we recognize that making pictures that refer to the world is not the only way we communicate, we can recognize other roles we ask language to play that can be just as intelligible as pictures. When we deal with aspects like the schematic cube and want to find out "what someone else sees, I can get him to make a model of what he sees, in addition to a copy, or to point to such a model" (*PI* 196.) We can build models that display the state we are in, just as we can compose pictures whose role is to tell me something consisting "in its own structure, in *its* own lines and colors" (*PI* 523).

The crucial point is that once we say we need a different explanation for "so," we also need a different method for applying that explanation. That is why the idea of making a model is inseparable from how we deal with the dawning of aspects. Now the important question becomes, what can models show—in life and in art or in casting the theory of poetry as the theory of life? Wittgenstein's thinking here sets display, and hence Kant's "presentation," against representation without treating the arts as somehow autonomous and irrelevant to the theory of life. Minimally, a model for the dawning of an aspect provides a framework for valuing momentary shifts in perspective, as if we could see our actual candle blaze with artifice. Or, to come closer to Stevens, these analyses involve the possibility not just of capturing images but also of producing a sense of value for them that honors their particularity. Yet because building models is involved, that particularity can be treated as exemplary of a way of seeing and so take on substantial public import.

Artworks can be models for the dawning of aspects. But most models for the dawning of aspects confine themselves to clarifying what is at stake in a particular expression. The model of models may not go far enough in satisfying possible interests regarding why an agent would develop this specific avowal as a response to the dawning of the aspect. The particular model helps us engage what the agent sees but does not give enough information about the participation of the agent's emotions in what is seen. And it does not allow a sufficient measure of the urgencies or scope of concern that the agent might reveal in second-order reflections. This is one reason that Wittgenstein developed a concept of "confession," which he was reluctant to employ philosophically because its use is to indicate the importance of a religious domain for our most fundamental choices, such as those involving concerns for authenticity.[11] Confession is the effort to make display function in much more capacious ways than in characterizing the dawning of single aspects. But confession is neither an argument nor a description of the self. It is the presentation of the deep concerns held by the self in contexts that insist on their singularity so that the agent can seek something closer to sympathy and indulgence than discursive understanding:

> The criteria for the truth of the *confession* that I thought such and such are not the criteria for a true *description* of a process. And the importance of the true confession does not reside in its being a correct and certain report of a process. It resides rather in the special consequences which can be drawn from a confession whose truth is guaranteed by the special criteria of *truthfulness*.[12]

> (*PI* 222)

The best analogy for confession in *The Rock* is the display of intimate involvement in extending the impact of aspect-seeing. That intimacy helps us focus on the personal stance making implicit judgments about the significance of the particular action displayed. The values at stake are not argued for. Rather, the reader is invited to ask why it might matter to see in a certain way and how we might value the stance toward experience that the seeing embodies. Indeed, the poems seem to involve a religious quest for ultimate meanings. It is by no means clear that the pressure the poet puts on the poems could be relieved by the answers proposed within traditional religious faiths. But it is clear that the poems we have been dealing with and will deal with in this chapter seek attitudes capable of responding to concerns that the world is a source of unrelenting pain and disappointment, lit by moments of grace. How can we find a mode of will to acceptance and even affirmation that is not the will to pleasure or the will to power?

VI

There is considerable second-order work in the end of "Lebensweisheitspielerei" because the poem so actively affirms its readiness to accept necessity. But I want to close with two poems that offer a fuller elaboration of hearing themselves find a way of treating "is" and "as" as necessary doubles of each other. I want to show how the entire process of aspect-seeing not only governs many of the poems but also becomes the center of an interpretation, or perhaps even a confession, of why Stevens thinks that way of seeing can matter for our sense of values. My choice of the poems to discuss has been a difficult one because there is a subgenre of poems in *The Rock* that all represent what I am after. This subgenre consists of poems that focus on specific characters seen from a respectful meditative distance, like "To an Old Philosopher in Rome" and "St. Armorer's Church from the Outside," as well as poems that represent particular persons in reflective states—quintessentially "Final Soliloquy of the Interior Paramour," but also "The World as Meditation." And then there is the magnificent reflection on the entire volume provided by "The Plain Sense of Things," which requires only a slight exaggeration to put the rat who comes out to see in the same class as Santayana and Penelope. I have settled on the last two of the poems that I have mentioned because they allow me to construct a dialogue between the sun and the rat.[13]

"The World as Meditation" begins with a passage of free indirect discourse offering Penelope's sense of the sun's "savage presence" as its form of fire approaches her cretonnes. This awakens her by also standing in for her intense hopes that her husband will return just as the sun does. Two stanzas suffice to spell out how Penelope lives in a doubled world, where the repetition of the sun's arrival brings more than hope for the singular event of her husband's return. Instead of an abstract hope, the sun brings a literal version of his presence, so absolutely does she see it as a version of the satisfaction he would bring. But here Stevens seems interested in the character of the speaker and not just in the quality of her reflections. Short, indicative sentences that forego syntactic pyrotechnics render Penelope's straightforward determination. Then the kind of intimacy that stems from identifying with a character's syntax allows Stevens also to develop projections that involve her state of will. He can appreciate what it takes to find satisfaction within oppressive conditions:

> She has composed, so long, a self with which to welcome him,
> Companion to this self for her, which she imagined,
> Two in a deep-founded sheltering, friend and dear friend.
>
> The trees had been mended, as an essential exercise
> In an inhuman meditation, larger than her own.
> No winds like dogs watched over her at night.
>
> She wanted nothing he could not bring her by coming alone.
> She wanted no fetchings. His arms would be her necklace
> And her belt the final fortune of their desire.
>
> But was it Ulysses, or was it only the warmth of the sun
> On her pillow? The thought kept beating in her like her heart.
> The two kept beating together. It was only day.

It was Ulysses and it was not. Yet they had met,
Friend and dear friend in a planet's encouragement.
The barbarous strength within her would never fail.

She would talk a little to herself as she combed her hair,
Repeating his name with its patient syllables,
Never forgetting him that kept coming constantly so near.

                                                        (CPP 442)

For me the most striking feature of these lines is how the syntax takes up past-perfect tenses in order to capture what for her is the basic condition of her plight—its condemnation to the same repeated desire for an end of repetition that would be Ulysses's homecoming. Through those tenses Stevens manages two fundamental achievements. First, he transforms Penelope's quest by in effect knowing her better than she knows herself. Her deep quest is not for change—that would be to succumb to romantic models of desire. Rather, she wants ultimately to come to complete terms with necessity, the necessity of loss and the necessity of repetition by which the sun reminds her of her loss. Only by accepting necessity will she be able to see the sun in another way. The sun can be transformed to become a mark of a quotidian reality with sufficient strength and intimacy for her to realize that "the barbarous strength within her would never fail."

The second achievement is more abstract. The three verbs "would be," "would never fail," and "would talk" seem intricately appropriate in a poem ultimately about time and projected identification. The first two have to be in the subjunctive; I do not know how to characterize the grammatical function of the third. Each verb has a different valence. The first "would" is pure wish. The second has the ring of something like a confident, indicative assertion about the future. In fact, it becomes a counterpart to "has composed" and "had been mended," as if the sense of the future was built on an awareness of what her persistence might have earned her. Although I cannot adequately characterize the grammatical function of the third "would," I think I can appreciate its affective role in the poem. "She would talk a little to herself as she combed her hair" expresses repetition in the past. But it also builds on that past to combine wish and fact as a condition shaping her future actions. This third "would' takes Penelope out of past time and provides a present and future with which the speaker can identify. Now what matters is her waiting under a new dispensation—not a waiting marked by loss so much as an adaption to what her intimacy with the sun promises for the future. Then "never forgetting him that kept coming constantly so near" does a marvelous syntactic and semantic job of transforming the situation from a narrative to a second-order willing of what she can project as her future. "Forgetting" modifies "she." But because it is the second participle, it has much of the effect of an absolute construction. Here that effect frees the poem from the past as burden, just as the last clause builds on what is close to a double negative in order to let the present and the future stand out.[14] The poem does not pursue intimacy with Penelope because of her state of desire so much as because of what she makes of that desire. The poem begins with a question and ends with this positive double negative, which allows her to align herself with something very close to Nietzsche's eternal return of the same. The fantasy of Ulysses shapes a consciousness that can find contentment in the simplest features of the sun because she knows now what desires such recurrence can satisfy. And that contentment marks a state of will surprising and compelling in its absolute concreteness. One need not go through humanist models of decision making to convince an audience that one has staked oneself deliberately on a direction for one's life.

VII

All the motifs of this chapter come together most fully in two gestures. The first is the kind of choice of the actual world and its spiritual double at the end of "To an Old Philosopher in Rome":

> It is a kind of total grandeur at the end,
> With every visible thing enlarged and yet
> No more than a bed, a chair and moving nuns, . . .
>
> Total grandeur of a total edifice
> Chosen by an inquisitor of structures
> For himself. He stops upon this threshold,
> As if the design of all his words takes form
> And frame from thinking and is realized.
>
> *(CPP 434)*

The second is the kind of "as" that concludes "The Plain Sense of Things." Both poems have been carefully read by many of Stevens's critics, so I have little to add to our knowledge of either. But clarifying that "as" will afford a more concrete foundation of the nature of the willing in *The Rock* than will whatever I can say about the grand theatrical peroration on Santayana's choice of a life and a death.[15] So I turn to "The Plain Sense of Things."[16] It provides a powerful second-order aspect of a process of "seeing as" that is asked to reconcile will and necessity:

> After the leaves have fallen, we return
> To a plain sense of things. It is as if
> We had come to the end of the imagination,
> Inanimate in an inert savoir.
>
> It is difficult even to choose the adjective
> For this blank cold, this sadness without cause.
> The great structure has become a minor house
> No turban walks across the lessened floors.
>
> The greenhouse never so badly needed paint.
> The chimney is fifty years old and slants to one side.
> A fantastic effort has failed, a repetition
> In a repetitiousness of men and flies.
>
> Yet the absence of imagination had
> Itself to be imagined. The great pond,
> The plain sense of it, without reflections, leaves,
> Mud, water like dirty glass, expressing silence
>
> Of a sort, silence of a rat come out to see,
> The great pond and its waste of lilies, all this
> Had to be imagined as an inevitable knowledge,
> Required, as a necessity requires.
>
> *(CPP 428)*

The best way to see what is distinctive in this poem is to contrast it with "The Snow Man." That poem had two basic commitments, starkly realized. One was to define as cleanly as possible a world reduced to what demands "a mind of winter." The other was to make manifest the continuing presence of some kind of synthetic force that in fact could serve as the minding of that winter because it has the power to contain the entire scene in an elaborate single sentence. "The Plain Sense of Things" offers neither that concentrated reduction of the scene nor that particular model of compositional power. Instead, the pacing is much slower, the language no longer driven by a single syntactic structure. Why? What about the absence of imagination can Stevens render in this mode that he could not in the earlier poem?

Both poems treat the "inert savoir" as if it were a response to the world in which it is impossible for adjectives to enhance being: being seems deprived of any qualities that relieve its absolute thereness. "The Plain Sense of Things" also has to contend with a sense of history ("a fantastic effort has failed") that prevents it from realizing the kind of timeless present tense established by the single synthetic sentence in "The Snow Man." So in the later poem the mind keeps on doing the work of comparison, unwilling or unable to give up on the possibility of still being able to choose adjectives even if they have to take negative form. Notice how in the beginning the focus is not on an observed scene but on trying to characterize the act of seeing. And even when the adjectives fail, the mind seems capable of varying the modes of "seeing as" by which it views this bleakness. At this negative center, even the silence turns out to elicit analogies.

None of these analogies has transformative power. Yet the entire series makes the absence of imagination less a fact to be registered than a transcendental condition to be inhabited by second-order reflection on what a way of thinking elicits. After choice is mentioned, the poem turns swiftly to the transformation of a "great structure" into a "minor house," a measuring of loss that soon generates a strange form of negation: "no turban walks across the lessened floors." Then there is a second comparison based on physical observation, and finally a bleak generalization about failure that in its turn generates further comparatives. Negatives populate scenes so that we can feel a nonpresence within them, but with none of the violence that we examined with previous instances of negation. Then with the abstract statement that "the absence of imagination had / Itself to be imagined," the mind tries to articulate its own heightened response to what turn out to be its own figures.

By the time the poem utters this abstract generalization, it is putting into the mode of necessity what it had already discovered on the order of simple description. It is entering the domain where will is called upon to make some kind of decision in relation to what is described. The discursive mode has to handle a shift from describing a situation to describing a mental state, while simultaneously maintaining the same distance and flatness it had directed toward the scene. Stevens's response to that challenge is magnificent. He turns to "the great pond, the plain sense of it," even though no pond has been mentioned. Consequently, the pond hovers between one imagined as actual and one that exists primarily as part of a metaphor for how the absence of imagination can be imagined. Projected description and self-referential metaphoric reach become strangely identical.

This identity is celebrated in the great figure of the "rat come out to see." Again the rat could be part of the imagined scene. But it also could be the mind's figure for its own pushing itself on the scene so as to find ways to figure the absence of imagination. Such doubleness provides a strange, otherworldly concreteness for the imagination. The rat parallels the mind's uncomfortable but somehow fated presence as witness to this desolation and as one more feature of the desolation that has to be imagined. In fact, appreciating the rat requires that one recognize why any analogue with a human observer would limit the poem. Confronted with this scene, the most the mind can do is compose an emblem for its own estrangement in a bizarrely intimate way. By having a figure for aspect-seeing that is also a figure of nonidentity with the self, the poem can encompass the scope of the poverty it confronts. Yet for this knowledge to take hold the poem also has to go beyond the figure of the rat to a more capacious mode of agency. The rat is a figure for contingency. The mind happens to come upon its way of seeing as just a contingent moment in this contingent world. But that level of contingency will not justify the poem's sense of poverty.

A full sense of dispossession requires something like the figure of necessity. Our being bound to that contingency seems not contingent at all: all this *had* to be imagined. And now self-consciousness has to grapple to hold in one thought both contingency and necessity. This is clearly a task for an imagination that is not put off by equivocation and contradiction. Imagination even has to develop a sufficiently broad view able to replace the rat's vision with a far more capacious relation to the impoverished scene. Needing to pursue a plain sense of things in this most unplain way is the price we pay for having the investments we do in recognizing and appreciating our situations. But this price seems worth paying, so long as we can imagine that such imagining provides an instrument for coming to terms with a fatality too comprehensive and abstract to be engaged by discursive reasoning. Figures are absolutely necessary for dealing with the plainest possible sense of things. And figures require a version of agency capable of directing these figures—both cognitively and affectively—hence the role that the second-order considerations about consciousness have to play in the poem.

"The Snow Man" could rely on its single sentence in order to establish how the mind might be adequate even to this bleak situation. Ultimately, a practical lucidity is possible. In "The Plain Sense of Things," the situation is quite different. There remains a parallel movement toward containing and recasting the series of reflections elicited by the plain sense of things. But even a mobile Stevensian sentence is not the appropriate vehicle. Rather than rely on a single sentence, this poem can only prevent the absence from dominating the sense of imagination by bringing to bear what for Stevens is a new use of equivalences. I know of no other place in Stevens where the subject of the "as" clause treats the relevant form of equivalence as an abstract noun.

Stevens has to be abstract here because he does not want to draw an equivalence with any concrete image. That would not be sufficiently general. It would not get beyond the mode of "seeing as" contributed by the rat. "As" itself turns out to have the power to engage the second-order task of characterizing the significance of how one sees what one sees in the landscape—not as the rat sees contingently but as the mind sees in terms of inescapable conditions. The equivalence "as" produces in time forces the agent to become a participant in what necessity requires. And the equivalences "as" produces in quality allow us both to name this bleakness and to identify with the metaphysical qualities that identification brings into focus. Our thinking and our figuring all become aspects of our recognizing that we are not so much describing the absence of imagination as ritually manifesting where we are positioned when we make that attempt. Here "as a necessity requires" is not simply a practical observation because "requires" takes on the cast of logical discovery grounded in poetic process. It turns out that the present tense of experience produced by the "as" clause cannot be separated from the eternal present of logical form.

Our sense of this ability for reasoning at this point in the poem proves most important for its giving sharp content to the "we" that begins as only a hopeful assertion in the poem's first stanza. This "we" evokes the ego's power to adjust to necessity, and it embodies the power to feel what one shares with others even as one is most sharply confronted with one's own isolation. The capacity to generalize proves inseparable from the second-order ability to see that it takes such an abstract mode of statement to stage the absence of imagination in its full theatrical presence. (One's own absence of imagination would be banal in comparison.) Yet for all this generalization, this power can be realized only by the individual's accepting the condition of our fully fleshing out the possibilities that "as" produces—namely that each of us aligns with the sense of necessity. "All this" parallels the function of the single sentence in "The Snow Man." It gathers the situation and simultaneously offers itself as provocation to take responsibility for the poverty involved by finding figures for everything the plain sense affords. Perhaps philosophy has found its own poetry in this demand to find a will capable of bearing the poverty of truth. The final figures give the feeling for what the scene had lacked—not as a fiction but as a bleak assessment that satisfies because it intensifies the level of sheer fact that can be taken into intimate being. That may be all that is left viable as a concept of the will, and it may suffice.

VIII

Stevens came to suspect modernist styles had become little more than means by which poets and painters without much talent hid their lack of originality in a difficult inventiveness.[17] Such art seemed to him willing to sacrifice the possibility of helping audiences "realize" what the necessary poverty of their lives might nonetheless afford them. Yet he remained an exemplary modernist in two important ways. The first is stylistic. He never wavered in the idea that poems are not rhetorical exercises in argument or in manipulating scenic details to elicit strong dramatic emotions. Poems are objective displays of acts of mind attempting to make concrete the processes of feeling that occur as we shift our positions in the world and toward the world. Ultimately, for Stevens modernist display could give us access to an activity of a central imagination inviting the participation of individual audience members.

The second way is his capacity to define a sensibility that would fully emerge only in philosophical work challenging the priority of epistemic and hence empiricist models of value—from Wittgenstein to Sartre, Cavell, and MacDowell. The great American modernists—Eliot, Pound, Williams, Crane, Loy, and Moore—all make central in their work the need to reconcile the powers of imagination with a recalcitrant and fundamentally alienating object world. Their nineteenth-century predecessors dreamed that somehow a stance toward knowledge would release the possibility of an inner harmony between at least the needs of mind for a home and the needs of the world for being seen in a way that it could be valued. For the modernists, no change in vision was possible to produce that harmony unless it could foster a cure of the self that would also become a cure of the ground. Eliot's conversion was repugnant to most of his peers. But it defined the ultimate logic of their enterprise. The world could open itself to being valued only if we brought a new way of looking at it; no mode of descriptive realism could sufficiently address our needs and our anxieties. Realism for modernity was inescapably a condition of all significant writing. But it could serve only as necessary condition, not as a sufficient condition for any making manifest of what spirit might become.

Harmonium was a great book exploring the fundamental tensions between an impoverished world that would not yield meaningfulness and an imagination that would not submit to any authority except the will to invention. Stevens's subsequent intense and capacious effort to escape those binaries relied on a conceptually sophisticated and imaginatively engaging sense of the powers of negation to force the recognition that bourgeois identity thinking simply could not produce any sense of values not limited to individual pleasures and release from need. But this sense of the negative itself had to be explained. Where did it get its energy, and why did it betray a persistent idealistic quest for states that humans could not adapt to practical life yet treat as satisfying in themselves? This is the underlying logic for his developing the fiction of "major man."

Stevens then realized that despite the problems this fiction caused in making connections to actual historical existence, it did not have quite to be rejected. It could be modified by ceasing to isolate this sense of creative power. This sense of creative power could be put within conditions of daily encounter with the recalcitrant facts of experience. Perhaps rather than project possible identification with the inner life of this heroic mode of existence, the poet could imagine a more mundane but also more constant participation in the forces abstracted by the figure of major man. The poet could give constant vitality to a will to change persisting within the fixed world of bourgeois practices. This, I think, was the cure of the ground promised by the ideal of participation and the activity of the play of equivalences.

The Rock staged itself as not satisfied by the poetics of participation. In its emphasis on living in change, this poetic stance risked forgetting just how much our lives have to face a condition that requires a different kind of imagination. In order to appreciate fully why and how change seems so vital we have also to have imagination realize how "the absence of imagination had itself to be imagined." Imagination had to learn to look at itself not as the power that drives art but as the source of artifice by which life manages to look at itself and then not look away. Then imagination can will that poverty as the condition of recognizing how its own activity binds itself to the world, as the world solicits a meaning into which it "wanted to enter" (*CPP* 438):

> The way some first thing coming into Northern trees
> Adds to them the whole vocabulary of the South,
> The way the earliest single light in the evening sky, in spring,
> Creates a fresh universe out of nothingness by adding itself,
> The way a look or a touch reveals its unexpected magnitudes.
>
> *(CPP 439)*

I love Stevens for taking us on this journey, for making that journey sensually and intellectually exciting, for not lying to us along the way, and for making it still possible to care about our own caring for the conditions that define our lives.

NOTES

Chapter 1: Philosophical Poetry and the Demands of Modernity

1. Bart Eeckhout, "Stevens and Philosophy," in *The Cambridge Companion to Wallace Stevens*, ed. John Serio, 109 (New York: Cambridge University Press, 2007). In criticizing the standard idea of Stevens's emphasis on epistemic issues I am pleased to ally myself with, I think, the best commentator on Stevens's poetics, Simon Critchley, *Things Merely Are: Philosophy in the Poetry of Wallace Stevens* (London: Routledge, 2005). I argue later with how Critchley reads the poems of *The Rock*.

2. Julianne Buchsbaum, "The Never-Ending Meditation: Wallace Stevens' 'An Ordinary Evening in New Haven' and Pragmatic Theories of Truth," *Wallace Stevens Journal* 32 (1) (2008): 94. I take my description of pragmatism as adapting nineteenth-century antifoundational strategies from Louis Menand's absorbing *The Metaphysical Club: A Story of Ideas in America* (New York: Farrar, Strauss, and Giroux, 2001).

3. Joseph Riddel, "Metaphoric Staging: Stevens' Beginning Again of the 'End of the Book,'" in *Wallace Stevens: A Celebration*, ed. Frank Doggett and Robert Buttel, 308–38 (Princeton, NJ: Princeton University Press). This is J. Hillis Miller's version of the same theme: "To identify this disrupting element in Stevens' poetry, if it is neither imitation nor 'Being' nor merely the play of language, would require a full reading of his work. Even then it may be that the identification would be a discovery of what cannot be named or identified in so many words, even figurative ones" (284). See "Theoretical and Atheoretical in Stevens," in Doggett and Buttel, *Wallace Stevens* (274–85).

4. See, for example, Krzysztof Ziarek's keen philosophical essay, "'Without Human Meaning': Stevens, Heidegger, and the Foreignness of Poetry," in *Wallace Stevens across the Atlantic*, ed. Bart Eeckhout and Edward Ragg, 79–94 (London: Palgrave Macmillan, 2008): "One can say, then, that Stevens' poems through their multiple registers . . . endeavor to understand, and to say how things are. What demarcates Stevens' approach is that he does not see beings as objects to be known, represented or described poetically; but instead accentuates their elusive manner of being" (81). Ziarek is not quite a deconstructionist, but he reads Heidegger to accord with deconstructive ontology and the ethics of "letting be." I argue for honoring Stevens's interest in metaphysics, in "Stevens and the Crisis of European Philosophy," in Eeckhout and Ragg, *Wallace Stevens across the Atlantic*, 61–78, note 2.

5. The book that follows will pursue in my own fashion Lensing's fundamental question in his *Wallace Stevens and the Seasons* (Baton Rouge: Louisiana State University Press, 2001): "How, his poems ask over and over again, can I possess the other as the *human* presence is made over into the other of the world? How can I possess her/it in such a way as to escape betrayal and disappointment" (4).

And this is Vendler in *Wallace Stevens: Words Chosen out of Desire* (Knoxville: University of Tennessee Press, 1984) on the opposition in Stevens between imagination and reality: "The cause of setting the two at odds is usually, in Stevens' case, passionate feeling, and not merely epistemological query" (10). And then on style: "It is one of Stevens' claims to greatness that he went on to invent a new style—the style of parts as parts, of words refusing to form a single word, of the many truths not part of 'a' truth, the style of many of the most interesting later poems" (19–22).

This attention to style leads her to what is after fifty years probably still the most sensitive attention to the large-scale shifts in Stevens's writing, which I address in my sixth chapter. I refer to her *On Extended Wings: Wallace Stevens' Longer Poems* (Cambridge, MA: Harvard University Press, 1969).

6. I realize that there are other ways of taking Stevens's poetry seriously without taking his ambitions to address philosophy to be as central as I take them. Criticism of Stevens has done a superb job of explicating poems, clarifying themes, and even showing how this apparently most unpolitical man had a lively sense of social realities. For a full and very intelligent survey of such work until 2002 see Bart Eeckhout, *Wallace Stevens and the Limits of Reading and Writing* (Columbia: University of Missouri Press, 2002). But I focus here on how criticism of his modes of thinking seems to me not to have fully addressed the intricacies or the value of such thinking, even in superb books like Critchley's and Edward Ragg, *Wallace Stevens and the Aesthetics of Abstraction* (Cambridge: Cambridge University Press, 2010). In the general body of criticism, I find two basic traits in dealing with Stevens's ideas that need addressing. First, there are those critics who do not find Stevens adequate as a philosophical poet—for his evasive aestheticism, for the pious domesticity of his later work, and for his refusal to extend his obsessions with the first person into dialogical spaces where philosophy, too, can be an affair of other people. Critics like Frederic Jameson and Gerald Bruns ("Stevens without Epistemology," in *Wallace Stevens: The Poetics of Modernism,* ed. Albert Gelpi, 24 [New York: Cambridge University Press, 1985]) are right to argue that a poetry obsessed with the mind's relation to reality will not have much appeal to audiences convinced that this is old philosophical song, as is the case for those now who envision reality established by practices and not by individual minds. Jameson, for example, complains about Stevens's language "calling attention to its own hollowness as that which is merely the image of the thing and not the thing itself." See his "Wallace Stevens," in *Critical Essays on Wallace Stevens,* ed. Steven Gould Axelrod and Helen Deese, 178 (Boston: Hall, 1988). But suppose Stevens is after something quite different, as both Ragg and Critchley appreciate. Suppose he is less interested in the division between mind and reality, than in the question of how the lyric imagination might be actively engaged in all sorts of valuing, including the decision to dismiss poetry mired in epistemology.

At the other end of the pole, we find critics who have clearly done admirable and important work in studying Stevens's relations to social and political forces, preeminently Alan Filreis and James Longenbach. However, I cannot see that work making a huge difference either in questions about how we value Stevens's poetry now as art or in how Stevens affects our understanding of how and why we might rely on imagination in shaping our actions. Very few nonprofessional readers turn to Stevens for his value as a commentator on society. Instead, I think they ask of criticism that it justify Stevens's elevated tone and sense of self-importance by elaborating how the poetry makes significant and plausible claims on our lives. Ragg is precise and, I think, right in his critique of social and political readings (8).

The possibility of reading Stevens as a philosophical poet also forces us to reconsider the ways that this prospect was once dominated by critics engaging deconstructive themes. I have already stated my view of the limitations of deconstructive work on Stevens. But I also have to comment on the way the popularity of deconstruction warped books that had the courage to address it critically because it forced the authors to argue on grounds established by what they were opposing. I address one important example of this trap in discussing Robert Leggett's *Early Stevens: The Nietzschean Intertext,* in my chapter on *Harmonium*. I must address another here because of its relationship to my entire project. Jacqueline Vaught Brogan's *Stevens and Simile: A Theory of Language* (Princeton, NJ: Princeton University Press, 1986) offers a brilliant account of why the domination of metaphor in literary studies is problematic and how Stevens manages by simile to balance two primary features of language—its capacity to establish unity in relation to variety and its capacity to break into fragments what seems capable of satisfying too readily the desire for unity. Brogan does this by adapting the capacity of a simile to make the gap or "différence" continually visible between our acts in language and our efforts to match language to the world while interpreting the necessity of balancing unity and fragmentation. See especially IX, 12–17, 119–26, 139–43, and 166. I also talk about the powers of simile, focused primarily on what I call "the grammatical resources of "as." And I share her critique of identity thinking. But my concern is adamantly not with epistemological questions and even more adamantly not with "as if." I want to examine how uses of "as" make it possible for Stevens to realize the kinds of values that stand as theoretically significant for certain aspects of living. I am much less interested in how language represents reality than I am in how the poet can establish surprising and compelling affective states that exemplify possible and plausible attitudes toward the world. I am also much less interested in what simile can undo than in the work equivalences and resemblances can do in quickening the world and in making us aware of our capacities and orientations when that quickening occurs. Eventually I even show how Stevens develops what we identify as a basic mode of thinking based on these grammatical resources. But even as I stress our differences I want to thank and honor Brogan for how carefully she attends to the critique of identity thinking, which makes these quickenings possible.

In general, I think criticism of Stevens has to develop richer concrete yet speculative accounts of what is at stake as his poetry attunes self-reflexively to the quickenings of sense it establishes. How can these processes of quickening and the significance projected for them appear now as more or as other than epistemological stances ready for the dump? How can what Stevens saw as resisting the pressures of reality cut deeply enough that we still find that resistance compelling and still can be led to trust in the imaginative reach provided by verbal equivalents of "the meeting of planes in the sunlight"?

7. Eeckhout is perhaps the best critic in summarizing how Stevens saw his relation to professional philosophy (*Wallace Stevens and the Limits of Reading and Writing,* 135–42). And the second half of his book is very good in proposing a "perception,

thought, language nexus" with variable interrelations among those nodes as a means of characterizing how Stevens's poetry comes to bear philosophical weight while maintaining its differences from professional philosophy. Also very helpful is Critchley's capacity to summarize Stevens's poetics in terms that draw on and extend the concerns of many philosophers.

8. I can be less glib on Stevens's understanding of the philosophical issues involved in the discourse about values if I refer to three thinkers he probably read or at least had conversations about, all of whom reflect common assumptions about the divide between facts and values. At the same time none of my three figures simply laments the separation of fact from value. Rather, they take that separation for granted and explore how it might be possible to develop a general theory of values on primarily psychological grounds. George Santayana (*The Sense of Beauty: Being the Outline of an Aesthetic Theory* [Cambridge, MA: MIT Press, 1896]) sets the stage by his claims that "values spring from the irrational part of our natures" (15): "the appreciation of beauty and its embodiments in the arts are activities that belong to our holiday life when we are redeemed for the moment from the shadow of evil and the slavery to fear, and are following the bent of our nature where it chooses to lead us" (19). Ivor A. Richards, *Principles of Literary Criticism* (2nd ed. [New York: Harcourt Brace,1926), engages the more sober task of describing value entirely in psychological terms. For Richards the science that set fact against value can ultimately demonstrate why we value and how we might best distribute those values. To make his case he begins by criticizing the concept of aesthetic experience (rightly in my view) because it imposes notions of contemplation and disinterest, which distort the psychological attitudes made possible in experiencing the arts. On the basis of this criticism, Richards argues for a discourse of values based only on the empirical study of the intensities and modes of organization characterizing these experiences. These became lively issues at the time because the New Critics, some of whom were friends of Stevens, were virulent in their attacks on Richards's psychologism, arguing that separating states of mind from the objects and activities that could distinguish them and connect them to the world was a major simplification of value theory. Finally, my third figure, Ralph Barton Perry, provided a much richer account than Richards, in part because he tried to incorporate pragmatist positions within a more general explanatory framework. Perry's massive and often brilliant tome offered a general theory of value with elaborate means of making experiences of value commensurate and so ranking their importance. To do this Perry had to acknowledge persistent tensions between "descriptions as attitudes on the part of subjects" and those ascribing character to particular objective conditions (*General Theory of Value: Its Meaning and Basic Principles Construed in Terms of Interest,* [New York: Longmans, Green, 1926], 3). Then he could go beyond the psychological experiences (see 615 ff) in order to develop comparative measures of intensity, particularity (the interests of the agent), and inclusiveness (how the value might find a place in more comprehensive reasonings). Stevens, as we will see, also provides a brilliant way of reconciling experience and world by defining imagination as involving the theory of values because it provides images of the mind's power over the possibility of things.

I also have to mention historical support for the centrality of these questions about value and fact from a book that in all probability Stevens did not read.

After I had submitted this manuscript, my colleague Dan Blanton gave me a copy of Wolfgang Köhler, *The Place of Value in a World of Facts* (New York: Liveright, 1938), dedicated to Perry. Köhler lays out the positivist case denying that philosophy can talk about values in any meaningful way, then the proponent of gestalt theory insists that "requiredness" is a basic phenomenon that entails our including value within philosophy. Facts are all equal. Doing things with facts requires seeing relations and hierarchies, and these constitute values. Then Köhler argues that we need a quite basic and general phenomenology to appreciate the place these values have within experience. For the discussion of phenomenology see chap. 3, 63–101.

I will be arguing in subsequent work that literary criticism tends to operate on problematic assumptions that it must be comprehensive general values that hold the discipline together. I think it much wiser to look phenomenologically for values in the various particular satisfactions that we find in criticism. That phenomenology will no longer ever try to posit single values for the study of literature or the experience of literary experience. Rather, it will explore the many ways that we can take seriously the immense range of psychological and practical values that can become present in our reading practices by producing experiences of precise attention and careful articulation, experiences of "realization," where an initial distance between mind and world becomes a sudden awareness of the possible mutual interpenetration within a particular way of seeing, experiences of sympathy with depth of character and of clever ways of engaging with superficiality, and experience of the plasticity of our caring that can have these various modes of encounter enter into conversation with each other—conversation that is itself exemplary of how capacious a conscious may become when we read completely for appreciation.

9. I am aware that there are several interesting, more technical treatments of Stevens's relation to phenomenology, especially the work of Krzysztof Ziarek. But I think such technical treatments are problematic for literary criticism because we end up spending most of our time translating a philosopher's technical vocabulary into what seems the more unstable and imprecise vocabulary of the poet. So I prefer to begin from the start to risk using more basic concepts in order to appreciate fully what the poet's labors can accomplish.

10. This definition is indebted to Dermot Moran's very clear and engaging *Introduction to Phenomenology* (London: Routledge, 2000).

11. This interest in drawing contemporary significance from Stevens greatly complicates my task. How he formulates the asymmetry between fact and value is quite different from how just about any contemporary philosopher would cast the issue. Indeed, even in Stevens's time James and Dewey were arguing against that simple bifurcation. But the Stevens of *Harmonium,* the volume closest to his Harvard years, simply and boldly prefers to engage the positivist treatment of the issue, probably because it made the contribution of poetry more striking. Late Stevens shares much more with James but places value primarily in the attitudes poems embody rather than in what shapes practical inquiries. Then further complications come in when we realize that despite our culture's increasing flexibility in reconciling fact and value, literary critics at least now call for materialist models of criticism that posit analogues of the old divide in their separating explanation of the work's

historicity from any discussion of its value as poetry (which is not quite the same thing as "aesthetic value"). I hope how I read Stevens makes that materialist position more difficult to maintain as a plausible end for criticism.

12. It would be nice if it could go without saying that I do not claim here to explain anything about Victorian culture. I simply want to illustrate how certain typical passages rendered the feel of the crisis and attributed it to problems of correlating facts and the desire for values.

13. I owe this observation to my colleague Steven Goldsmith in conversation.

14. Geoffrey Hartmann used this scene masterfully to argue that Wordsworth is best seen not as a poet merging imagination and fact but grappling with the unruly and usurping powers of an imagination only temporizing when it reconciles with fact. I argued thirty years ago, in "Wordsworth's Wavering Balance: The Thematic Rhythm of the *Prelude*" (*Wordsworth Circle* 4 [1972]: 226–40) that Hartman's case depends on ignoring the lines that follow the recognition he has crossed the Alps because Wordsworth finds there a reconciliation richer for the temporary disjunction.

15. I think the most moving aspect of this distraction takes place in Arnold's first Marguerite poem, which anticipates "The Love Song of J. Alfred Prufrock" in its registering of the lover's self-protective illusions about himself. I develop this reading of Arnold much more fully in my *Painterly Abstraction in Modernist American Poetry* (New York: Cambridge University Press, 1989, 96–98).

16. In the conclusion to this chapter I claim that the contemporary obsession with moral or ethical values in literary criticism is the direct heir of the Victorian attitudes represented by Arnold. Arnold no longer has a central role in our critical understanding of the roles morality can play in literary criticism (although he did substantially influence the generation for whom Lionel Trilling spoke). But philosophers and critics now do rely a great deal on the equally bleak figures of Charles Dickens and George Eliot as exemplars of literature's capacity to render moral values and influence moral decision making. Dickens is paradigmatic for the writer turning from the natural world as the model for romantic notions of value to the social world (except for occasional set pieces) in an effort to redeem an almost unbearable sadness and sense of alienation into extreme states of character (like Miss Havisham). Then he reconfigures the social by having forgiveness play the crucial ethical role that restores a human nature without nature. For Dickens, Wordsworthian values depend on humans' capacity to recognize their own shortcomings and the dependencies they impose upon us: at the least we could offer mutual acknowledgment of those shortcomings and build modes of recognition around them. And Eliot is bleaker yet because it is eventually primarily a sense of duty that allows one to yield to what sympathy one can muster in order to manage the self-suppression necessary to an adult moral order without God. Love and morality both have all they can do to find any values for an imagination deprived of any direct pleasures in his sense of elemental existence in company with a world of sensations.

17. There are many books on Nietzsche and modernism, so my only originality here is in the focus on value and in the selection of motifs from his work.

18. This Nietzschean context also helps explain why the concept of autonomy never took hold among the American poets (in contrast to what occurred in France)—probably because they could not align their own labors with disinterested

judgment. Autonomy at most meant the capacity not to be bound by the past: the poets did not seek disinterest but tried to enhance and realize their own interests in finer tones and more fluent evocations. I think Stevens's "The Idea of Order at Key West" an exemplary statement of the powers of art that refuse or redirect claims about autonomy for art. See my essay "Why Modernist Claims for Autonomy Matter" (*Journal of Modern Literature* 32[3] [2009]: 1–21).

19. There are two ways to adapt Nietzsche's account of art. One involves a Heideggerean mode, attentive to how being discloses itself, rather than the Hegelian mode, in which power thrives on destruction. The other is Dionysian, with its rejection of moral scruples and its absolute commitment to what can unfold in the present.

20. Sartre developed a version of this logic when he argued in *Being and Nothingness: an Essay on Phenomenological Ontology,* trans. Hazel Barnes (New York: Philosophical Library,1956) that one cannot be sincere and direct because the effort to be sincere requires fidelity to an idea that is not an aspect of the concrete situation.

21. As Nietzsche's "amor fati" indicates, self-expression earns praise and nobility only if it is carried out in alignment with the facts of a life. His difference from epistemic thinking is that he does not treat the facts as internal determiners of what the values might be. He would say that epistemic thinking sets conditions for valuing but only the individual provides the sense of need and significance that allows for determinations about value. Epistemic thinking requires a justification of values that is too demanding to allow for what creative individuals make of desire and too reductive to allow individuation to matter. These criteria are doomed to fail— hence producing either self-deception or nihilism.

22. Hugh Kenner, *The Pound Era* (Berkeley: University of California Press, 1971).

23. Dora Zhang, "Strange Likeness: Modernist Description in James, Proust, and Virginia Woolf" (PhD diss., Princeton University, 2012). In January 2012 I heard an excellent talk from this dissertation, which I want to summarize for two reasons. First, it gave a superb analytic account of how modernist fiction writers managed to resist the allure of epistemic foundations while developing an alternative to Nietzschean reconfigurations of the fact-value problem. Zhang begins with what Bertrand Russell misses in his theory of description. Russell uses the concept of knowledge by acquaintance to secure the possibility of an objective world that then can be used to measure the adequacy of propositions about that world. But we are not only acquainted with objects. We can also be acquainted with feelings that cannot be quite embodied in objects or defined by propositions. So the very concept of direct acquaintance also brings into play an unanchorable sense of "this," of particular qualities of being that do not resolve into knowledge. Think of the being locked into the self who has to respond to the command "Damyatta" in the *Waste Land.* Or think of Stephen Daedalus encountering the "ineluctable modality of the visible." For modernist writers, then, description cannot be just the fixing of a proposition. In its active form it becomes the work of a self to seek relief from everything Russell's theory of description tries to secure by its model of how we get names to fit the world. Description has to take on the job of addressing the person who feels the full force of a "this" that alienates us from what impersonal names can provide.

Zhang then extends this ironic twisting of Russell into what I think of as a non-Nietzschean way to see how modernist writing might resist the notion that either value is based on fact or is sheer fiction. Woolf and Proust, for example, often spoke of their disdain for traditional narrative description because it functioned primarily to establish settings and contextualize the writer's thematic concerns. Therefore it honored a pseudo-objectivity that ignored the domains of desire typical in how we apply descriptions to our concerns . Yet these novelists did not entirely reject the impulse to description. Rather, they psychologized it. Description could be a primarily first-person activity—based not on copulative assertions but on similes and so a logic of equivalence. Fiction could not only preserve description but also make it more dynamic by foregrounding the character's investment in the description. To describe, for these writers, is not to offer efforts at objective description but to say what something is "like" for a subject. And then subjectivity itself becomes somewhat altered. There is less need to posit a mysterious psyche revealing its unknowable depths as it is forced to stand apart from what can be described. Instead, the world and the psyche emerge together, each a function of the other. The emphasis is now not on the matter of what is seen but on the intricate relationships possible between the character's manner of caring and the world's manner of becoming within the auspices of the character's caring. Simile affords terms of caring. So the text's demand on the reader is to intensify that caring by attempting to attune to it. Character is no longer a kind of substance but a dynamic fluidity that has something like a Bersonian or Deleuzian flow. The second reason I found this talk so useful is that it allows us to understand the challenges Stevens faced as a poet who was developing similar understandings of the place of value in a world of fact. Lyric poetry does not allow for much development of character. Stevens had no Clarissa Dalloway to make a day in London come alive. Instead, he had to deal directly with the feelings of readers. For him the feelings of what states could be like had to be stated in general terms and thickened by mastering the resources of syntax and cadence. The example of Proust and Woolf made it impossible to think of simile simply as ornament. But Stevens had to be abstract if he was to have his audience develop a taste for the power of simile as such, as an element of syntax that provided an alternative to the work of copulative verbs. I want to tell the story of what this abstraction made possible for engaged readers.

24. This is Nietzsche's image of Dionysius in section 295 of *Beyond Good and Evil:*

> [T]he genius of the heart, who makes everything loud and self-satisfied falls silent and teaches it to listen, who smooths rough souls and gives them a new desire to savor—the desire to lie still as a mirror, that the deep sky may mirror itself in them—; the genius of the heart who teaches the stupid and hasty hand to hesitate and grasp more delicately; who divines the hidden and forgotten treasure, the drop of goodness and sweet spirituality under thick and opaque ice, and is a divining-rod for every grain of gold which has lain long in the prison of much mud and sand; the genius of the heart from whose touch everyone goes away richer, not favored and surprised, not as if blessed and oppressed with the goods of others, but richer in himself, newer to himself than before, broken open, blown upon and sounded out by a thawing wind, more uncertain perhaps, more delicate, more fragile, more broken, but full of hopes that as yet have no names . . .

Pound would have been especially drawn to Nietzsche's linking Dionysius with genius that directly produces states of mind. That vision makes the god appear because of his own nature rather than any kind of beneficence or duty.

25. Edward Ragg has many important things to say about Stevens's understanding of abstraction. But, like most critics of Stevens, he for the most part confines himself to thinking about abstraction as a way of handling the relation between imagination and reality, with very few comments on Stevens's concern for the power of making evaluations that accord with and go beyond what our best instruments take as truth.

26. Pound's three spirits and his figure of a triumphant Dionysius would seem to Stevens trapped within the set of images that are now on the dump because they are inadequate to modern needs. Yet these figures also provide powerful emblems for forces that the conditions of modernity bring out as desperate, recurrent needs for principles of value not reducible to concepts or to images.

27. It is interesting to compare Heidegger in *Being and Time,* trans. John Macquarrie and Edward Robinson (New York: Harper and Row, 1962), to Stevens on possibility and value:

> As understanding, Dasein projects its Being upon possibilities. . . . Nor is interpretation the acquiring of information about what is understood; it is rather the working out of possibilities projected in understanding. . . . If we tell what it is for [des Wozu], we are not simply designating something; but that which is designated is understood *as* that *as* which we are to take the thing in question. . . . The "as" makes up the structure of the explicitness of something that is understood. It constitutes the interpretation. . . . When we merely stare at something , our just-having-it-before-us lies before us *as a failure to understand it any more.* (188–90)

My thanks to David Nowell-Smith for pointing out the possible importance to my reading of Stevens of sections 32 and 33 of *Being and Time.* These chapters not only show how close Stevens and Heidegger are in their concern for possibilities but also demonstrate how my own fascination with the grammar of "as" later in this study has something like its ontological roots in these parallels. Stevens does not use a language of "disclosure" by which to ground his sense of possibilities, but both thinkers clarify ways language need not just describe the world but can also charge it with significance.

28. There is a possible third general model of value pursued by modernist poets, but I think its centrality occurs somewhat later than in high modernism—in the objectivists and then most powerfully in Oppen. As I develop later when I speak of Peter Nichols's book on Oppen, there is the possibility that poetry can revitalize the world by expanding and sharpening the possible uses of the copulative verb. Positivism claims authority over and through the copulative. But Heidegger mounts a powerful challenge to positivism on this front since his thinking offers a competing version of the copulative that offers direct senses of possible value. The full power of "is" allows the direct light of being as emergence. One can claim an aspect of Heidgeggeran thinking for Williams and even for Pound since realizing emergent properties is basic for both poets. But I think both poets also want to register the

force of the will of the artist in this process of realization. This is why I align them with Nietzsche. And this is why I ultimately cannot use Heidegger as a model. He shares Nietzsche's critique of the epistemic. But I cannot be sure to what degree he stresses the unmediated presence of which the "is" is capable and to what degree there is presupposed something like an act of will or mode of seeing and making that allows the copulative its claim to transcend its uses in empiricist thinking. Given this uncertainty and given the absence of reference to the unmediated "is" in the generation of modernist American poetry preceding objectivism, I think it safer and cleaner to use only the models of Nietzsche and the work of likeness. But see the preceding footnote for a complication involving Heidegger that I cannot yet handle. There is much more of the "as" in Heideggerean ontology than I had thought. Yet the more clearly I recognize this the more I feel oppressed by confusion about whether "as" is a result of our frameworks for thinking or primarily the creative use of something like authorial will.

29. This is why I believe Stevens's thinking about value takes a very different path from that of most philosophers and critics who turn to literature so that they can speculate on how the literary imagination produces those actionable values we can honor as contributions to ethics. The tendency in those philosophers interested in literature, like Martha Nussbaum and Alice Crary, is to stress how literary works, almost always realistic novels, exemplify a moral reasoning that is more sensitive to detail and nuance than the work of professional philosophy. These philosophers manage to chide their fellow philosophers for their insensitivity while often demonstrating their own insensitivity to some modes of awareness these texts solicit. These philosophers rarely attend to states like intensity or precision or the capacity to dwell in fascination without having to make practical judgments, and they are not at all interested in formal questions as figures for the roles artifice plays in our lives. Because of such insensitivity they remind me of the desperate need for ethics driving Victorian culture, on whose costs Nietzsche is so eloquent. At the other end of the spectrum there are literary critics like J. Hillis Miller who treat ethics as the cult of just these idiosyncratic particulars. Here the emphasis is on drawing connections between aesthetic singularity and what is claimed as an ethics of letting be that has the capacity to release phenomena from concepts so that they can partake of the sublime. Stevens is certainly individualist enough to appreciate how the distinctive ways that the arts present themselves challenge the authority of concepts. But his critique of the quest for the abnormal suggests that the normal and so what is opposed traditionally to the sublime also rest on practices of intuition and exemplification that deflect the authority of concepts. There is nothing heroic about setting intuition against the conceptual: concepts and intuitions are simply two separate kinds of practices, each with its own uses and abuses. The only basic contrast to the conceptual that matters to Stevens is poetry's ability to foreground processes and so allow audiences to participate in how the poems intensify our capacities to realize values. So there is nothing metaphysically noteworthy about particulars except that they tempt us to a romantic satisfaction in the content of our ideals rather than in what the processes make us realize we are capable of. Locating the sublime in the difference between particulars and concepts amounts to a romantic reduction of the sublime struggle against mere fact to something doomed to become only a fact.

I elaborate these arguments against Nussbaum in chapter five of my *The Particulars of Rapture: An Aesthetics of the Affects* (Ithaca, NY: Cornell University Press, 2003) and in two essays: "Lyrical Ethics and Literary Experience," *Style* 32 (1998): 272–97, and "The Riches of Value and the Poverty of Moral Theory in Literary Criticism," *Soundings* 94 (2011): 35–54. I engage Crary in "The Poverty of Moral Theory in Literary Discourse: A Plea for Recognizing the Multiplicity of Value Frameworks," *Soundings* 94 (2011): 35–54.

30. This is Wittgenstein in *Culture and Value,* trans. Peter Winch (Chicago: University of Chicago Press, 1984, 50):

> How small a thought it takes to fill someone's whole life!
>
> Just as a man can spend his life traveling around the same little country and think there is nothing outside of it!
>
> You see everything in a queer perspective (or projection): the country that you keep travelling around strikes you as enormously big; the surrounding countries all look like narrow border regions.

If you want to go down deep you do not need to travel far; indeed, you don't have to leave your most immediate and familiar surroundings.

31. Siobhan Phillips, *The Poetics of the Everyday: Creative Repetition in Modern American Verse* (New York: Columbia University Press, 2009, 87), usefully connects the line "he is and is and as are one" (406) from "Ordinary Evening in New Haven" to a letter in which Stevens explains "tournamonde" as referring to "a world in which things revolve" and so is "appropriate in the collocation of is and as" (*LWS* 699).

32. My interest in naturalism crossed with this concern for values requires that I address Joan Richardson's *A Natural History of Pragmatism: The Fact of Feeling from Jonathan Edwards to Gertrude Stein* (Cambridge: Cambridge University Press, 2007) even though I do not know how to judge that book. On the one hand it is superbly written and at least as well informed about Stevens as any criticism of his work. On the other hand there is a boldness of assertion that makes me very defensive and suspicious, as if I were encountering one of the characters in Melville's *Confidence-Man*. Richardson sees no problems in tilting pragmatism so that it seems a secularizing and naturalizing extension of Edwards and Emerson, then in associating Stevens's religious yearnings as a young man with his treatments of values as a mature poet, without much attention to context or to what close reading of poems might contribute to getting the nuances of his imaginative activity. There is also an inordinate stress on what is claimed to be Stevens's knowledge of science on the basis of very little evidence (e.g., notice the gulf between Whitehead's and Stevens's statements on 182). Yet such assertions are employed to set a stage for claims about what "Stevens surely would have concluded," although there is no evidence in his writing that he made any such conclusion (e.g., 208, 210).

33. There are two very good recent essays addressing what Stevens means by "Supreme Fiction" that I want to acknowledge: Raina Kostova, "Deleuzian Underpinnings: The Affective Emergence of Stevens' Concept of a Supreme Fiction," *Wallace Stevens Journal* 35 (Spring 2011): 33–55; and Milton J. Bates, "Stevens and Modernist Narrative," *Wallace Stevens Journal* 35 (Fall 2011): 160–73. I think one has

to see Stevens changing the valence of this idea—from something close to a metaphysical concept replacing God to something close to the Deleuzian concept Kostova elaborates, stressing the continual place of artifice in the possibility of there being a world at all. This explains how he can use the notion in letters near the end of his life to refer to poetry quite different in spirit from his work in the early 1940s and can claim that the concept applies to his *Collected Poems.*

34. Here I go over ground ably explored by Edward Ragg.

35. The relevant passage here makes clear that evasion is not an escape from reality but the maintaining of an "unreal" on which depends the power of poetry to bring out what feeling for reality might be. Notice how even the lineation almost torturously brings weight and "intricate" expansiveness to what can be acclaimed as real:

> This endlessly elaborating poem
> Displays the theory of reality
> As the life of poetry. A more severe,
>
> More harassing master would extemporize
> Subtler, more urgent proof that the theory
> Of poetry is the theory of life,
>
> As it is, in the intricate evasions of as,
> Things seen and unseen, created from nothingness,
> The heavens, the hells, the worlds, the longed-for lands.
>
> *(CPP 415)*

36. It is not that Stevens refuses to use images but that he refuses to treat the image as an idealized state with the power to unify the poem by conferring a distinctive concreteness upon it. Stevens tries to suffuse his images with thought rather than treat them as an alternative to thought, even in early poems like "The Emperor of Ice Cream" and "Anecdote of the Jar," which stress their resistance to conceptual frameworks.

37. Phillips's *Poetics of the Everyday* offers a powerful analysis of some of these traits in Stevens's late poetry. But I think she is not sufficiently attuned to the second-order power that Stevens's concern for artifice brings to these poems. The poems celebrate less the actual conditions of ordinariness than the discipline of imagination that makes valuing inseparable from recognizing what is involved in fully participating within conditions of "normality."

Chapter 2: *Harmonium* as a Modernist Text

1. The most important documents in this tradition of challenging Stevens's capacity to engage a distinctively modern world are Hugh Kenner, *The Pound Era,* who linked Stevens with Eliot's fidelity to symbolism (Berkeley: University of California Press, 1971, 131–41), and Marjorie Perloff, "Pound/Stevens: Whose Era?" (*New Literary History* 13 [1982]: 485–514). But that judgment of his conservatism also runs through critiques of Stevens's idealism such as Cary Nelson, *Repression and Recovery: Modern American Poetry and the Politics of Cultural Memory, 1910–1945* (Madison: University of Wisconsin Press, 1989), and Alan Filreis, *Wallace Stevens and the Actual World* (Princeton, NJ: Princeton University Press, 1991). For that charge and additional

claims about Stevens's emotional cowardice, see Frank Lentrichia, "Patriarchy against Itself: The Young Manhood of Wallace Stevens" (*Critical Inquiry* 13 [1987]: 742–86), and for claims that Stevens represses the dialogical as the grounding for his solipsistic meditations see Gerald Bruns, "Stevens without Epistemology," in *Wallace Stevens: The Poetics of Modernism,* ed. Albert Gelpi, 24–40 (New York: Cambridge University Press, 1985). If we go back to the prototype for such attacks, Frederic Jameson, "Wallace Stevens," in *Critical Essays on Wallace Stevens,* ed. Steven Gould Axelrod and Helen Deese (Boston: Hall, 1988), we see clearly that these criticisms stem in large part from failures on the part of more traditional critics to cast Stevens's idealism in a way that allows it to bear significant content. Jameson offers a superb formulation of the odd richness of Stevens's writing as the "tension between an astonishing linguistic richness and a hollowness of content, each capable of drawing the other into its force field" (10). But then, rather than ask what Stevens might have intended by such emphases and such loops, Jameson leaps to historical explanation. To do that he must treat Stevens in terms of the social formations of the 1960s, thereby offering remarkable testimony to how much criticism can bend reality in order to maintain political melodrama. Thus, while Jameson understands Stevens's critiques of dramatic modes, he does not take up Stevens's own claims about the importance of poetry as statement. And he fails to see how Stevens might put that critique of his fellow modernists to the purposes that I describe here.

2. Later in this chapter I address the best of these accounts of the relation between Stevens and Nietzsche, B. J. Leggett's *Early Stevens: The Nietzschean Intertext* (Durham, NC: Duke University Press, 1992).

3. I do not want to overstate Nietzsche's influence on Stevens. I am torn between wanting to document influence and wanting to invoke Nietzsche here simply because the parallels dignify and bring out the sharpness of Stevens's intellectual work. So I propose the following compromise: we know Stevens read a fair amount of Nietzsche, whose first collected edition in English came out in 1908. So if one can independently establish significant parallels or stylistic emphases, one can reasonably assume that the parallels derive from what the poet could have attributed to the philosopher. And if that does not suffice, it may suffice just to treat Nietzsche as one element in the public sphere that helps explain the vitality of Stevens's early poetry. Later I argue that I do not trust references to specific intertexts because I do not think that is how poets typically read philosophers, and it would take strong evidence to convince me that Stevens goes against type in this respect.

4. I cannot prove Stevens connected empiricism's commitment to fact with the idea that death is the ultimate submission to the rule of fact. But I can go a long way toward demonstrating Stevens's own obsession with death from a strange letter he wrote to Harriet Monroe, apologizing for "my gossip about death at your house." He goes on to explain, "The subject absorbs me, but that is no excuse: there are too many people in the world, vitally involved, to whom it is infinitely more than a thing to think of" (*LWS* 206: Apr. 8, 1918). The route from the absoluteness of death to the absoluteness of fact is a well-traveled one.

5. It should go without saying that the fundamental statement of this attitude toward metaphor is Nietzsche's early essay "Truth or Falsity in an Extra-Moral Sense." It also might almost go without saying that Williams might already be ironic

in "El Hombre," the poem Stevens refers to. But if Williams is ironic, Stevens chooses not to see the irony because of his own purposes. Lisa Steinman, "Lending No Part: Teaching Stevens with Williams," in *Teaching Wallace Stevens: Practical Essays,* ed. John Serio and B. J. Leggett, 169–78 (Knoxville: University of Tennessee Press, 1994), argues that both poets are being ironic in their respective poems, but I just do not see why Stevens would bother to write the poem if he were to undercut himself.

6. I hear echoes of Kant's saying "concepts without intuitions are empty; intuitions without concepts are blind." I would also like the reader to notice how the poem's failure to sustain any classical connection between sense and meaning seems to warrant a third alternative, which Rancière calls the aesthetic regime's elaboration of the "sentence image": "The sentence is not the sayable and the image is not the visible. By sentence image I intend the combination of two functions that are to be defined aesthetically—that is by the way in which they undo the representative relation between text and image. . . . The sentence image reins in the power of the great parataxis and stands in the way of its vanishing into schizophrenia or consensus" (Jacques Rancière, *The Future of the Image,* translated by Gregory Eliot, New York: Verso, 2007, 46).

7. For a brilliant general treatment of ellipsis in Stevens see Bart Eeckhout, "When Language Stops . . . Suspension Points in the Poetry of Hart Crane and Wallace Stevens," in *Semantics of Silences in Linguistics and Literature,* ed. Gudrun M. Grabher and Ulrike Jebner, 257–70 (Heidelberg: Universitätsverlag C. Winter, 1996).

8. The satisfaction I refer to could derive from how the spirit of play might seem to deploy the full energies of the mind while managing to create an imaginative site that did not lie or adapt sentimental and nostalgic postures.

9. Natalie Gerber, "Stevens's Mixed-Breed Versifiying and His Adaptations of Blank Verse" (*Wallace Stevens Journal* 35 [2011]: 188–223) does a beautiful job of comparing the quite different "competing prosodic strategies" (190) in these opening two poems.

10. The particular speakers in "The Plot against the Giant" use the first person, but that speaking is not linked to the role of the maker or underlying intentional presence in the same way that it is in "Domination of Black."

11. Eeckhout devotes a whole chapter to an intelligent analysis of readings that have been given to "The Snow Man."

12. Richard Wollheim's *Thread of Life* (Cambridge: Cambridge University Press, 1985) affords a useful definition of intentionality that helps us make intelligible the imaginative shift I am seeking. He defines intentionality as the aspect of a mental phenomenon that captures and preserves "not just what the thought is of, or its object, but how the thought presents its object" (35.) This "how" need not lead us to a particular human speaker. All poems can be interpreted as modes of intentionality for which the work itself models the intention and dictates the opaqueness conditions. But most poems link that orientation, making a *this* of a *that,* to a specific expressive agent-speaker, literal or ironic. Early Stevens emphatically denies that expressivist model for grounding consciousness and its investments. See also on the general question of intentionality in literature Paisley Livingstone's persuasive analysis of intentions in "Authorial Intention and the Varieties of Intentionalism," in *A Companion to the Philosophy of Literature,* ed. Gary Hagberg and Walter Jost, 401–419 (Malden, MA: Wiley-Blackwell, 2010).

13. Let me try one more way of making the same point since these experiments with intentionality also resurface in *The Rock*. These opening poems impose a considerable opaqueness of reference. But they do so in order to shift attention to the source of the utterance—not in what some person intends but in the capacity of a given utterance to evoke a particular relation to the world because of how it disposes the intending mind. "Intentionality" need refer only to that orientation of consciousness by which *a* situation becomes *this* situation for a particular point of view. Then we can see that although concerns for intention lead us to focus on what an agent might be trying to express, concerns for intentionality focus our attention on how consciousness is structured and affect explored in bringing about the sense of "this situation." Correlatively, the emphasis on how situations are composed brings with it a complex set of questions about both the projected satisfactions that elicit the particular orientation and the actual satisfactions that explain why it persists. Because the focus is not on situations but on stances, the volume as a whole has to deal on a second-order level with how the range of intentional positions can be seen as weaving consciousness into the world and so enabling a particular range of possible identifications. The volume must provide the sense of context that we conventionally derive from projections about expressive intentions in particular situations.

These links between intentional states and possible identifications are important in all aspects of life, but they seem to me especially pressing concerns for poets of Stevens's generation. For these poets seemed always forced to engage both the particular structure of lyric investments and the constant general pressure of justifying to themselves the identifications by which they staged themselves as genuinely modernist. Were poets to rely on narratives about how individual intentions were shaped, they would find it very difficult to avoid the dominant cultural order, an order that obviously reinforced the very conventions on every level that modernism wanted to unsettle and transform. Narrative accounts of selves were fundamental to that order. The conditions evoked by the stories typically sustained roles and identifications continuous with the dominant practices.

Putting all one's reflective energies into the articulation of intentional states enabled poets to treat lyrics as pure moments for engaging aspects of the world and of seeing how consciousness might be altered by its efforts to draw out what it could from such moments. On such a basis poets might be able to pursue identifications that could satisfy the psyche at its most intense without subjecting it to conventional forms of reflection ill suited to such intensities. Dominant culture has substantial interests in poets making the kinds of simple identifications that find satisfaction simply in the fact that one can claim to be acting as a poet and so demonstrating a certain kind of approved sensitivity. There might be a certain *frisson* possible within this marginal mode of production, but the *frisson* remains an aspect of the licensing by which society maintained its authority. Fully embracing modernity required pursuing quite different modes of identification, modes based not on the role of "poet" but on the sense of embracing a task whose practical consequences had yet to be defined.

14. I need a word about why "The Comedian as the Letter C" plays no role in my argument about the volume despite the pronounced "as" in the title. I do not

feel I understand this poem well enough to talk about it. Yet if pressed I could say that the poem seems to grapple with mortality from the point of view of narrative rather than lyrical poetry. In that genre the poem can deal with various kinds of "realism," and it can track changes in attitude more thoroughly than can lyrics limited largely to figural resources. This poem does appear to reach a rapprochement with death as it projects itself into the future at the end. But it remains a rapprochement that seems less to resolve than to mock the work of lyric. "Comedian" explores a time-based alternative to the work of something closer to pure imagination trying out what of its resistance to realism can take hold in the modern world.

15. Adorno's clearest statements about identity thinking and the negative dialectic capable of exposing the mistakes caused by that thinking are in his and Horkheimer's *Dialectic of Enlightenment,* trans. John Cumming (New York: Continuum, 1998).

16. I owe Leggett at the least a substantial footnote in response to his brilliant book. Leggett's *Early Stevens* is especially persuasive on Stevens's interest in three Nietzschean concepts: that "truth" is an abstraction serving primarily as the institutionalization of power for given perspectives, that the way to avoid such abstraction is to replace concepts of "being" with emphasis on the innocence of becoming provided by constant changes in appearances, and that the source of tragedy is the tension between Apollonian efforts to establish order and Dionysiac reveling in its deconstruction. Leggett also argues powerfully that one can find in major poems like "Sunday Morning," "Peter Quince at the Clavier," and "Thirteen Ways of Looking at Blackbird" specific evidence for relying on a model of "intertextuality" intended to preserve "authorship" in a critical epoch (the 1980s) committed to the death of the author.

Compelling as these arguments are, they do not in my view provide an adequate picture of what Stevens probably thought he was taking responsibility for when he published his poems, so I will elaborate a little on what I claim in the main text. Like most of the major modernists (even Eliot after 1914), Stevens does not seem to be the kind of reader of philosophical texts that would engage closely with the specific arguments or, on a regular basis, think of basing poems on particular philosophical passages. Certainly Stevens read Nietzsche, but he does not have a philosopher's grasp of Nietzsche's work. Rather, it seems that his knowledge was largely a matter of internalizing cultural conversations, probably from the intellectual magazines that he did love to read. I say this in part because Stevens does not seem bound to specific fealties or to marking when he does and does not follow Nietzsche. Rather, he takes several stances that echo Nietzschean ideas. He combines various elements from Nietzsche that do not follow the philosopher's specific arguments; he remains faithful to Nietzsche's general principles while shifting the emphases within these principles; and he treats Nietzsche as an ideal interlocutor imaginatively present as the poet tries variations of or even alternatives to the philosopher's basic positions.

Take, for example, Stevens's attitude toward Nietzsche's naturalism, which is the concern of this chapter. Stevens would probably agree with Nietzsche's specific critiques of "truth" and his treatments of "becoming." Following Nietzsche at all requires engaging a naturalism shorn of all idealism and insistent on showing empiricism the consequences of its arguments. Yet for Stevens naturalism seems more of a metaphysical condition one addresses than a theoretical position to be refuted or even to be the object of Nietzschean critique. That indeed is why Stevens so fluently moves from the problem of reducing the world to fact to issues of mortality (while struggles with mortality do not seem so central to Nietzsche because the focus is on the heroic domain of tragedy). And Stevens seems less concerned with the formulation of ideas than the testing of attitudes. This is why he pursues such an intricate connection to the senses rather than to ideas about the senses. Stevensian attitudes color the world more than shape its specific conceptual contours. Such coloring fosters attention to the style by which ideas are presented rather than to the analyses by which they might be confronted.

Conversely, there is no obligation for the critic to connect these attitudes to other prevailing ideas of the philosopher. Nietzschean concepts of eternal return, "laughing ecstatic destruction," and (more controversially) the will to power do not seem important for how Stevens understands his own intellectual situation. We must even recognize that Stevens's gaiety is not Nietzsche's. There is little sense of tragedy in *Harmonium*. It seems as if the poems offer compensations for the fact that we must die rather than specify ways tragedy can become a joy to the man who dies. In the face of mortality, Stevens marshals an intricate sensualism indebted to the freedoms of postimpressionist painting for the task of engaging the consequences of Nietzsche's naturalism. Perhaps most important, Stevens could not give up the individual, whatever the appeal of a Dionysiac cult of becoming. In my view even the end of "Sunday Morning" is less the affirmation of becoming than the testing of an attitude of rueful acknowledgment that one tries to hold to life by extending the wings that bring us to darkness. Here I think the proposed intertext for the poem leads us to recognize how far Stevens is from Nietzsche's particular attitude toward mortality. Leggett cites this passage from Nietzsche: "Before the Dionysian process can be fully experienced one must surrender the belief that continuity means only *individual* consciousness, only the permanence of oneself. . . . Death is the very *source* of becoming" (*Early Stevens* 108). But it seems to me that the final section of "Sunday Morning" replaces the Dionysiac fantasies of section seven with a tone that is accepting but not celebratory at all. The poem can come to terms with having to die but not see this as anything other than a moment of steeling oneself ruefully to inescapable truth. Stevens is less concerned with overcoming mortality by evading individualism than with articulating how individual mourning over that mortality can be performed and transmuted.

Finally, I want to use Leggett to extend a more general observation about even the best criticism of Stevens in the seventies and eighties, which I present in the notes to my first chapter. Like Brogan and other conscientious and careful critics of the seventies and eighties, Leggett felt an obligation to address the climate of poststructuralist criticism even while resisting its enthusiasms. Brogan's instrument was to historicize deconstruction and show its many parallels with traditional nominalist themes about language. Leggett's compromise is to propose an idea of definite meaning from the conjunction of two texts, which is always open to interpretation. In his eyes the conjunction is objective because it is a matter of textual parallels not dependent on any claim about authorial intentions or the critic's will to truth, which will emerge as the conjunction gets interpreted (*Early Stevens* 252). So even when authorship is being deconstructed there is concrete evidence of some purposiveness in authorial activity.

It is amazing to me that despite my skepticism Leggett's particular claims about intertexts usually seem completely persuasive whenever he spends a great deal of time developing a reading, as he does with "Peter Quince at the Clavier" and "Thirteen Ways of Looking at a Blackbird." But even then, I am almost persuaded only that Stevens knew the passage in question but not that this involves a distinctive mode of intertextual authorship that can be adapted across a poet's œuvre. And when Leggett is more casual, the intertext invoked sometimes seems more arbitrary and occasionally misleading. A good example of the problems with intertexuality occurs when Leggett cites approvingly an argument by Milton Bates about Nietzsche's influence on Stevens's "concept of major man" (*Early Stevens* 14). In my view no claim based on a specific intertext can outweigh the contextual and textual evidence that Edward Ragg musters to demonstrate that the lineage of this idea is from philosophical idealism. "Major man" is a feat of abstraction, of locating the possibility of a transcendental and idealized form of subjectivity that appeals by inviting agreement. It echoes Hegel's "Spirit" or Bradley's "Absolute" because Stevens wants to make it an abstracted teleological force rather than a dynamic and dominating one. In fact, echoes of Nietzsche's "Übermensch" would destroy Stevens's vision that everyone with an imagination can participate in the sensibility of major man. That is perhaps the background to what is for Leggett the puzzling fact of Steven's uneasiness in the 1940s, when Frank Church proposes to Stevens that they read Nietzsche together (*Early Stevens* 35). I think Stevens did not want Nietzsche anywhere near his basic ideas at the time. (Similar problems occur with Leggett's claims about intertexts; *Early Stevens* 237 and 245.)

17. For support of my claim about Eliot and Bradley, see my "Reading Bradley after Reading Laforgue: How Eliot Transformed Symbolist Poetics into a Paradigmatic Modernism" (*Modern Language Quarterly* 72 [2011]: 225–52).

18. See the appendix to this chapter for an account of how *Harmonium* makes use of the symbolist tradition.

19. Let us define "style" in the simplest way: style is the demand to pay careful attention to what the manners of expression bring to the matter implicated by the poem's assertions about an imagined world.

20. Nietzsche, *Twilight of the Idols,* trans. Richard Polt (Indianapolis: Hackett, 1997), 6. I cannot resist another passage from the same text: "The Church and morality say, 'A race, a people is destroyed by vice and luxury.' My *reconstituted* reason says: when a people is perishing, psychologically degenerating, the *effects* of this are vice and luxury" (31).

21. The point is sufficiently important for modernist art to warrant two more examples:

> We have been spun into a severe yarn and shirt of duties and *cannot* get out of that—and in this we are "men of duty," we, too. Occasionally . . . we dance in our "chains" and between our "swords"; more often, . . . we gnash our teeth and feel impatient with all the secret hardness of our destiny. (*BGE,* sec. 226)

Their fundamental faith simply has to be that society must *not* exist for society's sake but only as the foundation and scaffolding on which a choice type of being is able to raise itself to its higher task and to a higher state of being—comparable to those sun-seeking vines of Java . . . that so long and so often enclasp an oak tree with their tendrils until eventually, high above it but supported by it, they can unfold their crowns in the open light and display their happiness. (*BGE*, sec. 258)

22. This is a rather awkward way of bringing the late poem "The Plain Sense of Things" into play.

23. Here I disagree with Leggett, who argues that "the relation between music and scene in the poem is not that between lyric and narrative but rather between two resources of the lyric"—the language of feeling and the form given to feeling (*Early Stevens* 81). See also Joan Richardson, *A Natural History of Pragmatism: The Fact of Feeling from Jonathan Edwards to Gertrude Stein* (Cambridge: Cambridge University Press, 2007), 216–31, who says many intelligent things in her effusion about music in "Peter Quince," the central poem for her argument. Unfortunately, she insists on binary oppositions—music must replace painting as a mode of thought rather than serve particular purposes painting cannot serve.—and she treats this poem as the climax of what becomes a quite homogenous intellectual career for Stevens devoid of doubt and tension.

24. Jon Cook and Rupert Read, "Wittgenstein and Literary Language," in *A Companion to the Philosophy of Literature,* ed. Gary Hagbert and Walter Jost, 467–91 (Malden, MA: Wiley-Blackwell, 2010), use "Thirteen Ways" as an example of Stevens's foregrounding the "intransitivity of literature" by presenting a series of scenes of looking that in fact do not have clear objects for sight without complex mediations by the mind. The authors put their case more strongly: "Stevens encourages one to form a kind of belief about what one can succeed in imagining [like an eye of a blackbird moving], and then facilitates one's learning from the collapse of that belief under its own weight. . . . Stevens discloses the sensical through 'violating' the limits of language" (482; see also 485). I prefer to see Stevens simply making us aware of how much seeing takes place by having the mind complete possible pictures. But even if one accepts their argument, I think one has to recognize that there seems a movement in the poem from states that are actually difficult to visualize to the almost automatic cooperation of mind with natural process in the last two sections (first concretely and then metaphorically by extending the significance of the blackbird's waiting). This reinforces my sense of the distinctive resolving power of the poem's final two sections, although I doubt Cook and Read would agree that sections XII and XIII successfully naturalize how the mind complements looking: see 480–81 of their essay.

25. This poem fits my concerns so well that I have used similar terms to write about it in *The Art of Twentieth-Century American Poetry: Modernism and After* (Malden, MA: Wiley-Blackwell, 2009) and "Why Modernist Claims for Autonomy Matter" (*Journal of Modern Literature* 32(3) (2009): 1–21). I hope I adjust my interpretation sufficiently for this context.

26. I want to acknowledge the significance for me of Jennifer Gurley's "Emerson's Politics of Uncertainty," *ESQ* 53(4) (2007) (Nos. 209 O.S.): 322–59. Gurley's essay

shows how Emerson uses Plato's ideal of participation in being as an alternative to any empiricist notion of mind representing an independent world of objects. That argument enabled me to appreciate how fully this concept applies to the poet who wrote *Parts of a World* and "The Latest Free Man," with its intense desire to escape from envisioning language as caught up in practices of description. A very very short version of Stevens's poetics would claim that he adapts an Emersonian ideal of participation to the Cézannian ideal of "realization." I cite Stevens's uses of "participate" in chapters 4 and 5.

27. I make this claim in my Williams chapter in *Painterly Abstraction in Modernist American Poetry* (New York: Cambridge University Press, 1989).

28. I am delighted to be able to use Henry Weinfield's fine verse translation of Stéphane Mallarmé, *Collected Poems* (Berkeley: University of California Press, 1996):

Tired of the sad hospital and the fetid smell
That rises from the banal whiteness of the drapes
Toward the large crucifix bored of the empty wall,
The dying man straightens his old back and creeps

Slyly from bed, less to warm his carcass
Than to see the sunlight on the stones,
To press his white hair and the bones of this thin face
Against the windows, which a lovely ray of light wishes to bronze.

And his mouth, feverish and starved for the clear
Blue air—just as, when young, it drank in the bliss
Of a virginal skin long ago—smears
The warm golden panes with a long, bitter kiss.

Drunk, he lives! Forgetting the horror of the holy oils,
The medicine, the clock, the obligatory bed,
The cough, and when the evening bleeds along the tiles,
His eye, on the horizon of light, is fed

With golden galleys, beautiful as swans,
Wafted on purple and perfumed streams,
The tawny, rich light of their sinuous lines
In a vast nonchalance charged with memories!

(11)

Chapter 3: "Ghostlier Demarcations, Keener Sounds"

1. I especially like the play between plural "philosophers" and singular "man," as well as the possibility that history can be subsumed simply under the assertion "has had the time to think enough." In the first case "man" becomes a single term built up by all these philosophers. In the second case thinking itself takes on a dimension to which history contributes yet cannot dominate.

2. One of the generative forces for this book was my admiration for what Peter Nichols does with the force of "is" in his terrific book on *George Oppen and the Fate of Modernism* (Oxford: Oxford University Press, 2007). I had a problem with it, nonetheless, because I do not much like most of Oppen for reasons that I could see

from Nichols's book involved my not liking much an emphasis on copulative verbs even after they have been properly made robust by a substantial infusion of Heidegger and Hegel. This book is my Wittgensteinian response to Nichols's version of the course of modernism.

3. See Edward Ragg, *Wallace Stevens and the Aesthetics of Abstraction* (Cambridge: Cambridge University Press, 2010), chapters three and four, for an engaging discussion of the imperative for abstraction in relation to history. Both Ragg and I think that Stevens uses "abstraction" in two fundamental ways, but neither of us is quite capable of always keeping the differences in view. In his poetry of the 1930s the primary role of abstraction is to escape the vulnerability of the image to history by placing images within more fundamental and concrete conditions of desire. But in "Notes toward a Supreme Fiction" abstraction is primarily a state poets achieve when they identify with their own creativity as something more powerful and more distinctive than anything that they can claim for their empirical personal selves. In this regard abstraction is Stevens's final way of constructing his idealist version of the hero and "major man" by defining it as a second-order relation to one's own creativity:

He is and may be but oh! he is, he is,
This foundling of the infected past, so bright,
So moving in the manner of his hand.

Yet look not at his colored eyes. Give him
No names. Dismiss him from your images.
The hot of him is purest in the heart.
                    (CPP 335–36)

4. Because I am fascinated by how much typical critical prose relies on the equivalences enabled by "as" I italicize those uses of "as" that allow my writing to engage the movements of mind in Stevens's texts.

5. "As we stand gazing at the rounded moon" offers a great example of some of the resources of "as" that I elaborate in my next chapter. The lines suggest that the gazing and the moon share certain qualities, if only the emphasis on "rounded" as evidence of the filter an observer provides. And that equivalence between states of the subject and states of the object becomes inseparable from a suggested temporal equivalence among all the subjects reading the poem and so constituting this "we." To these semantic equivalences Stevens adds a rich set of sensual equivalences that deepen what the agents can share. The play of long *a* and *u* sounds abstract the "gazing" and "the rounded moon," respectively, into a dramatically shared activity. The voice pregnant within proves to be in total correspondence with that rounded moon—in space and then in the time of the gazing. It is as if the moon and the pregnant imagination were living one another's lives.

6. The ellipses in the last line of this and the previous stanza are Stevens's; the rest are mine.

7. In his lengthy chapter on "The Snow Man," Eeckhout makes the reasonable argument that the poem is self-reflexive because it presents the experience of a specific state of caring. Most lyrics have some element of this kind of self-reflexivity. But even the title "Farewell to Florida" suggests attention to the specific speech-act qualities by which the poem accomplishes what it asserts. So this introductory

poem seems to establish not just a self-reflexive dimension but also the very condition of performativity as the promise of a new style.

8. See for the relation between "I" and "one" Anne Luyat, "The Meditation of Wallace Stevens on Nothing," *English and American Studies Journal* (2001)[0] (Shanghai, China: Shanghai International Studies University Press).

9. Ragg (*Wallace Stevens* 55–69).

10. That same logic occurs much more bleakly in the world of war represented by *Parts of a World*. Look there at "No Possum, No Sop, No Taters" (*CPP* 261–62) for the sense that Stevens cannot build on this logic of equivalences because differences seem to prevail.

11. One might say that here Stevens's incipient idealism betrayed itself by its choice of heroic action. But at the same time the quest for possibilities of poetic action made possible a repudiation of that idealism.

12. For strong visual examples, see Pablo Picasso's landscapes like *Reservoir at Horta de Ebro*. These multiple contending perspectives then generate cubist experiments in still life, probably because this genre was most in need of revivifying to make visible the painterly energies possible within restricted forms. I take up this issue in my *Painterly Abstraction in Modernist American Poetry* (New York: Cambridge University Press, 1989) and in "Why Modernist Claims for Autonomy Matter," *Journal of Modern Literature* 32(3) (2009): 1–21. But even I have to admit the reader would do much better to consult the chapter on Picasso in T. J. Clark, *Farewell to an Idea: Episodes from a History of Modernism* (New Haven, CT: Yale University Press, 2001). I also want to point out the close analogy to protocubist bold multiplicity of perspective in "Delightful Evening," the concluding poem of *Ideas of Order* and perhaps one point of genesis for "The Man with the Blue Guitar." One can read the title "Delightful Evening" as only ironic. But it makes more sense to me to treat it as a serious modernist statement because the imagination can revel in the opening up of possible figures for bleak multiplicity in the final stanza:

> The spruces' outstretched hands;
> The twilight overfull
> Of wormy metaphors.
>   *(CPP 131)*

13. It may be important that the paraphrases do not always match, most visibly in the accounts of "sea of ex" in the crucial section XVIII (*LWS* 360, 783). For a more general defensiveness, probably produced by an uneasiness with the level of generalization and the taking up of motifs fundamental to modernist painting, see *LWS* 788: "This is the general scope of the poem, which is confined to the area of poetry and makes no pretense of going beyond that area."

14. Eleanor Cook is one critic who recognizes the disjunction between Stevens's paraphrases and the actual dynamics of the poem. See her *A Reader's Guide to Wallace Stevens*, 112–29 (Princeton: Princeton University Press, 2007).

15. I hear "keening" in "keener" because I think death is rarely far from Stevens's imagination.

16. Let me be more precise on Stevens's relation to modernist painting and to modernism in general. On the one hand he continued to honor it for developing a new relation to reality by showing how to equate substance with subtlety. For that

line of thinking see Stevens's essay "The Relations between Poetry and Painting." But he also grew frustrated by the theatricality of an inventiveness that rarely justified itself by conveying what he saw as the significant experience people needed from poetry. For that thinking see *LWS* 647: "In painting, as in poetry, theory moves very rapidly and things that are revelations today are obsolete tomorrow, like things on one's plate at dinner. . . . After about an hour of it you say the hell with it. Is all this really hard thinking, really high feeling or is a lot of nobodies running after a few somebodies?"

Chapter 4: How Stevens Uses the Grammar of *As*

1. These statements date from almost the same time even though one is a development of Stevens's rhetoric of the hero, the other an early version of what I call aspectual thinking. I point this out because during the early 1940s and probably at most periods, Stevens, like most poets, was not confined to any one style but kept exercising his entire imaginative repertoire although the ratios of frequency change within that repertoire.

2. Because I want to call attention to how the grammar of "as" works *as* embedded in the language, I again resort to an awkward but, I hope, telling orthographic device for the rest of this book. When I deliberately refer to "as" *as* a grammatical feature I put it within quotation marks. But when I need *as* in my own work at explanation I put it in italics so that those readers who care can have the small *frisson* of recognizing a degree of suppleness afforded by our grammar to even all-too-ordinary prose.

3. The key Emerson passage for me is in the chapter on "Spirit" in *Nature* cited at the end of the appendix in this chapter. Again I want to acknowledge the significance of Jennifer Gurley's work on Emerson's Platonic sense of participation and partaking. See "Emerson's Politics of Uncertainty," *ESQ* 53(4) (2007) (Nos. 209 O.S.): 322–59.

4. See my discussion of "Bouquet of Roses in Sunlight" later in the chapter for a more elaborate version of this interplay between subject and object.

5. Stevens borrows the phrase "compresence" from Samuel Alexander to define a close parallel to the form of participation that I am describing (*CPP* 859–60).

6. One can say simply that by offering a concrete embodiment of imagination the text exemplifies its own fictionality. But then we would be in the realm of Vaihinger's *as if* and Derrida's "différance." And then we find a very hard time getting back to any version of the "real" or the describable and testable. Eeckhout's very good summary of the idea of "fiction" in his sixth chapter of *Wallace Stevens and the Limits of Reading and Writing*, Columbia: University of Missouri Press, 2002, (150–55) does not quite recognize this. Consequently, Eeckhout seems stuck with two problematic ancillary concepts. He adapts a view of pleasure (119) that depends on the reader's interpretive activity rather than on a much more teleological reading of the term in accord with the thinking of Wordsworth and Emerson. That thinking emphasizes a mode of pleasure that takes the form of self-aware extension of the self to act in accord with what seems something like laws of our higher nature: pleasure is the affective discovery of the good that makes us align with law. And Eeckhout attributes Stevens's commitment to producing open-ended sites of possible multiple

meanings to a pluralistic and democratic spirit respectful of the audience's differences. I will show that this multiplicity simply derives from Stevens's view of what affords the richest possibilities for thinking with the instruments poetry provides. There is no theoretical commitment to a particular view of the slipperiness of language or to the democratic spirit. But this love of multiplicity is why I argue that gradually "as if" in Stevens becomes subordinated to the equivalences produced by "as." "As" has the capacity to bring the imagination so close to the plane of description that the fullness of this presence simply beggars the role of the hypothetical. As-ness is not so much a hypothetical state as a fundamentally lyrical one exploring how imagining and attending to the world enter dynamic partnership. (On the evidence of Eeckhout's subsequent chapters I think he would ultimately agree with me.)

7. I will be citing in particular items 592, 624, and 628–43 in R. W. Zandvoort, *A Handbook of English Grammar*, 6th ed. (London: Longman, 1972).

8. For me the most useful essays by linguists have been Misha Becker, "*Is* Isn't *Be*," *Lingua* 14 (2004): 399–418, and, on *as,* Gerhard Jäger, "Towards an Explanation of Copula Effects," *Linguistics and Philosophy* 26 (2003): 557–93. Jäger points out the possible complexities even when "as" functions as a predicate adjunct. For although we would usually interpret this expression as referring to John by specifying various attributes that can make the sentence true, we have to recognize that the picturing function is paralleled by a potential theatrical function indicating that John is only playing the doctor since there is this strong orientation toward the present tense (569). That is, "as" evokes here both terms that specify qualities and terms that suggest temporal relations (when John performs as a doctor). In addition, Jäger is very good on the distinction between "Being a blonde, Mary might look something like Jane" and "As a blonde, Mary might look something like Jane." The difference shows how "as" adjuncts are always weak and "be" adjuncts produce strong individuation (562–63). His summary insists that, because "as" produces only small situations, it can be adequate to perception reports. But the copula projects "world size eventuality," which has to be read as a proposition rather than a perception report (571; cf. 588).

9. I modify Zandvoort's examples to put them in the present tense because Stevens's use of this grammar is mostly confined to the present. Zandvoort points out that "'when' indicates a point of time; *as* introduces a clause describing an action in progress" (*Handbook of English Grammar,* 630).

10. Lyn Hejinian, "Figuring Out," *Kiosk* 1 (2002): 195–206.

11. I cite Stevens's note on his "Les Plus Belles Pages" to exemplify how Stevens idealizes imaginings that stress interrelationship:

> Apparently the poem means that the conjunction of milkman and moonlight is the equivalent of the conjunction of logician and saint. What it really means is that the inter-relation between things is what makes them fecund. Interaction is the source of potency. . . . But the title also means that les plus belles pages are those in which things do not stand alone but are operative as the result of interaction, interrelation. . . . The interrelation between reality and the imagination is the basis of the character of literature. The interrelation between reality and the emotions is the basis of the vitality of literature, between reality and thought the basis of its power. (*CPP* 867)

12. By stressing this undermining of authority we can see concretely how grammar itself resists the exclusive rule of identity thinking. In addition to the abstract targets put in our sights by Adorno, I have two particular antagonists in mind here. One is Helen Vendler's pointing out the importance of "is" in Stevens's poetry without acknowledging his parallel interest in its counterpart. The other is Peter Nichols's book on Oppen that I have already discussed. Nichols makes a powerful case that Oppen reconfigures modernism from within by stressing fact, not image and syntax or form as the vehicle for poetry's developing a "materiality" that offers "resistance to the mind's embrace" (*George Oppen and the Fate of Modernism* 10). This is certainly a reconfiguring of modernism but not one that faces the full power of how the mind can be woven into that materiality.

13. Perhaps we can say that each aspectual force transforms a copulative condition. The psychological and temporal dimensions transform "I am"; the qualitative dimension transforms "it is"; and the second-order domain of assent/dissent has at least the possibility of transforming "I will."

Were we to use Zandvoort, the category of temporal simultaneity would stay the same. Stevens does not make much use of "clauses attributing reasons" or of "clauses introducing concessions," probably because they are conceptual and do not emphasize the function of equivalence. On the other hand, because Stevens does stress equivalents, we will see that he combines Zandvoort's other three types of clauses to call attention to parallel properties more than logical distinctness.

14. See Eeckhout's discussion of "sense" in chapter 9 of *Wallace Stevens and the Limits of Reading and Writing*, with this poem as a prime example.

15. It is interesting to me that Stevens often uses "as" to modify the subject rather than the object. This is consistent with his manifest narcissism. What is not consistent with typical narcissism is how the poems can reshift the modification to incorporate the object, as I show later.

16. William Bevis, *The Mind of Winter: Wallace Stevens, Meditation, and Literature* (Pittsburgh: University of Pittsburgh Press, 1989), calls this the will not to will, but I prefer a more flexible and positive capacity to distinguish states and processes that are worth pursuing from those that are not.

17. Actually, in retrospect one can divide modernist traditions in the United States by the contrary roles "as" and "is" play in the development of competing poetics. That division somewhat matches Hugh Kenner's contrast between Eliot's symbolism and Pound's commitment to fact. But I would put at one end of the pole Williams and Oppen and at the other Stevens and Eliot. Pound's most glorious moments are when he joins fact with a commitment to participation in what beauty affords.

18. Jacqueline Brogan makes this point, and has many other parallel interests to my argument in her quite intelligent *Stevens and Simile: A Theory of Language* (Princeton, NJ: Princeton University Press, 1986). However, her focus is quite different from mine. She casts the primary role of simile in Stevens and mediating between a metaphoric discourse that seeks unity and a catachrestic discourse aiming at continuous decreation: "Stevens increasingly came to rely on similes and the related form of 'as if' to sustain this difficult relation that he desired, as they afforded him a way to sustain simultaneously the interplay and inter-dependence of the possibilities of language as metaphor and language as fragmentation" (125). For her the hypothetical

"as if" is continuous with simile. I agree that the hypothetical can be used that way, but for Vaihinger and the critics who invoke him, the hypothetical functions primarily as a suspension of epistemic objectivity. I want to emphasize how the fullest uses of simile tend to evade entirely the demands of epistemic discourse.

19. Perhaps it will take another lifetime, but I would like to show how late twentieth-century culture offers several enterprises based on this possibility of indeterminacy as a positive state—from the art of Johns to the philosophy of Deleuze and later Derrida, to the music of Boulez, to much of the poetry produced to counter the relentless ironies of "language poetry."

20. Cleanth Brooks, *The Well Wrought Urn* (New York: Harvest Books, 1947). I am simplifying the story by not considering two supplemental features. First, I underplay an important connection between Brooks's Christianity and his faith in metaphor because the Word is in the Flesh and not merely "like" the flesh. And I ignore the importance for the New Critics of warding off the psychologism of I. A. Richards, who saw metaphor as contributing to complex experiences of identity in the minds of readers. The New Critics charged that Richards substituted the reader for the poem and so wanted something closer to Ransom's "miraculist" view of metaphor, by which metaphors actually altered our views of what the substance of the world could be. That power to alter relations was ultimately metaphor's connection to the life of Spirit.

21. Ransom, "Poetry: A Note on Ontology," in *Critical Theory since Plato,* ed. Hazard Adams, 879 (New York: Harcourt Brace Jovanovich, 1971). Alan Tate is more secular but fascinated by the same phenomena. In *Essays of Four Decades* (New York: Morrow, 1969) he points out that, although metaphor for the Greeks was a matter of rhetoric, metaphor from the seventeenth century on in England has become "a metaphysical problem to be investigated" (490). And the nineteenth century did not do well in the investigations because its sentimentality led it to have the vehicle overwhelm the tenor (337ff).

22. Not surprisingly, Adorno and Benjamin both notice this quality of resistance to abstract "meaning" in the classical epic—Benjamin through the figure of the storyteller and Adorno through simile. But Adorno does not develop any specific power of simile or bother to close read. Instead, he aligns simile with the power for event rather than the imposition of meaningfulness: "It is only by abandoning meaning that epic discourse comes to resemble the image, a figure of objective meaning emerging from the negation of subjectively rational meaning" (Theodor Adorno, "On Epic Naiveté," in *Notes to Literature,* vol. 1, trans. Shierry Weber Nicholsen, 29 (New York: Columbia University Press, 1991). I doubt that the epic texts sought the status of an image of fact. It is more likely they wanted life at the limit of what could be represented by the image.

23. I cannot resist pointing out that similes drawing on infant orality are pervasive in Dante's text and recur almost at the very end (Dante Alighieri, *Paradiso,* trans. Robert Hollander and Jean Hollander (New York: Random House, 2008), 33: 106–8.

24. The peroration of Emerson's essay offers an even more elaborate movement from the equivalences found in nature between nature and spirit to the possibility of spirit emerging as the self-conscious will to participate where it finds itself. Spirit here actively transforms description into an identification with proliferating correspondences.

Chapter 5: Aspectual Thinking

1. A second reason for Stevens's writing these essays, especially the later ones, was his taking responsibility for his increasing stature in the poetry world. This stature also almost requires his reflecting seriously on the course his work might take.

2. I am indebted to a conversation with Anne Luyat for the observation that Stevens's essays in the thirties show him trying to articulate what the commitments would be for his new poetry.

3. I fear that my use of both "analogical thinking" and "aspectual thinking" may produce some confusion. I want to say that analogical thinking is the basic strategy by which the poetry captures the role of subjectivity taking its place within the flow of the experience rendered by the poetry. "Aspectual thinking" is an account of the values that become possible because of the deliberate commitment to analogies. The concept of aspectual thinking allows us to talk about the analogies as the means to an end, albeit an end that emerges as the process of constant attunement.

4. For example, much of *Parts of a World* is driven by the sentiment made explicit in "The Poems of Our Climate." This text begins with an elaborate indoor scene that could take place in a poem by Amy Lowell if not quite in one by Pound or Williams or H. D. But by the sixth line the speaker reflects that "one desires / so much more than that" (*CPP* 178). In Stevens's view it is simply not enough to have objects sustain metaphors like the figure of snow the poem insists (painfully) on establishing. While the work done by metaphor is crucial to putting the subject into the world, the poem enters the world most fully for Stevens when it expresses its awareness of this need for metaphor and reflects on what conditions that need. In this case what conditions the need is "the evilly compounded vital I" (*CPP* 179). So, rather than idealize sheer presence, Stevens projects a mode that internalizes bitterness and recognizes that form can never be simply united with content. Form has to be a Cézannian making visible of the artist's decisions that render presence imperfect and solicit our reflections on what is involved in inhabiting a world from which we remain alien:

> There would still remain the never-resting mind, . . .
> The imperfect is our Paradise.
> Note that in this bitterness, delight,
> Since the imperfect is so hot in us,
> Lies in flawed words and stubborn sounds. *(CPP 179)*

5. For one recognition of Mallarmé's naturalizing of rhetoric see Jacques Rancière, *The Future of the Image,* trans. Gregory Elliot (London: Verso, 2007), p. 19.

6. I think this is Mallarmé's richest statement on equivalences: "We renounce that erroneous esthetic . . . which would have the poet fill the delicate pages of his book with the actual and palpable wood of trees, rather than with the forest's shuddering or the silent scattering of thunder through the foliage" Stéphane Mallarmé, *Mallarmé: Selected Prose Poems, Essays, and Letters,* ed. Bradford Cook, 40 (Baltimore: Johns Hopkins University Press, 1956).

7. Lisa Goldfarb is very helpful on Stevens and Valéry. See especially her "Philosophical Parallels: Wallace Stevens and Paul Valéry," *Wallace Stevens Journal* 29 (Spring 2005): 163–70.

8. Stevens's talk of rhetoric and "attitude" in this essay fits his citing of Kenneth Burke (*CPP* 721) and makes me think Burke may have had a substantial influence on his thinking that the critics have not sufficiently addressed.

9. There are moments where analogical thinking does merge with aspectual thinking as early as "Description without Place" and the use of "Now" in "Credences of Summer."

10. Here Stevens is not writing explicitly about symbolism, but I suspect his interest in that lyric tradition made a major contribution to his isolating of the imagination as a value that has at best an uneasy relationship to meaning:

> Poetic value is an intrinsic value. It is not the value of knowledge. It is not the value of faith. It is the value of imagination. The poet tries to exemplify it, in part, . . . by identifying it with an imaginative activity that diffuses ourselves throughout our lives. . . . We cannot very well speak of spheres of value and the transmission of value . . . without reminding ourselves that we are speaking of a thing in continual flux. . . . It is as if the painter carried on with himself a continual argument as to whether what delights us in the exercise of the mind is what we produce or whether it is an exercise of a power of the mind. (*CPP* 735)

11. I imagine this chapter engaged in a continuous conversation with Rancière's *Future of the Image*. Rancière repeatedly breaks the ordering of the fine arts into three large regimes: ethical, representative, and aesthetic. There was first an ethical regime for the arts shaped by Platonic thinking, where all art was political because it was seen as directly affecting the life of the community and immediately judged by its effects on that life (*PA* 12–18).

With Aristotle there emerged the representative regime that offered an art devoted to holding together a threefold relation among "a productive nature, a sensible nature, and a legislative nature" (Rancière, *Aesthetics and Its Discontents,* trans. Steven Corcoran. Cambridge: Polity, 2009, p. 7). This art posits the correlation of a poesis or way of doing, an aesthesis or way of sensing, and a way of interpreting the interplay of these two as a demonstration of something exemplary about human nature (*AD* 7). Finally, the aesthetic regime can be seen as working with these same three categories, but now there is a tension between its images of productive nature and of the sensible nature because poesis and aesthesis have to occupy the same plane without the mediation of any legislative function beyond the individual work of art. Without this stable legislative function, poesis must seek not exemplary representativeness but a singularity that uproots stable orders of perception. Then, in *Future of the Image,* Rancière focuses on the image in the aesthetic regime by pointing out how it gets defined in terms of "relations between a whole and parts; between a visibility and a power of signification and affect associated with it" (*FI* 3). This enables him to foreground possible tensions between claims to visual presence and demands that the image be itself a mode of intelligibility because it makes writing the means of affording presence to the sensible world. Hence the basic tensions between what I call imagist and symbolist modes of thinking.

Rancière also makes interesting claims about how the image takes on multiple meanings that indicate basic tensions between two large domains. There are two basic means of staging this confrontation. The sentence image casts the image as "leap," and the sentential element becomes a register of how passively meanings come to coexist with things without being able to impose authority upon them (*FI* 46–47). In contrast, the montage offers a mode of connection that divides into dialectical tensions and symbolist fluid analogy (*FI* 57–60, 77–79). Finally, we see the historical payoff of this way of dividing the cultural field when Rancière suggests that ultimately the aesthetic regime lays the "the groundwork of its own undoing": "The shared surface on which forms of painting simultaneously become autonomous and blend with words and things is also a surface common to art and to nonart" (*FI* 106). That surface then will invite a new relation between art and politics that may be the next major regime.

I cannot envision not being impressed by Rancière's dexterity of mind and supple way with abstraction. Moreover, he clearly captures an intricacy in the concept of image that helps us see Stevens's need to recast this important term for modernist poetry in English. But I do not think Rancière's is the best way to divide the history of art or to account for the variety of modernisms. In general, rather than having one regime, with its connotations of mysterious constraints, I prefer a sense of multiple modes of thinking all capable of being evaluated and reconfigured. For Rancière, Mallarmé and Flaubert reign supreme in representing the aesthetic regime. This inevitably suggests that all that comes after or comes with other national labels is either derivative or deluded. One way of combating such generalization is to offer Stevens's discontent with the passive states that the sentence image embodies. He does acknowledge the priority of the prose world, but it is a prose world made up not of parataxis but of objective laws. And then the task of the imagination, or of an imaginative meaning not identical to other kinds of meaning, is somehow to restore the possibility of seeing how we can be active and confer at least individual value within this condition. The very flatness of modernity as a regime of value makes it strikingly clear when modes of imaginative activity that are in no way mystical succeed in making a difference in how the landscape comes to appear.

12. "A generation ago we should have said that the imagination is an aspect of the conflict between man and nature. Today we are more likely to say that it is an aspect of the conflict between man and organized society" (*CPP* 735).

13. In this pursuit of his version of the antiartifact Stevens helps make thinkable experiments that would have appalled him—from the work of Frank O'Hara to that of the "Language poets." For a superb discussion of the impulse to the antiartifact see Oren Izenberg, *Being Numerous: Poetry and the Ground of Social Life* (Princeton, NJ: Princeton University Press, 2011). Izenberg's basic argument is that there is a "tradition of poets for whom our century's extreme failures to value persons adequately—or even to perceive persons as persons—issue to poetry a reconstructive philosophical imperative that is greater than any imperative to art; indeed it is hostile to art as such" (2). Ultimately, this tradition resists the poem as artifact because the poets want "our concepts of personhood to identify something real" so that there might be "a ground on which the idea of a 'we' might stand" (3). Izenberg does not include Stevens because it seems he would not grant Stevens's distinction between the

artificial, which helps distinguish aesthetic value, and artifice, which calls attention to what we make in becoming who we are moment by moment. Stevens would treat this sense of becoming as also what art can accomplish.

14. I survey these in "Rhetoric and Poetics: How to Use the Inevitable Return of the Repressed," in Walter Jost and Wendy Olmstead, eds., *A Companion to Rhetoric and Rhetorical Criticism,* 473–93 (Oxford: Blackwell, 2004).

15. I refer primarily to the work on this concept by Nelson Goodman and its modifications by Richard Wollheim, although the relevant philosophical framework goes back to Kant on "presentation." For Wollheim's argument against Goodman's extensionalist commitments see his two essays in Catherine Z. Elgin, ed., *The Philosophy of Nelson Goodman: Nelson Goodman's Philosophy of Art,* 18–42 and 73–92 (New York: Garland, 1997). Goodman's *Languages of Art* (New York: Bobbs-Merrill, 1968) argues that examples are not labels for the world but models that enable us to select features of the world because they possess certain properties that attract our interest. His most useful gloss for his position is his pointing out how there are two routes to reference for examples. One can point to the redness of a sweater with an interest in finding the right name for the appropriate shade, or one can point to the color the sample possesses in order to ask someone else to find similar shades in a group of sweaters. In my essay "Exemplification and Expression," in Gary Hagberg and Walter Jost, eds., *A Companion to the Philosophy of Literature,* 491–506 (Oxford: Wiley-Blackwell, 2010) I use Wittgenstein to elaborate this second option, which I consider the basic way art implicates the world.

For Stevens on example and exemplification see especially the rest of *CPP* 734–35. In *Auroras of Autumn* and especially in *The Rock* Stevens is distinctive because of his attention to the dimension of possibility within the work of exemplification. Possibility is not a fiction. Rather, it results from making visible how participation is not just in the moment but also opens into the implications or possibilities of that moment. In Goodman's terms, one becomes aware of the possibility of this shade of sweater in the world. And for Stevens's "The House Was Quiet and the World Was Calm," the summer is inseparable from the reader leaning late and reading there, so this figure of fusion becomes also the image of possibility of what night can be for consciousness.

16. I quote Stevens again because the role possibility plays is so important and Stevens so sharp on it: "Nietzsche walked in the Alps in the caresses of reality. We ourselves crawl out of our offices and classrooms and become alert at the opera. Or we sit listening to music as in an imagination in which we believe. If imagination is the faculty by which we import the unreal into what is real, its value is the value of the way of thinking by which we project the idea of God into the idea of man" (*CPP* 735–36).

17. By this logic "Owl's Clover" failed because it sought success as allegory and so trapped the mind within its own desires for the consistency of figural construction. The poem lost all sense of mystery and so of the mind's capacity to live fully in constant change.

18. I think the language of "satisfaction" provides a basic element for developing a completely secular poetics without echoes of the Word in the flesh and also without submission to the notion that the secular equals the political. See on the concept

of satisfaction in the lyric the fine essay by Rachel Cole, "Rethinking the Value of Lyric Closure: Giorgio Agamben, Wallace Stevens, and the Ethics of Satisfaction," *PMLA* 126 (2011): 398–411.

19. One could see expressions like "clanging at its make" and "the removes must give, including the removes toward poetry" as just plain bad, vague poetry. But the expressions are so clumsy within an otherwise masterful rhetorical performance that I think the awkwardness must be purposive. We can after all make semantic sense of these expressions. "Clanging at its make" seems to me a rough parallel to "kicking against the pricks" who force us to try to make poetry of mortality. And "removes" can be read as referring to the imagination's abstraction having to recognize the difference between perception and imagination. The important point is that the poem is trying to hear through its own painful evasiveness a cause for that evasiveness that it can accept. See also Eleanor Cook's heroic attempt at making sense of "its make" (Reader's Guide, 253).

20. It is an especially keen move to use the natural figure of "branchings" to explain how the mind fosters desires that take it away from what could be its home.

21. One could make the same point more technically by pointing out that "sight and insight as they are" is a tautology. The statement is true for any specification of "sight and insight." However, this complaint makes sense only if we treat this statement as an instance of description. Stevens wants us to see that this treatment is not called for. Readers can project a range for "sight and insight as they are" if they treat the phrase as suggesting that the equivalence between sight and insight is relative to the degree of participation the speaker has in the analogies and the audience has in the reverberations. This expression joins subject, object, and audience all within what the processes directed by the poem can make articulate—both in the order of apprehension and in the second-order possibilities of identification. We make sight and insight as they are, but we do it only because we participate with varying degrees of intensity in what it can mean to have a "cry of its occasion." The cry itself indicates how far expression can stray from description. It also makes possible modes of apprehension engaging what it might mean to be fully a part of the world, freed from traces of one's verbality.

Chapter 6: Stevens's Tragic Mode

1. I will honor these distinctions as I proceed. But the important thing about the variety of terms—suffering, tragedy, evil—is their traditional resistance to imagination because they are indices for the kind of power that resides in fate and chance and error rather than in any plausible figure for human desire. It would be foolish for him to be more conceptually sophisticated and intricate here because the major purpose of this discourse is to produce a version of solidarity with a general sense of humanity.

2. James Longenbach, *Wallace Stevens: The Plain Sense of Things* (New York: Oxford University Press, 1991), 279. Longenbach is referring strictly to *Auroras of Autumn*.

3. I defend my claims for the relative slightness of this poem by pointing to its neighbors: "Ordinary Evening in New Haven" and "Things of August." It uses its slightness beautifully.

4. Perhaps the richest version of Stevens's ideals about how one casts one's individual life is his "Two or Three Ideas," a discourse about men appropriating the gods in a possible perfectionism.

5. In addition to the essays I mention later, I found Bruce Lawder ("Poetry and Painting: Wallace Stevens and Pierre Tal-Coat" [*Word and Image* 18 (2002): 348–56]) especially helpful on the presence of Wordsworth and Whitman in the poem. Lawder also gives a fine, sophisticated account of Tal-Coat's career.

6. Costello defines "megalography" as presentation on a grand scale, while "rhopography" is "mediation on small-scale decorative and domestic objects" or "low-plane reality" (Costello, Bonnie. "Effects of Analogy: Wallace Stevens and Painting," in *Wallace Stevens: The Poetics of Modernism,* ed. Albert Gelpi, 477 [New York: Cambridge University Press, 1985]).

7. Alan Filreis, "Still-Life without Substance: Wallace Stevens and the Language of Agency," *Poetics Today* 10 (1989): 345–46. See also his superb "Beyond the Rhetorician's Touch," *American Literary History* (Spring 1992): 230–63. As good as Filreis is on abstraction in both his essays, though, he does not address the specific force of the abstraction in "Angel" beyond the issue of how relations become primary. More precisely, Filreis does not thematize the work of abstraction in this particular act of poetic thinking. I should add two observations about these essays. Clearly the emphasis on relations rather than substance prefigures my argument about aspectual thinking as resisting the force of copulative verbs, although I cannot say it influenced my development of that idea. (It probably should have.) Second I want to note that I am not persuaded by Filreis's argument that the "impulse" behind Steven's choosing to redo the still life as a poem about angels and paysans comes from his correspondence with Thomas McGreevey (365ff.). That hypothesis seems to me to depend on overreading the correspondence with McGreevey and underreading the resonance of the poem.

8. Beverly Maeder, *Wallace Stevens' Experimental Language: The Lion in the Lute* (New York: St. Martin's, 1999), 185.

9. The rarely noticed poem "Imago" (*CPP* 377) is more elaborate on this point and so close in spirit to "Angel with Paysans" that I feel secure in seeing both poems as asking how poetry can deal with the tragic. "Imago" is even explicit on the role of the lightness, which, I think, is the central feature of "Angel." But "Angel" makes lightness a property of the action rather than an abstract lyrical motif.

10. Helen Vendler, *On Extended Wings: Wallace Stevens' Longer Poems* (Cambridge, MA: Harvard University Press, 1969), 207. Vendler's psychological language insisting on a "refusal to feel" makes it impossible for her to grapple with the underlying problem or see any intellectual dialectic as Stevens returns to the difficulty of the issues involved.

11. For slight evidence of Stevens's own dissatisfaction see *LWS* 472.

12. These cantos enact an ascetic turn from three basic ideas of how the observer might be a participant. They reject in turn the Cézannian sense that there can be a visibility of the visible satisfying to the imagination, the space of a fantasized union with the mother, and the illusion of patriarchal mastery forced to accommodate the world of observation by saying "yes to no" and so saying farewell to any satisfaction even in the acts of observation.

13. *The Cavell Reader* succinctly explores the many ways Cavell engages the consequences of skepticism.

14. Vendler is superb in showing how "Ordinary Evening" elaborates the figure of the eye (*On Extended Wings*, 285–88).

15. Notice how section IX in particular resolves the tension between particularity and generality in "Auroras" by insisting that "We seek / Nothing beyond reality. Within it, / Everything, the spirits alchemicana / Included" (*CPP* 402). See also the end of canto XXVII.

16. "Longed-for lands" for me echoes the indulgent nostalgias of "Academic Discourse at Havana." But here Stevens sounds the melancholy and makes it a powerful operator in the play between symptomatic and metaphorical readings that I try to elaborate. Let me also offer two further comments on these closing lines. I am not sure what "as" is evading beyond perhaps the power of the copulative verb to fix identities. So "evasions" is probably closer to a verb of sheer movement than the evocation of something deliberately not addressed. (Geoffrey O'Brien pointed out in conversation that the most outlandish of the realizations "as" makes possible may be the presence of the conjunction at the core of "ev*as*ion.") And "lands" might have pride of place in part because the next canto makes present a version of those lands.

17. I qualify "empiricist" by "traditional" here to honor the way James's "radical empiricism" would welcome Stevens's multiplying of possible perspectives within experience.

Chapter 7: Aspect-Seeing and Its Implications in *The Rock*

1. Even Simon Critchley, whose book is by far the clearest and most sophisticated effort to explain Stevens's poetics, seems to me to undervalue the imaginative implications of the artifice in these poems. He sees *The Rock* as driven by two basic correlated desires. Stevens wants to show one can give up a sense that the ego matters while retaining the assertive powers of poetry: "the moment of the ego's assertion, in swelling up to fill a universe without god, is also the point at which it shrinks to insignificance" (*Things Merely Are: Philosophy in the Poetry of Wallace Stevens* [London: Routledge, 2005], 87). (No more oxen out of ants.) And given this diminishing of the ego, the status of the object in lyric poetry has to change. Reading Stevens's "cure of the ground" as "the desire to be cured of the desire for poetry" (83), Critchley argues that in a new realism "poetry can be brought closer to the plain sense of things, to things in the remoteness from us and our intentions" (84):

> We see things in their mereness, in their plainness and remoteness from us, and we accept it calmly, without the frustrated assertions and juvenile overreachings of the will. Such calm is not thoughtless, but rather thoughtful, the contemplative insight that comes from having things in sight. At its best, poetry offers an experience of the world as meditation, the mind slowing in front of things, the mind pushing back against the pressure of reality through the minimal transfigurations of the imagination. (88)

I am suspicious of this account because it does not correlate with either the pau-
city of reference to actual things in late Stevens or the marvelous outflow of lyrics
(which is hard to explain as motivated by emerging disbelief in the lyric). These
poems are much less about things than about people accommodating themselves to
the mode of being they share with things, as in "Lebensweisheitspielerei":

Each person completely touches us
With what he is and as he is,
In the stale grandeur of annihilation.
                    (CPP 430)

Analogously "An emerging disbelief in the lyric" is difficult to correlate with
Stevens's continuing efforts to establish figures of capable imagination. And this insistence on disbelief becomes a reason for ignoring both the formal aspects of the
poems and the vision of second-order reflection connecting these formal aspects to
the "theory of life." In my view these poems do not want to escape poetry but to
test its power to build modes of response adequate to the stripped-down world the
poems confront. That is why I want to stress the degree of artifice as an aspect of
the poems' efforts to correlate will for the world with the givenness of its inhuman
plenitude.

More generally, Critchley's reading of Stevens's late poems seems to me driven
by the only model of value on which many contemporary philosophers trained in
European traditions can agree. I refer to the Levinasian ideal of "letting be," with its
eagerness to celebrate what manages to resist the ego's demands and the rhetorician'
skills. I think this model is neither sufficiently rich in its affirmations nor sufficiently
dark in its sense of tragedy to be adequate to late Stevens. (The appropriate sense of
tragedy has to involve finding an aspect of the will, and hence the ego, that can
come to terms with necessity.)

2. In conversation Ted Alexander pointed out to me that the vowel sound in
"drowsy" also seems to give the sonorous structure of the line a palindromic character, with the *r, i,* and *o* (in "motion") sounds reversing their order after "drowsy"
appears at the center of the line.

3. One of the best accounts of *The Rock* is by Siobhan Philips (*The Poetics of the
Everyday: Creative Repetition in Modern American Verse* [New York: Columbia University Press, 2009]), because she connects the poems beautifully to a respect for the
relation of poetry to ordinary life, with the concept of the ordinary based on the
poem's willingness to embrace repetition and hence the temporal nature of experience. But I think even this sophisticated way of talking about ordinary experience
underplays Stevens's philosophical intelligence in this volume. His "ordinary" is not
an empirical category or even necessarily a familiar one. His sense of the elemental
world is based much less on time and repetition than on the spatial figure of centrality. I have already cited his ideal of a normal existence where even images pass away
so I will rely now on just one other passage to support my point:

He sees without images. But is he not seeing a clarified reality of his own?
Does he not dwell in an analogy? His imageless world is, after all, the same
sort as a world full of the obvious analogies of happiness or unhappiness . . .
In any case these are the pictorializations of men, for whom the world exists

as a world and for whom life exists as life, the objects of their passions, the objects before which they come and speak, with intense choosing, words that we remember and make our own. Their words have made a world that transcends the world and a life livable in that transcendence. (*CPP* 722)

The important feature of the ordinary for Stevens is not its social condition but the metaphysical possibility of what can be entailed by someone's pursuing this ordinariness as the reason for accepting necessity and thus willing one's fate. The poems try to make visible what in humanity is both elemental and ineluctably transpersonal. So here Stevens has significant parallels with the Husserl of "Crisis of the European Sciences," which I study in my essay "Stevens and the Crisis of European Philosophy" (in *Wallace Stevens across the Atlantic,* ed. Bart Eeckhout and Edward Ragg [London: Palgrave Macmillan, 2008]).

4. I cannot entirely defend Stevens's fascination with Berkeley. But perhaps I can mitigate the risks of his figure of doubling if I explain how it culminates in address. Stevens seems to believe that there is an inner picture of an outer world, something Wittgenstein sharply opposes. But the inner picture is not psychological in the sense that it has independent existence built up by interpretations composed by the subject. The inner picture seems simply a place in which consciousness dwells so that description itself becomes a matter of response and responsibility for what can be described. I cannot argue that this idea is philosophically defensible, but I can suggest that it is not naïve or stupid.

5. One could of course insist that imaginative possibilities are additions to the scene rather than participants within it. But this would betray a methodologically driven demand to reduce an emotional event to the abstract world of sheer perception. It would be inattentive to what the life lived in the scene invites us to see and to feel.

6. Ted Alexander again: "It is as if 'his' is not a properly 'possessive' pronoun but an adjective connoting election or appointment (e.g., 'he was summoned to his assigned seat'), which would play off of the simultaneity of making/finding in the demonstrative assertion of a place doubled between world and image in the mind."

7. Eleanor Cook translates the title as "Practical Wisdom's Amusement" 281). But I think the elements are to be left more fluid and so free to interact. Tying the German to one translation is probably ill advised. The important thing is that the poem promises to correlate the seriousness of the study of life with the artfulness of play, both in art and as an attitude toward how we maintain distance from that life.

8. I am adapting here arguments I have made at greater length in quite different contexts, "Style," in *The Oxford Handbook of Philosophy and Literature,* ed. Richard Eldridge, 420–41 (New York: Oxford University Press, 2009), and "Exemplification and Expression," in *A Companion to the Philosophy of Literature,* ed. Gary Hagberg and Walter Jost, 491–506 (Oxford: Wiley-Blackwell, 2010).

9. John Verdi, *Fat Wednesday: Wittgenstein on Aspects* (Philadelphia: Paul Dry Books, 2009) is very helpful both for construing Wittgenstein and for applying his model of "seeing as" to works of art.

10. In fact, late Stevens does not like exclamations. I think he thought exclamation rhetorically tries to force the audience to feel and hence is embarrassingly forward. His dream is to have indicatives function with the force of exclamations.

11. Wittgenstein uses style as another means of making models, but this topic would take us too far afield now. Let me just cite the relevant passage and comment on it: "'Le style c'est l'homme,,' 'Le style c'est l'homme même.' The first expression has cheap epigrammatic brevity. The second, correct version opens up quite a different perspective. It says that a man's style is a picture [Bild] of him" (*CV* 78). The second formulation says that style is a picture of the person because the self-reflexive dimension by which it frames the world makes visible how the language has been worked. One might say that style implies ownership but does not entail discursive self-consciousness about ownership or the possibility of describing the terms of that ownership. Style accomplishes this framing by accepting and displaying the individual's differences from others and not seeking any normative justification: "You have to accept the faults in your own style. Almost like the blemishes in your own face." (*CV* 76).

I have written on the relation between style and confession as an alternative to moralizing views of expression in "The Riches of Value and the Poverty of Moral Theory in Literary Criticism" (*Soundings* 94 (2011): 35–54) and "Cavell and Wittgenstein on Morality: The Limits of Acknowledgment," in *Stanley Cavell and Literary Studies: Consequences of Skepticism,* ed. Richard Eldridge and Bernie Rhie (New York: Continuum, 2011).

12. The passion behind this formulation emerges in Wittgenstein's private writing:

The Christian Faith—as I see it—is a man's refuge in this ultimate torment. Anyone in such torment who has the gift of opening his heart, rather than contracting it, accepts the means of salvation in his heart. Someone who in this way penitently opens his heart to God in confession lays it open for other men too. In doing this he loses the dignity that goes with his personal prestige and becomes like a child. . . . A man can bare himself before others only out of a particular kind of love. A love which acknowledges as it were, that we are all wicked children. We could also say: Hate between men comes from our cutting ourselves off from each other. (*CV* 46)

13. Actually, "To an Old Philosopher in Rome" best represents the conjunction between a continually doubled world and attributed second-order reflection on the significance of being able to see how aspect-seeing affords that doubling. But the poem is too long to do justice here, and I have little even remotely original to say about it (with the exception, I hope, of endnote 15 here). One reason I have nothing to say is that this poem is for Stevens surprisingly direct. That indeed may be its deepest testimony to what Santayana has achieved in his simple and direct choice of life simultaneously in two worlds.

14. Siobhan Phillips is more precise with this great statement: "Penelope turns the terrified farewells of 'The Auroras of Autumn' into the peaceful routine of 'An Ordinary Evening' (*Poetics of the Everyday* 107–8). Phillips is also very good on will in these poems: "The fact of one's lack may provide one's greatest assurance" (109).

15. I cannot fully resist saying at least something in a note about these closing lines. Choice here is how thinking and realizing become one, raising the activity of knowing to theater while simultaneously reducing the world to transparency. Therefore it is not a major exaggeration to suggest that Stevens's entire career might be summarized as the exploration of the founding difference between "real" and

"realized." One basic change in Stevens's career takes the form of a gradual shift from stressing what imagination does to stressing what people can do because of the imagination's power to create theater while resisting the temptation to let that theater present fictional plots.

16. This discussion is somewhat revised from a version published in my essay on Husserl. I am indebted to the readings by Longenbach, Critchley, and Ragg and especially to Eeckhout's engaging with the history of scholarship on the poem.

17. See *LWS* 622. More memorable is *LWS* 647: "I rather resent professional modernism the way one resents an excessively fashionable woman."

Bibliography

Adorno, Theodor. "On Epic Naiveté." In *Notes to Literature*, vol. 1, translated by Shierry Weber Nicholsen, 24–29. New York: Columbia University Press, 1991.

———, and Max Horkheimer. *The Dialectic of Enlightenment*. Translated by John Cumming. New York: Continuum, 1998.

Alighieri, Dante. *Paradiso*. Translated by Robert Hollander and Jean Hollander. New York: Random House, 2008.

Altieri, Charles. "Aesthetics." In *Modernism and Theory: A Critical Debate,* ed. Stephen Ross. London: Routledge, 2008.

———. *The Art of Twentieth-Century American Poetry: Modernism and After.* Malden, MA: Wiley-Blackwell, 2009.

———. "Cavell and Wittgenstein on Morality: The Limits of Acknowledgment." In *Stanley Cavell and Literary Studies: Consequences of Skepticism,* ed. Richard Eldridge and Bernie Rhie, 62–77. New York: Continuum, 2011.

———. "Exemplification and Expression." In *A Companion to the Philosophy of Literature,* ed. Gary Hagberg and Walter Jost, 491–506. Oxford: Wiley-Blackwell, 2010.

———. "Lyrical Ethics and Literary Experience." *Style* 32 (1998): 272–97. Reprinted in Todd Davis and Kenneth Womack, eds., *Mapping the Ethical Turn,* 30–58. Charlottesville: University of Virginia Press, 2001.

———. *Painterly Abstraction in Modernist American Poetry.* New York: Cambridge University Press, 1989.

———. *The Particulars of Rapture: An Aesthetics of the Affects.* Ithaca, NY: Cornell University Press, 2003.

———. "Reading Bradley after Reading Laforgue: How Eliot Transformed Symbolist Poetics into a Paradigmatic Modernism." *Modern Language Quarterly* 72 (2011): 225–52.

———. "Rhetoric and Poetics: How to Use the Inevitable Return of the Repressed." In *A Companion to Rhetoric and Rhetorical Criticism,* ed. Walter Jost and Wendy Olmstead, 473–93. Oxford: Blackwell, 2004.

———. "The Riches of Value and the Poverty of Moral Theory in Literary Criticism." *Soundings* 94 (2011): 35–54.

———. "The Sensuous Dimension of Literary Experience: An Alternative to Materialist Theory." *New Literary History* 38 (2007): 71–98.

———. "Stevens and the Crisis of European Philosophy." In *Wallace Stevens across the Atlantic,* ed. Bart Eeckhout and Edward Ragg, 61–78. London: Palgrave Macmillan, 2008.

————. "Style." In *The Oxford Handbook of Philosophy and Literature,* ed. Richard Eldridge, 420–41. New York: Oxford University Press, 2009.

————. "Why Modernist Claims for Autonomy Matter." *Journal of Modern Literature* 32(3) (2009): 1–21.

————. "Wordsworth's Wavering Balance: The Thematic Rhythm of *The Prelude.*" *Wordsworth Circle* 4 (1972): 226–40.

Arnold, Matthew. "Dover Beach." In *The Norton Anthology of English Literature,* 8th ed., vol. 2, ed. Steven Greenblatt and M. H. Abrams, 1368. New York: Norton, 2006.

————. "The Scholar Gypsy." In *The Norton Anthology of English Literature,* 8th ed., vol. 2, ed. Steven Greenblatt and M. H. Abrams, 1361–67. New York: Norton, 2006.

Balakian, Anne. *The Symbolist Movement: A Critical Appraisal.* New York: New York University Press, 1977.

Becker, Misha. "*Is* Isn't *Be.*" *Lingua* 14 (2004): 399–418.

Bevis, William. *The Mind of Winter: Wallace Stevens, Meditation, and Literature.* Pittsburgh: University of Pittsburgh Press, 1989.

Brogan, Jacqueline Vaught. *Stevens and Simile: A Theory of Language.* Princeton, NJ: Princeton University Press, 1986.

Brooks, Cleanth. *The Well-Wrought Urn.* New York: Harvest Books, 1947.

Bruns, Gerald. "Stevens without Epistemology." In *Wallace Stevens: The Poetics of Modernism,* ed. Albert Gelpi, 24–40. New York: Cambridge University Press, 1985.

Buchsbaum, Julianne. "The Never-Ending Meditation: Wallace Stevens' 'An Ordinary Evening in New Haven' and Pragmatic Theories of Truth." *Wallace Stevens Journal* 32(1) (2008): 94.

Buttel, Robert. *Wallace Stevens: The Making of Harmonium.* Princeton, NJ: Princeton University Press, 1967.

Chipp, Herschel. *Theories of Modern Art: A Source Book by Artists and Critics.* Berkeley: University of California Press, 1984.

Clark, T. J. *Farewell to an Idea: Episodes from a History of Modernism.* New Haven, CT: Yale University Press, 2001.

Cole, Rachel. "Rethinking the Value of Lyric Closure: Giorgio Agamben, Wallace Stevens, and the Ethics of Satisfaction." *PMLA* 126 (2011): 398–411.

Cook, Eleanor. *A Reader's Guide to Wallace Stevens.* Princeton, NJ: Princeton University Press, 2007.

Cook, Jon, and Rupert Read. "Wittgenstein and Literary Language." In *A Companion to the Philosophy of Literature,* ed. Gary Hagbert and Walter Jost, 467–91. Malden, MA: Wiley-Blackwell, 2010.

Costello, Bonnie. "Effects of Analogy: Wallace Stevens and Painting." In *Wallace Stevens: The Poetics of Modernism,* ed. Albert Gelpi, 65–85. New York: Cambridge University Press, 1985.

Critchley, Simon. *Things Merely Are: Philosophy in the Poetry of Wallace Stevens.* London: Routledge, 2005.

Eeckhout, Bart. "Stevens and Philosophy." In *The Cambridge Companion to Wallace Stevens,* ed. John Serio, 103–117. New York: Cambridge University Press, 2007.

————. *Wallace Stevens and the Limits of Reading and Writing.* Columbia: University of Missouri Press, 2002.

————. "When Language Stops . . . Suspension Points in the Poetry of Hart Crane and Wallace Stevens." In *Semantics of Silences in Linguistics and Literature,* ed. Gudrun M. Grabher and Ulrike Jebner, 257–70. Heidelberg: Universitätsverlag C. Winter, 1996.

Emerson, Ralph Waldo. *Nature.* In *The Norton Anthology of American Literature,* 6th ed., ed. Nina Baym, 1106–34. New York: Norton, 2003 [1836].

Filreis, Alan. "Beyond the Rhetorician's Touch." *American Literary History* (Spring 1992): 230–63.

————. "Still-Life without Substance: Wallace Stevens and the Language of Agency." *Poetics Today* 10 (1989): 345–46.

————. *Wallace Stevens and the Actual World.* Princeton, NJ: Princeton University Press, 1991.

Gerber, Natalie. "Stevens' Mixed-Breed Versifying and His Adaptations of Blank Verse." *Wallace Stevens Journal* 35 (2011): 188–223.

Goldfarb, Lisa. "Philosophical Parallels: Wallace Stevens and Paul Valéry." *Wallace Stevens Journal* 29 (Spring 2005): 163–70.

Goodman, Nelson. *Languages of Art.* New York: Bobbs-Merrill, 1968.

Gurley, Jennifer. "Emerson's Politics of Uncertainty." *ESQ* 53(4) (2007) (Nos. 209 O.S.): 322–59.

Heidegger, Martin. *Being and Time.* Translated by John Macquarrie and Edward Robinson. New York: Harper and Row, 1962.

————. *Introduction to Metaphysics.* Translated by Ralph Manheim. New Haven, CT: Yale University Press, 1974.

Hejinian, Lynn. "Figuring Out." *Kiosk* 1 (2002): 195–206.

Homer. *The Iliad.* Translated by Robert Fitzgerald. New York: Farrar, Strauss, and Giroux, 2004.

————. *The Odyssey.* Translated by Robert Fitzgerald. Garden City, NJ: Doubleday Anchor, 1963.

Izenberg, Oren. *Being Numerous: Poetry and the Ground of Social Life.* Princeton, NJ: Princeton University Press, 2011.

Jäger, Gerhard. "Towards an Explanation of Copula Effects." *Linguistics and Philosophy* 26 (2003): 557–93.

Jameson, Frederic. "Wallace Stevens." In *Critical Essays on Wallace Stevens,* ed. Steven Gould Axelrod and Helen Deese, 177-91. Boston: Hall, 1988.

Kenner, Hugh. *The Pound Era.* Berkeley: University of California Press, 1971.

Köhler, Wolfgang. *The Place of Value in a World of Facts.* New York: Liveright, 1938.

Lawder, Bruce. "Poetry and Painting: Wallace Stevens and Pierre Tal-Coat." *Word and Image* 18 (2002): 348–56.

Leggett, B. J. *Early Stevens: The Nietzschean Intertext.* Durham, NC: Duke University Press, 1992.

Lensing, George. *Wallace Stevens and the Seasons.* Baton Rouge: Louisiana State University Press, 2001.

Lentricchia, Frank. "Patriarchy against Itself: The Young Manhood of Wallace Stevens." *Critical Inquiry* 13 (1987): 742–86.

Livingstone, Paisley. "Authorial Intention and the Varieties of Intentionalism." In *A Companion to the Philosophy of Literature,* ed. Gary Hagberg and Walter Jost, 401–19. Malden, MA: Wiley-Blackwell, 2010.

Longenbach, James. *Wallace Stevens: The Plain Sense of Things.* New York: Oxford University Press, 1991.

Luyat, Anne. "The Meditation of Wallace Stevens on Nothing." *English and American Studies Journal* (2001): 21–28. Shanghai, China: Shanghai International Studies University Press.

Maeder, Beverly. *Wallace Stevens' Experimental Language: The Lion in the Lute.* New York: St. Martin's, 1999.

Mallarmé, Stéphane. *Collected Poems.* Translated by Henry Weinfield. Berkeley: University of California Press, 1996.

———. *Mallarmé: Selected Prose Poems, Essays, and Letters,* ed. Bradford Cook. Baltimore: Johns Hopkins University Press, 1956.

Menand, Louis. *The Metaphysical Club: A Story of Ideas in America.* New York: Farrar, Strauss, and Giroux, 2001.

Miller, J. Hillis. "Theoretical and Atheoretical in Stevens." In *Wallace Stevens: A Celebration,* ed. Frank Doggett and Robert Buttel, 274–85. Princeton, NJ: Princeton University Press.

Moran, Dermot. *Introduction to Phenomenology.* London: Routledge, 2000.

Mulhall, Stephen, ed. *The Cavell Reader.* Oxford: Blackwell, 1996.

Nelson, Cary. *Repression and Recovery: Modern American Poetry and the Politics of Cultural Memory, 1910–1945.* Madison: University of Wisconsin Press, 1989.

Nichols, Peter. *George Oppen and the Fate of Modernism.* Oxford: Oxford University Press, 2007.

Nietzsche, Friedrich. *Beyond Good and Evil: A Prelude to a Philosophy of the Future.* Translated by Walter Kaufmann. New York: Random House, 1966.

———. *The Birth of Tragedy.* In *Basic Writings of Nietzsche,* edited and translated by Walter Kaufmann, 3–144. New York: Modern Library, 1968.

———. *Twilight of the Idols.* Translated by Richard Polt. Indianapolis: Hackett, 1997.

Perloff, Marjorie. "Pound/Stevens: Whose Era?" *New Literary History* 13 (1982): 485–514.

Perry, Ralph Barton. *General Theory of Value: Its Meaning and Basic Principles Construed in Terms of Interest.* New York: Longmans, Green, 1926.

Phillips, Siobhan. *The Poetics of the Everyday: Creative Repetition in Modern American Verse.* New York: Columbia University Press, 2009.

Pound, Ezra. *The Cantos.* New York: New Directions, 1996.

———. *Gaudier-Brzeska: A Memoir.* New York: New Directions, 1970.

———. *Literary Essays of Ezra Pound.* New York: New Directions, 1968.

———. *Personae: The Shorter Poems.* New York: New Directions, 1990.

Ragg, Edward. *Wallace Stevens and the Aesthetics of Abstraction.* Cambridge: Cambridge University Press, 2010.

Rancière, Jacques. *Aesthetics and Its Discontents.* Translated by Steven Corcoran. Cambridge: Polity, 2009.

———. *The Future of the Image.* Translated by Gregory Elliot. London: Verso, 2007.

————. *The Politics of Aesthetics.* Translated by Gabriel Rockhill. London: Continuum, 2004.

Ransom, John Crowe. "Poetry, A Note on Ontology." *Critical Theory since Plato,* ed. Hazard Adams, 871–80. New York: Harcourt Brace Jovanovich, 1971.

Richards, I. A. *Principles of Literary Criticism,* 2nd ed. New York: Harcourt Brace, 1926.

Richardson, Joan. *A Natural History of Pragmatism: The Fact of Feeling from Jonathan Edwards to Gertrude Stein.* Cambridge: Cambridge University Press, 2007.

Riddel, Joseph. "Metaphoric Staging: Stevens' Beginning Again of the 'End of the Book.'" In *Wallace Stevens: A Celebration,* ed. Frank Doggett and Robert Buttel, 308–38. Princeton, NJ: Princeton University Press.

————. "Theoretical and Atheoretical in Stevens." In *Wallace Stevens: A Celebration,* ed. Frank Doggett and Robert Buttel, 274–85. Princeton, NJ: Princeton University Press.

Santayana, George. *The Sense of Beauty: Being the Outline of an Aesthetic Theory.* Cambridge, MA: MIT Press, 1896.

Sartre, Jean-Paul. *Being and Nothingness: an Essay on Phenomenological Ontology.* Translated by Hazel Barnes. New York: Philosophical Library, 1956.

Scheler, Max. *The Constitution of the Human Being: From the Posthumous Works, Volumes 11 and 12 / Max Scheler.* Translated by John Cutting. Milwaukee: Marquette University Press, 2008.

Steinman, Lisa. "Lending No Part: Teaching Stevens with Williams." In *Teaching Wallace Stevens: Practical Essays,* ed. John Serio and B. J. Leggett, 169–78. Knoxville: University of Tennessee Press, 1994.

Stevens, Wallace. *Collected Poetry and Prose,* ed. Frank Kermode and Joan Richardson. New York: Library of America, 1997.

————. *The Letters of Wallace Stevens,* ed. Holly Stevens. Berkeley: University of California Press, 1996.

Symons, Arthur. *The Symbolist Movement in Literature.* With an introduction by Richard Ellman. Whitefish, MT: Kessinger, 2004.

Tate, Alan. *Essays of Four Decades.* New York: Morrow, 1969.

Vendler, Helen. *On Extended Wings: Wallace Stevens' Longer Poems.* Cambridge, MA: Harvard University Press, 1969.

————. *Wallace Stevens: Words Chosen out of Desire.* Knoxville: University of Tennessee Press, 1984.

Verdi, John. *Fat Wednesday: Wittgenstein on Aspects.* Philadelphia: Paul Dry Books, 2009.

Wittgenstein, Ludwig. *Culture and Value.* Translated by Peter Winch. Chicago: University of Chicago Press, 1984.

————. *Philosophical Investigations,* 3rd ed. Translated by G. E. M. Anscombe. Upper Saddle River, NJ: Prentice Hall, 1958.

————. *Tractatus Logico Philosophicus.* Translated by D. F. Pears and B. F. McGuinness. London: Routledge and Kegan Paul, 1961.

Wollheim, Richard. "Are the Criteria of Identity That Hold for a Work of Art in the Different Arts Aesthetically Relevant?" In *The Philosophy of Nelson Goodman: Nelson Goodman's Philosophy of Art,* ed. Catherine Z. Elgin, 73–92. New York: Garland, 1997.

————. "Nelson Goodman's *Languages of Art.*" In *The Philosophy of Nelson Goodman: Nelson Goodman's Philosophy of Art,* ed. Catherine Z. Elgin, 18–42. New York: Garland, 1997.

————. *The Thread of Life.* Cambridge: Cambridge University Press, 1985.

Wordsworth, William. *The Major Works,* ed. Stephen Gill. Oxford: Oxford University Press, 1984.

————. *The Prelude: A Parallel Text,* ed. J. C. Maxwell. Baltimore: Penguin, 1971.

Zandvoort, R. W. *A Handbook of English Grammar,* 6th ed. London: Longman, 1972.

Zhang, Dora. "Strange Likeness: Modernist Description in James, Proust, and Woolf." PhD diss., Princeton University, 2012. Print.

Ziarwek, Krzysztof. "Without Human Meaning: Stevens, Heidegger, and the Foreignness of Poetry." *Wallace Stevens across the Atlantic,* ed. Bart Eeckhout and Edward Ragg, 79–94. London: Palgrave Macmillan, 2008.

Zukofsky, Louis. *Bottom: On Shakespeare.* Berkeley: University of California Press, 1987 [ca 1963].

Index